D1156773

THE
PROFESSIONAL DEVELOPMENT
OF
GRADUATE TEACHING ASSISTANTS

THE
PROFESSIONAL DEVELOPMENT
OF
GRADUATE TEACHING ASSISTANTS

Michele Marincovich
Jack Prostko
Frederic Stout

Stanford University

Editors

ANKER PUBLISHING COMPANY, INC.
Bolton, MA

**The Professional Development
of Graduate Teaching Assistants**

ISBN 1-882982-24-X

Composition by Deerfoot Studios
Cover design by Deerfoot Studios

Anker Publishing Company, Inc.
176 Ballville Road
P.O. Box 249
Bolton, MA 01740-0249

To our parents

Francis L. and Betsy F. Slavich

Eleanora and John Prostko

Elvira Magaz Stout and the late Harry Leon Stout

ABOUT THE EDITORS

MICHELE MARINCOVICH is assistant vice provost at Stanford University and director of its Center for Teaching and Learning, one of the oldest faculty and TA development offices in the country (founded in 1975). Shortly after finishing her Ph.D. in history, she joined the center as assistant director and initiated the campus's first videotaping and consultation programs for TAs. With a fellow lecturer from the department of linguistics, she also inaugurated Stanford's first course on teaching for international TAs. Since 1979 she has concentrated on work with faculty as well; her efforts brought her the university's prestigious Dinkelspiel Award for Outstanding Service to Undergraduate Education in 1988. Equally active off campus, she is a past president of the Professional and Organizational Development (POD) Network in Higher Education and a frequent presenter at campuses and conferences in the U.S. and abroad. Her most recent publication is (with Nira Hativa) *Disciplinary Differences in Teaching and Learning: Implications for Practice* (Jossey-Bass, 1995).

JACK PROSTKO is the associate director of the Center for Teaching and Learning at Stanford University. He coordinates the university's TA training efforts and assists with faculty development. His Ph.D. is in English, and he has directed a peer writing tutor program for undergraduates and worked closely with graduate students and departments to improve writing skills and instruction. In 1982 he received the university's Gores Award for Excellence in Teaching.

FREDERIC STOUT is a lecturer in the program on urban studies at Stanford University and the coauthor/coeditor of *The City Reader* (the leading anthology in the field) and the nine-volume *Early City Planning, 1870–1940*. Since 1994, he has been the coordinator of teaching assistant training at the Center for Teaching and Learning.

ABOUT THE CONTRIBUTORS

MICHAEL J. ALBRIGHT is an instructional development specialist in the Center for Instructional Technology, Iowa State University, with a joint appointment in the ISU college of family and consumer sciences. He has more than 25 years of experience in instructional development and instructional technology management, having served as director of the campus media centers at the University of South Dakota and the University of Hawaii, Manoa. Michael was coeditor of the Fall 1992 issue of New Directions for Teaching and Learning, entitled *Teaching in the Information Age: The Role of Educational Technology*, and has authored numerous other publications related to instructional technology and university teaching. His list of more than 40 presentations at national and international conferences includes keynote addresses in the U.S., Canada, and South Africa. He received his Ph.D. in instructional technology from Iowa State in 1988.

BEVERLY BLACK is an instructional consultant at the University of Michigan's Center for Research on Learning and Teaching. She has been working with TA development since 1983 and currently heads the team that works with graduate student instructor programs. During the past four years, she has worked half-time in the department of mathematics to help integrate cooperative learning into the introductory courses and to develop an extensive training program and support system for graduate students and faculty teaching in those courses.

NANCY VAN NOTE CHISM is director of faculty and TA development at The Ohio State University and an adjunct faculty member in the college of education. In her work supporting teaching at Ohio State, she has paid special attention to the needs of teaching assistants through organizing the orientations, TA coordinators' conferences, forums, and personal consultation services that have served more than 7,000 teaching assistants at Ohio State. In 1986, she coordinated the first national conference on teaching assistant issues. Since then, she has continued to participate in national dialogue on teaching assistants by serving on national planning committees for subsequent national conferences, consulting on more than 20 campuses, and making regular presentations and contributions to the literature on teaching assistant development. She was co-coordinator, with Marilla Svinicki, of the National Consortium on Preparing Graduate Students to Teach, funded by The Pew Charitable Trusts, and has served as president of the Professional and Organizational Development Network in Higher Education.

PATRICIA H. FEATHERSTONE is the assistant director of the TA program at Syracuse University. She is involved in planning, implementing, and assessing the university-wide orientation program for new teaching assistants and year-round professional development seminars and colloquia. She coordinates the English language courses that are offered to international teaching assistants. Patricia has made several presentations about TA professional development and is a coeditor of *University Teaching: A Guide for Graduate Students.*

JERRY G. GAFF is vice president of the Association of American Colleges and Universities, which supports high quality, purposeful, and coherent education at its nearly 700 member colleges and universities and which serves as the national voice of liberal learning. Jerry received a B.A. from DePauw University in 1958 and a Ph.D. in psychology from Syracuse University in 1965. Through his publications, projects, and related professional activities, he has contributed to many efforts to improve undergraduate education. He has directed national projects to strengthen undergraduate general education programs and to foster the professional development of faculty members. He is the founding director of the Network for Academic Renewal that assists administrators and faculty members to improve their academic programs in such ways as internationalizing the curriculum, using diversity and technology to aid learning, and developing more quality and coherence in general education curricula. He also directs the Preparing Future Faculty program, which has awarded grants to research universities to develop new programs that prepare graduate students for research, teaching, and service roles in a diversity of colleges and universities. His most recent book is *Handbook of the Undergraduate Curriculum: A Comprehensive Guide to Purposes, Structures, Practices, and Change* (1996).

PAT HUTCHINGS is a senior scholar with the Carnegie Foundation for the Advancement of Teaching, a position she moved to in the spring of 1998 after 10 years at the American Association for Higher Education. Her Ph.D. is in English, and she continues to teach creative writing on a part-time basis.

HOWARD C. JOHNSON is a nationally recognized mathematics educator who has held a number of major leadership positions in higher education. Dean of the graduate school and professor of mathematics and mathematics education, Johnson also serves Syracuse University as associate vice chancellor for academic affairs and chair of the mathematics education program. His areas of specialization include the acquisition of mathematical concepts and processes, problem solving, teacher education, and the development of materials for students and teachers that emphasize technology. He has worked to strengthen interdisciplinary initiatives, to create excellent academic services, to improve diversity of the graduate student body, to bring new efficiencies to the graduate school operations, and to improve tracking and attention to processes between graduate admission and degree certification, including graduate student professional development.

MATT KAPLAN is an instructional consultant at the University of Michigan's Center for Research on Learning and Teaching. For the last five years he has conducted workshops, developed orientation programs for centralized TA training programs, and worked with individual academic units as they develop departmental training programs. He is the editor of the 1998 edition of *To Improve the Academy*.

VIRGINIA MAURER is international faculty coordinator at the Derek Bok Center for Teaching and Learning at Harvard University. She directs the teaching in English program and develops individual and group training programs for ITAs. She has worked with international graduate students, faculty, and scholars in the United States and abroad since 1983. One of her areas of interest and expertise is oral proficiency testing.

JACQUELINE A. MINTZ directs the Graduate Student Instructor (GSI) Teaching and Resource Center and teaches in the department of comparative literature at the University of California, Berkeley, where she received her Ph.D. After living and teaching in London, she returned to Berkeley and created the center in 1989. An interdisciplinarian by design, she brings anthropology, religious studies, psychology, sociology, and history into her chosen specialty of theater and into her work as an educational developer. She has written articles on literary criticism, on values in teaching, on involving students in their own course design and peer teaching, and on the role of professional developers in North American higher education. She has served on the Professional and Organization Development Network in Higher Education (POD) core committee, is on the editorial board of *The Journal of Graduate Teaching Assistant Development*, and serves as the chair of the professional development committee of POD.

JODY D. NYQUIST is assistant dean of the graduate school and director of the Center for Instructional Development and Research at the University of Washington, Seattle. Drawing heavily on her own disciplinary roots in communication, she was among the first scholars to advocate discipline-specific instructional development and TA preparation and has advanced that philosophy consistently in her professional work. Jody is an international scholar and leader in the area of TA development, having written and edited several books and numerous articles on the topic and having been instrumental in the national consortium that has worked to advance the preparation of TAs as future faculty in the United States. She has presented keynote addresses and workshops on TA preparation across the United States and in England, Australia, Saudi Arabia, and New Zealand, where she served as a Fulbright Senior Scholar in 1992. In December 1994, she keynoted the first British National Conference "Using Graduate Teaching Assistants Effectively" at the University of Warwick in the U.K. She is currently a principal investigator for a national research study funded by Pew Charitable Trusts and the Spencer Foundation that is following graduate students over a four-year period to chart their development as teachers.

MATHEW L. OUELLETT is the associate director of the Center for Teaching at the University of Massachusetts, Amherst, and serves as an adjunct professor in the school of social work, Smith College. Mathew completed his doctorate in education with a focus in multicultural organization development and social justice education at the University of Massachusetts, Amherst.

ANNE S. PRUITT-LOGAN is scholar in residence at the Council of Graduate Schools where she codirects the Preparing Future Faculty program. Professor emerita of educational policy and leadership at The Ohio State

University, she served as associate provost, associate dean of the graduate school, and director of the Center for Teaching Excellence. Prior to joining Ohio State, she was a professor of education at Case Western Reserve University.

SHIRLEY A. RONKOWSKI is an instructional specialist in the Office of Instructional Consultation and the academic coordinator for the campus-wide TA Development Program at the University of California, Santa Barbara. Her published articles, book chapters, and conference papers focus on instructional design, the scholarship of teaching, cooperative learning, and instructional technology for both current and future faculty.

ELLEN SARKISIAN is associate director of the Derek Bok Center for Teaching and Learning at Harvard, where she began an ITA training program in 1981, and currently collaborates with several departments on a broad range of activities training graduate students and reflecting on teaching with experienced teachers. As educational consultant at the Harvard School of Public Health, she is responsible for several initiatives supporting teaching and learning, including English for Professional Education for incoming international graduate students. She spent several years teaching in Nigeria, Taiwan, and Hong Kong. Her most recent publication is a new edition of *Teaching American Students: A Guide for International Teaching Assistants in Colleges and Universities.*

JO SPRAGUE, a professor of communication studies at San Jose State University since 1971, is currently serving as associate dean for faculty affairs. For most of her career since receiving her Ph.D. from Purdue University, she has worked with teaching associates who teach the basic communication courses. She has also held several different leadership roles in faculty development. Her research interests include the pedagogy of teaching speech communication and the role of communication in all instructional settings. Besides coauthoring a public speaking textbook and a teaching methods book for secondary teachers, she has written several chapters and articles that take a critical perspective on teaching and learning. The social construction of meaning through communication informs her current funded research on the development of teaching assistants as members of the professoriate.

MARY DEANE SORCINELLI is associate provost for faculty development, director of the Center for Teaching, and adjunct associate professor,

University of Massachusetts, Amherst. Mary Deane has consulted with hundreds of individual faculty members on teaching and has worked at departmental, school, and campus-wide levels to encourage support and recognition for good teaching. She has published widely in the areas of faculty career development and teaching development and evaluation.

MARILLA D. SVINICKI received her Ph.D. from the University of Colorado, Boulder, in the area of experimental psychology. Upon graduating, she taught at Macalester College in St. Paul, Minnesota, before going to the University of Texas at Austin, where she joined a research team on computer-based instruction. At the same time, she joined the staff of the Center for Teaching Effectiveness, where she currently serves as director as well as being a senior lecturer in the department of educational psychology.

STACEY LANE TICE is an assistant dean of the graduate school and director of the TA program, Future Professoriate Project, and Preparing Future Faculty Program at Syracuse University. She is coeditor of *Preparing Graduate Students to Teach* and *University Teaching: A Guide for Graduate Students,* as well as several articles related to preparing graduate students for faculty positions. She has also served on the faculty of the two National Workshops on Preparing Graduate Students to Teach, sponsored by the National Consortium on Preparing Graduate Students as College Teachers.

TABLE OF CONTENTS

FOREWORD

The title "teaching assistant" is possibly one of the most ambiguous in higher education. The assistantship is a form of financial aid for the graduate student. In return for tuition reimbursement and a modest stipend, the university receives the assistance of someone who sets up labs or computer workstations, leads a discussion section as part of a large lecture course, or designs and teaches courses, often unsupervised. Yet for many graduate students, work as a TA is also a kind of apprenticeship, preparation for careers as faculty members. Many have teaching loads equal to those of their full-time, tenured faculty colleagues. It is no wonder that courts hearing labor cases involving graduate teaching assistants are wrestling with the question of whether a TA is a student or an employee.

Graduate teaching assistants provide instruction for roughly 40% of the undergraduate courses in research and comprehensive universities, and they have teaching responsibilities in approximately 60% of the introductory courses taken by first- and second-year undergraduates. Debate continues about the wisdom, fairness, or practicality of graduate programs that enroll many more students than might complete an advanced degree or find jobs in the academy or other professions. Legislators and regents urge universities to staff lower division courses exclusively with full-time, tenured, or tenure-track professors. Nonetheless, the fact remains that universities rely heavily on graduate students to cover courses or handle instruction-related work that they cannot afford to cover otherwise, and they are likely to continue to use TAs, especially universities in the states that are expected to see significant growth in higher education enrollments in the coming decade.

Enrollment growth may be only one of many changes that higher education will see in the coming decades. In a seminal article published in *Change* magazine in December 1995, Barr and Tagg describe the deep changes that colleges and universities are making—and have yet to make—as higher education undertakes the enormous shift "from teaching to learning." The role of the instructor is changing from one who imparts information to one who guides students to knowledge and understanding. Investment in faculty development (already undersupported) will become even more critical to both the current quality and the future improvement of the education that the institution offers, particularly to its undergraduates. With graduate students so deeply involved in their institutions' undergraduate programs, it is necessary to include the graduate TAs in university efforts to implement new curricula, pedagogies, uses of technology, peer evaluation of teaching, and assessment of student learning.

The broad acceptance of Ernest Boyer's (1990) notion of the scholarship of teaching and the national discussions of faculty roles and work prompted by the American Association for Higher Education suggest a new understanding of the profession. In colleges and universities that are focused on student learning, faculty members' discipline-based inquiry is but one professional pursuit; research on student learning in and across disciplines also forms the basis for scholarly inquiry. This leads to questions about the appropriateness of the traditional requirements for the Ph.D. Are a series of courses, exams in subspecialties, and an extended research project sufficient preparation for a career as a faculty member (or many of the other professions which Ph.D.s enter)? Graduate deans and department heads are seeing the value of integrating formal preparation for teaching into the graduate study of those who aspire to become faculty members, and they appreciate the strong foundation of high quality TA development. Yet none of these important changes can be effected through the half-day TA orientations that have passed for "training." If brief and episodic workshops are insufficient to prepare TAs for their immediate teaching duties, they are even more inadequate to launch a professional career in a changing environment.

Among the authors of this book are leaders in faculty development who are helping higher education to understand the importance of providing ongoing instruction and guidance for graduate students who teach. Through their work, these national leaders remind us that universities have a responsibility to their students to ensure that all instructors are prepared for and supported in their teaching and that universities must take responsibility to support graduate TAs in fulfilling their duties. They show us why it is necessary that TAs, as well as full- and part-time faculty, have access to the resources of university teaching and learning centers, departmental expertise, and regional and national organizations that advance teaching. We also learn from these authors that as graduate teaching assistants gain experience, their professional development needs do not diminish but simply change.

As Nancy Van Note Chism explains in Chapter 1, Preparing Graduate Students to Teach: Past, Present, and Future, the idea and practice of professional development for graduate teaching assistants have been gathering force over the past 20 years. A survey by Leo Lambert and Stacey Lane Tice (1993) revealed that many universities in the United States have carefully constructed programs that provide TAs with a strong understanding of student learning and the professional responsibilities of those who teach undergraduates. Some of these programs are designed to take the graduate students through a series of teaching assignments over several semesters. Many introduce graduate teaching assistants to a variety of pedagogies, assessment of student learning, peer evaluations of teaching, and scholarly inquiry about the acts of teaching and learning.

However, for all too many graduate students assigned to teach a course or to assist in teaching a course, a brief orientation is the extent of their formal preparation for the semester and beyond. The fact that this wide range in the quality of programs can exist within the same university is one of the continuing frustrations of those who work in TA development. In their research, Lambert and Tice had to overcome a major obstacle: finding the many people who run TA development programs and identifying the person or people on a campus with information about the full range of TA training and development taking place on that campus. Where these programs are located in an institution varies with the culture and structure of both the university and the departments making use of graduate teaching assistants. Responsibility for preparing graduate teaching assistants may be claimed by (or fall to) the graduate school, a center for teaching and learning, and individual departments. Who is assigned to design and run the programs also varies, even within the same university: senior faculty, junior faculty, experienced graduate students, and professional faculty developers. The resources—human and financial—available for these programs vary accordingly. Some departments are just now becoming aware of the need to prepare their graduate students for the teaching they do; all too often they try to build a program from scratch when across campus there is a strong program with years of history among its many resources.

The commitment of top administrators and graduate faculty to the importance of taking time to prepare graduate teaching assistants for their duties varies as well. Some programs flourish because of the policies and support of key administrators. Yet the meager resources of many programs reflect an all too slowly dying notion that teaching does not take much work or thought, or else is an inherent ability. Too many program directors have needs—and creative and well-informed ideas about meeting those needs—that far outstrip their small budgets or the amount of time they are allotted to do their work.

Much of the good news about the growing number and vitality of these programs can be attributed to the work of the researchers and practitioners authoring this volume. As the citations and bibliography in this volume attest, there is a growing body of literature about professional development for graduate teaching assistants. Since 1986, these authors have shared their ideas, experience, and research directly with the field through a series of national conferences on the training and employment of graduate teaching assistants. More recently, a core group of leaders in TA development have held intensive three-day workshops for other developers.

The conferences and workshops have allowed TA developers—from graduate deans to graduate students—to voice their need for information on tested theory and practice. One important resource for all programs is information about making their efforts more effective and more connected to other campus activities, theories of professional development, and policies that support TA development. Because responsibility for TA development can vary so widely among and within institutions, it is difficult to reach pertinent deans, faculty, and practitioners through the usual channels of national organizations. Michele Marincovich, Jack Prostko, and Frederic Stout conceived of a book which would draw together the important theories informing practice in graduate student professional development and the practical aspects of building and running a program.

Assembled in this book are the collective experience, wisdom, vision, and skills of the leading researchers and practitioners in graduate student professional development. The design of their own TA programs and the research they have contributed to the field are grounded in a variety of disciplines: Among them are psychology, communication, organizational development, sociology, education, history, English, and rhetoric.

This volume is an important resource for deans and other key administrators, faculty, practitioners, and teaching assistants themselves. It also represents an important step in the growth of the field of TA development itself: For the first time, the various strands of work have been joined. The assembled pieces, the opportunity to view TA development as a maturing field, suggest all sorts of possibilities for new directions, new questions. Should TA programs carry with them some form of certification in college and university teaching? In what ways must the faculty reward system change to encourage greater faculty participation in TA development? What professional preparation should TA developers have for their responsibilities? How can administrative leadership for TA development be increased? What alliances and information will yield new resources for programs?

It is the hope of the editors and authors that, in using this book, administrators, faculty, practitioners, and graduate students will become engaged with this national conversation and lend their experience and creativity to moving TA development to a new stage.

Ellen Wert
Program Officer, Education
The Pew Charitable Trusts

REFERENCES

Barr, R. B., & Tagg, J. (1995, November/December). From teaching to learning: A new paradigm for undergraduate education. *Change, 27* (6).

Boyer, E. L. (1990). *Scholarship reconsidered: Priorities of the professoriate.* Lawrenceville, NJ: Princeton University Press.

Lambert, L. M., & Tice, S. L. (Eds.). (1993). *Preparing graduate students to teach: A guide to programs that improve undergraduate education and develop tomorrow's faculty.* Washington, DC: American Association for Higher Education.

PREFACE

Although this might appear to be a specialist book, written by specialists and addressed to a specific audience, its subject—the training and professional development of graduate teaching assistants—is of very broad and general relevance to all those concerned with the future of the university and the society which it serves. Indeed, the way universities prepare their graduate students as classroom teachers and future academic professionals is a clear measure of what contemporary society regards as the meaning and importance of higher education itself.

The mission of higher education has traditionally been expressed as a trinity: teaching, research, and service. Over the centuries, the service function of education has been variously conceived, sometimes as guild-service to the university itself, sometimes as service to a broader social community. But teaching and research, the indisputable core functions of education, have perpetually existed in a state of delicate and self-correcting balance. And today, the increasing attention being paid to the pedagogical training of the graduate teaching assistants who carry out so much of the undergraduate teaching mission of the university is an important part of that self-correcting, self-balancing process.

Higher education has always been, in the words of philosopher-activist Paul Goodman, "an instrument of social needs." In the 19th and early 20th centuries, the modern university developed a highly specialized disciplinary/departmental structure that responded to the needs of an urbanizing, industrializing society by preparing elites in specific areas of expertise to help govern and manage an increasingly complex society. And during the mid- to late 20th century, that part of the university devoted to basic and applied research—in technology, science, and the social sciences—was harnessed to the corporate and national security needs of a dominant Cold War culture. Today, the Cold War is over, the postulates of modernism are giving way to postmodernism, and a new, if still uncertain sense of globalism—in economics, politics, technology, and culture—poses dramatic challenges to both the university and society at large. Today's graduate students face futures much less defined by their narrow specialist skills as research professionals and much more defined by their ability to communicate, generalize, and synthesize information that is increasingly interdisciplinary in nature.

In this context, the new emphasis on the training and professional development of teaching assistants is important for two reasons. First, it redresses a previous imbalance between the values of teaching and research that many had begun to see as extreme. Second, and even more important, it reasserts the centrality of teaching to the entire educational enterprise in a way that fundamentally changes some of our basic preconceptions about the functions of the university itself. The new ideas and sense of urgency that have been brought to the training and professional development of TAs in recent years respond to a widely felt institutional need to reemphasize a "culture of teaching" within the university as a whole. TA training also serves to recognize and valorize what the late Ernest Boyer called "the scholarship of teaching," the notion that research and teaching are not polar opposites after all but interdependent, mutually reinforcing parts of a larger whole. In fact, in 1997, two major reports—one by the Committee on Professional Employment of the Modern Language Association, another by the Center for Instructional Development at Syracuse University—indicate that the focus of both graduate education and the academic job market is increasingly turning toward issues of teaching rather than research.

This book, then, addresses a most timely issue and one with broad implications for the university as a social institution. Preparing our graduate students to be teachers as well as researchers—and to combine those functions in new and creative ways—is an important, even crucial part of the ongoing evolution of the university as a transmitter of culture and a servant of society. This volume brings together the most widely recognized practitioners in the field to trace the history, examine the theoretical bases, review the practical applications, and speculate about the future of a process that has long been conceived narrowly as "TA training" but which is increasingly being seen as "the comprehensive professional development of teaching assistants for their roles as future academic professionals."

The foreword, by Ellen Wert, locates TA training within the history of the modern university and the larger context of contemporary movements for social and educational reform. And Chapter 1, by Nancy Van

Note Chism, provides an overview of the history of teaching development programs, examining prominent, essential ideas shaping current efforts and their probable future direction.

Although much TA training is carried out by centralized programs serving the whole university, important aspects of pedagogy are discipline-specific. Chapter 2, by Jacqueline A. Mintz, describes the components of centralized programs—their mission within the university, their organizational structures, advantages, and disadvantages—and Chapter 3, by Shirley A. Ronkowski, describes the equally important role of initiatives at the department level.

The next several chapters address broadly applicable commonalities of TA training. In Chapter 4, Jody D. Nyquist and Jo Sprague update, refine, and extend their work on the stages of TA development and describe how to design effective programs that correspond to these stages. Chapter 5, by Marilla D. Svinicki, reviews the research on learning and cognitive development that underlies all pedagogy, outlining specific ways that TAs can help students learn more effectively. Chapter 6, by Mathew L. Ouellett and Mary Deane Sorcinelli, reviews how diversities of background and learning styles affect the classroom experience of students and suggests strategies for TA offices to pursue in making TAs and faculty more aware of the implications of diversity for effective teaching. And Chapter 7, by Frederic Stout, outlines some practical steps to consider in developing successful TA training programs from the ground up, with suggestions and resources for adapting documented models to existing campus cultures.

Narrowing the focus, another four chapters address specific aspects of TA training and their appropriate methodologies. In Chapter 8, Michele Marincovich examines a specific aspect of successful TA training programs—the course on teaching—looking at the kinds of courses offered and their goals, content, and benefits, with suggestions for implementing such courses. In Chapter 9, Ellen Sarkisian and Virginia Maurer explore issues relevant to the training of international TAs, especially the need to prepare them for the interactive American classroom, perhaps through work with undergraduates who can provide frank but helpful feedback during the initial stages of training. Chapter 10, by Jack Prostko, describes how TAs can help undergraduates improve their writing skills and examines the difficulties TA trainers face in addressing graduate students' own writing concerns while proposing ways they can assist undergraduate writers. And in Chapter 11, Michael J. Albright looks at the ever-changing nature of the new communications technologies as it affects pedagogy, highlighting the need to involve TAs in understanding the use of technology to solve instructional problems.

The next three chapters address issues of assessment and evaluation. Chapter 12, by Beverly Black and Matt Kaplan, explores various ways of ensuring systematic and fair formative and summative evaluations of classroom teaching by TAs. In Chapter 13, Pat Hutchings describes the teaching portfolio—its history, design, and benefits—as a tool for professional self-development and self-evaluation. In Chapter 14, Nancy Van Note Chism reviews the issues in, and uses of, program evaluations, offering recommendations for documenting program effectiveness.

Finally, two concluding chapters look to the future of TA training as an increasingly important and professionalized process central to the mission of the contemporary university. Chapter 15, by Stacey Lane Tice, Patricia H. Featherstone, and Howard C. Johnson, reviews the experience, the purposes, and benefits of formal certification programs for graduate teaching assistants. And Chapter 16, by Stacey Lane Tice, Jerry G. Gaff, and Anne S. Pruitt-Logan, describes the Preparing Future Faculty programs on various campuses that look well beyond TA training to a more comprehensive and integrated process of academic professional development that begins with the TA experience and continues on through full faculty membership.

ACKNOWLEDGMENTS

No undertaking of this magnitude could have been successfully completed without the assistance of many colleagues whose efforts have not been acknowledged elsewhere in this volume. We extend our thanks to all of the staff members of the Center for Teaching and Learning whose support and patience have been invaluable, and most particularly to Tiffany Haas for the admirable proofreading and to Stephanie Bazirjian for the steady project management. We also want to note the research assistance of Gary Lichtenstein of Quality Evaluation Design, whose efforts allowed us to complete our labors in a timely and efficient manner. Special thanks also go to the Pew Charitable Trusts and the National Consortium on Teaching Assistant Training for their support of the Summer Institute on TA Training held at Stanford in July 1997, a rewarding get-together of experienced and novice TA developers that served as both meeting ground and nurturing medium for many of the ideas included in this book. Thanks as well go to Robert Weisberg, vice-provost for faculty affairs at Stanford, whose ongoing support for this and other CTL activities is greatly appreciated. Above all else, we wish to express our deepest gratitude to all of the dedicated faculty members and teaching assistants with whom we have worked over the years. It is they who have made the movement for improved preparation of TAs as future faculty a meaningful part of a larger project to re-instill a culture of teaching in the academy of the future.

Michele Marincovich
Jack Prostko
Frederic Stout

1

PREPARING GRADUATE STUDENTS TO TEACH: PAST, PRESENT, AND FUTURE

Nancy Van Note Chism

During the 20th century, teaching development programs for graduate students have moved through several stages of conceptualization and implementation. The original emphasis on the development of teaching assistants (TAs)—both for their immediate tasks in teaching undergraduates and for the career development of those who intended to become faculty members—has now given way to a broader conception of preparing all graduate students for the teaching aspects of their professional careers, whether as faculty or in other walks of life. Notions of the range of skills and the knowledge base required for professional life have also expanded, as have approaches to providing preparation effectively. This chapter highlights the history of the progression, describes current thinking on preparing future professionals for teaching, and looks at trends that might suggest new directions and realities.

PAST

A chronological overview of graduate student professional preparation from its origins to the present can be divided into four phases. Using conversation as a theme, these phases in the history of graduate student professional development are titled: "Nothing to Say," "Private Conversations," "Can We Talk?," and "Extending the Conversation." During these four phases, the focus has been on teaching preparation for TAs;

only during recent years has it broadened to include other graduate students and other aspects of their future work.

Nothing to Say

This initial phase encompasses the first appearance of teaching assistants and extends until about 1960, although the state of affairs at some institutions still warrants this description. The label, "Nothing to Say," refers to a period when it did not seem to occur to most of those working with graduate students that preparation to teach was an issue worth considering.

Attempts to pinpoint the first use of graduate students as teachers have provided only sketchy information. Rudolph (1977) refers to the use of tutors at Yale in the 1700s. Minkel (1987) talks about the existence of TAs at the University of Tennessee as early as 1823 but suspects that counterparts to TAs existed as far back as early Greece. Eble (1987) cites a source dating TAs at Johns Hopkins from 1876. Certainly, teaching while studying is an idea not original to the present time. Generally, however, sources identify the postwar years of increasing college enrollments as the beginning of the large-scale employment of graduate students as teachers (Eble, 1987; Lewis, 1997).

Even less seems to be known about how early graduate student teachers were prepared for their teaching responsibilities. These first hundred years or so of TAs in the United States appear to have been the "rugged individualism" era of starting a teaching career: Faculty reminiscences invariably recount the directive, "Here's the textbook. There's the class," as the standard induction into teaching. Individual mentoring likely took place as faculty were so moved, but stories of drudgery, such as Ken Eble's (1987) account of a Harvard TA in 1912 who complained of the "brain fagging" work of grading endless freshman compositions, lead to the suspicion that TAs then, as now, were most often doing the routine, repetitive tasks that were thought to require little training.

The "Nothing to Say" phase is associated with prevailing ideas about teaching that have been the common heritage in college settings for some time, ideas that profess that there is nothing to teaching; that teachers are born, not made; that teaching is telling. Beliefs in these conceptions would hardly support development work, and there is record of very little. Some exceptions during this phase are noted by

Nyquist, Abbott, and Wulff (1989a), who detail a few instances from 1930, 1949, and the late 1950s when administrators at least raised the topic of preparing graduate students as teachers during conference deliberations on the role of graduate education.

Private Conversations

In the 1960s and the roughly 20 years that followed, a phase that could be called "Private Conversations" took place. Universities began to employ more and more TAs in increasingly independent teaching roles, student criticism of the quality of education escalated, and institutions began to respond. During this time, formal efforts to prepare graduate students to teach began, largely at the department level and largely in the departments with many TAs. Parrett's survey (1987) of 36 programs described in the literature between 1976 and 1986 showed that the majority (31) were discipline-specific and only five were campus-wide. In 1966, MacAllister's survey of foreign language departments showed that 40% had some TA training (broadly defined, which might include once-a-semester pep talks), while by 1980 Schultz's figures showed that 78% of foreign language, linguistics, and comparative literature departments were reporting development programs. Yoder's 1982 survey showed that 50% of speech communication departments had some training for their TAs. Other areas with documented programs during this period include writing, mathematics, and some large physical science programs.

The term "Private Conversations" is descriptive of this era because dialogue was, by and large, within individual departments or programs; public sharing about these efforts was mostly in disciplinary journals—when it was shared at all. Much of the literature contained program descriptions with titles on the order of "What We Do at State U," and many were prescriptive, on such topics as "Why We Should Train TAs," "How to Motivate TAs," and "How to Be a Physics TA." Protocols, which involved watching and then imitating ideal teaching behaviors modeled on videotape or by a demonstrator, were the training device of choice.

A major exception to the trend during this period was the work of the Carnegie Foundation for the Advancement of Teaching to promote the Doctor of Arts degree, designed to prepare graduates for teaching in college settings (Richlin, 1995). Another bright spot were the centers to support faculty growth that were funded by the Danforth and Kellogg Foundations—centers such as those at Stanford, Northwestern, and

Harvard—that grew to encompass efforts toward teaching assistant development as well.

There were some research studies, mostly centering around evaluation of TA performance, such as the effectiveness of TAs as teachers compared with faculty, as well as the ever-popular student ratings research. A few studies centered on the effectiveness of training. Carroll in 1980 dismissed most of these as nonrigorous, noting a pattern of weak treatment and no significant effects.

In 1982, Ervin and Muyskens attempted to find out what TAs in foreign language needed in their training; this was one of the first published studies that speculated that there might be phases of developmental and individual needs. The talk on international TAs centered largely on language issues and which test—TOEFL, TSE, or SPEAK—was most useful.

Can We Talk?

In 1986, with the first national conference on TA issues at The Ohio State University, and in the five years that followed, with a training institute at Syracuse and the second and third national conferences at Washington and Texas, a phase began that could be titled, after Joan Rivers, "Can We Talk?" During this phase, large institutions came together to publicly talk about a situation that they had previously treated cautiously: the fact that TAs were carrying a large part of the undergraduate load and that efforts to prepare these graduate students to teach were in their infancy. National professional groups, such as the Council of Graduate Schools and the American Association for Higher Education, became partners in the conversation.

Much of the dialogue at first dealt with policy issues. An example is Ken Eble's keynote address at the first national conference, "Defending the Indefensible," in which he questioned why and how institutions employ TAs. Eble (1987) recommended that we "get the TAs off their knees," and "put the education of teaching assistants first and their exploitation second, or last" (p. 9).

During this "Can We Talk?" phase, there was an interest in how TAs are selected and assigned, concern with "time to degree," and a discussion of stipends, workloads, and unionization. In terms of the preparation of TAs, the descriptions of interventions during this phase show a broader range than the previous protocol approach. More centralized programs arose to complement departmental ones. Buerkel-Rothfuss and Gray (1991) found in a 1986 survey that half of the responding department chairpersons reported having training programs, and one-fourth of responding graduate deans reported centralized training programs at their institutions. Awards, certificate programs, newsletters, handbooks, new TA orientations, courses on pedagogy, and consultation services all became popular during this period. Conference proceedings from each of the national conferences (Chism, 1987; Heenan & Jerich, 1995; Lewis, 1993; and Nyquist, Abbott, Wulff, & Sprague, 1991) detail these developments.

In international TA development, this phase marked a new focus on the cultural component of training and the first talk of the intolerance of the U.S. undergraduate as a dimension of the issue (vom Saal, 1987). In addition, the use of tutors, speech partners, and mock testing, as well as other approaches, arose during this period.

During this phase, research on stages of TA development began and became a much stronger theme in the literature. Examples include Sprague and Nyquist's study (1991) and work by Darling (1987) and Ruiz (1987). Research on the effectiveness of training and how TAs fare as teachers also continued. The publication of *Teaching Assistant Training in the 1990s* (Nyquist, Abbott, & Wulff, 1989b) provided an overview of the state of the art.

Extending the Conversation

An undercurrent during the "Can We Talk?" phase that became much more prominent in the early 1990s led to a phase of multiple constituencies, ideas, and initiatives, titled here as "Extending the Conversation." One group of constituents that became quite influential during this time included legislators and other public officials, investigative reporters, and citizens who focused on attempting to regulate the language proficiency of ITAs and curtailing the widespread employment of teaching assistants. At the 1993 national conference on TA development, held in Chicago, one presenter's description of a session on responding to state legislative and regional accreditation mandates reads: "Accountability to public entities that support and validate higher education has joined death and taxes as one of life's certainties" (Brown, 1993). Regulations, legislation, budget reduction, and internal policies from this period have continued to impact TA development efforts.

A major new emphasis at the Chicago conference was the inclusion of professional association leadership; five disciplines and organizations participated: the American Chemical Society, American Sociological Association, Modern Language Association of America, Speech Communication Association, and a joint effort of the American Mathematical Society, Mathematical Association of America, and the Society of Industrial and Applied Mathematics. The focus on disciplinary differences also manifested itself in an emphasis on discipline-specific training for ITAs. The theme of collaboration between central and departmental programs emerged at other conferences and in the literature during this period as well.

At both the 1993 Chicago and 1995 Colorado conferences, attention continued to escalate on issues affecting college teaching, such as technology and multiculturalism. At the Colorado conference, sustained discussion of a broader notion of professional development, which included the research and service roles of faculty, was introduced by several campuses, including Bowling Green, Minnesota, Florida State, Virginia Tech, and Syracuse. The national Preparing Future Faculty Program (see Chapter 16), funded by the Pew Charitable Trusts and jointly coordinated by the American Association of Colleges and Universities and the Council of Graduate Schools, offered first reports on its accomplishments toward these same goals on the 17 campuses that were a part of the program. Syracuse University, the American Association of Colleges, and the Council of Independent Colleges had taken a similarly broad perspective on future faculty preparation in projects they had previously initiated. The focus on partnerships—between departments and central programs, between research faculty and faculty from liberal arts and comprehensive institutions, between universities and industry—was just becoming prominent during this period. The idea of a developmental continuum for graduate students—from initial teaching experiences to more complex responsibilities under the mentorship of others to documentation through portfolios—was central to new projects. These were captured by the Colorado conference theme, "The Professional Apprenticeship." Attention focused as well on the job market and professional ethics.

PRESENT

The themes that led up to the present have coalesced into six central ideas prominent in the literature and national discussion today.

- *Professional development efforts center on teaching in the broader sense of the term.* They can focus not only on teaching in formal settings but also on the kind of teaching that occurs when engineers train new professionals to use the office's computer-assisted design system or research chemists brief a corporation on a commercial application for their work. Further, even those who will be in faculty positions will have to learn to teach in nontraditional settings and to apply their talents in different roles, such as instructional designers of electronic resources or teachers in a "virtual campus" environment.

- *Professional development efforts encompass other aspects of future careers besides teaching.* The responsibility for graduate education to provide background for the full range of skills and knowledge needed for future professionals has been increasingly recognized. While some programs that have a mission focused on teaching continue to specialize in this area, other programs have expanded their scope. For example, the Preparing Future Faculty (PFF) Program is addressing the totality of the faculty career, including the research and service dimensions. Other programs increasingly offered by graduate schools are addressing ethics, communication skills, teamwork skills, and the multiple dimensions of preparation for nonfaculty careers.

- *Professional development efforts are for all graduate students.* Although the main participants are likely to be teaching assistants, graduate students who are research fellows, administrative associates, or who are on their own also need professional development. Many of these will aspire to academic careers, and most will be in careers where they will be teaching others in some way.

- *Professional development efforts go beyond training.* One reason for resistance to teaching preparation is the belief that such preparation will consist only of skills training, which seems trivial. Formal attention to teaching preparation involves cultivating habits of reflection and developing conceptualizations and frameworks for practice to organize and evaluate skills and experiential knowledge gained prior to employment or on the job.

- *Professional development efforts should extend over the course of the graduate student program and into the early faculty/professional years.* Ongoing scholarship (see Chapter 4, for example) is describing stages in the experience of learning to teach. Each stage has different issues and ways of fostering growth in teaching. For example, the new college teacher needs survival skills, ways of conceptualizing teaching and learning, frequent feedback, close mentoring and encouragement, and limited responsibilities. As graduate students become more experienced, they need collegial dialogue with mentors and peers that focuses on problematic assumptions. They also need to have more independent responsibility.

- *Professional development efforts require a team effort.* The work of preparing future faculty belongs not only to the advisers, the beleaguered course supervisor, the faculty developer, the peer, but to all. It requires collaboration of multiple offices on campus, from offices that deal with English as a Second Language to those that deal with student development. And, as the PFF Project has advocated, those who will be hiring these teachers in the future, such as small liberal arts colleges, community colleges, and other kinds of postsecondary institutions, should help in the preparation of these teachers. A similar situation exists in informal educational settings as students do co-ops, internships, and other learning experiences outside the college setting.

Recent interventions that have stimulated thinking and action include the continuing work of the PFF (Gaff & Lambert, 1996) and the Consortium on the Preparation of Graduate Students as College Teachers, both funded by the Pew Charitable Trusts; the continuation of the national TA conferences, including the 1997 Minnesota offering; and the increased work of professional associations, campus development programs, and graduate schools. Developments in higher education that are looking more generally at the future of the professoriate, such as the New Pathways project of the American Association for Higher Education and the work of the National Center on Postsecondary Teaching, Assessment, and Learning, have also been influential.

The literature on graduate student professional development is also beginning to expand, with the appearance of *The Journal of Graduate Teaching Assistant Development,* publications devoted to graduate student professional issues, such as the proceedings from the two most recent national TA conferences (Border, 1998; Heenan & Jerich, 1995) and Lambert & Tice's 1993 guide to programs, and publications for teaching associates themselves, such as Lambert, Tice, and Featherstone (1996). More research-based pieces are also appearing in these sources.

Many institutions, such as the University of California at Berkeley and Stanford University, have also expanded their focus on faculty who work with graduate student professional development issues and regularly have conferences or workshops for TA coordinators, graduate chairs, and others. The publication of Nyquist and Wulff's *Working Effectively with Graduate Students* (1996) has formalized and encouraged this work. Work on documenting preparation for faculty careers has been enhanced by the popularity of portfolios, notations on transcripts, and certificate programs (see Chapters 13 and 15).

FUTURE

Literature on change and the future proliferates. Such trends as the increasing diversity of the student population, advances in instructional technology, competition from private industry to provide education, and combining work and study hold the potential for dramatically changing the roles of future faculty. Several essays (Barr & Tagg, 1995; Cox & Richlin, 1993; Dolence & Norris, 1995; Oblinger & Rush, 1997; Smith & Waller, 1997) identify patterns in the way in which education has been structured and delivered and predict changes that will take place in the future:

- From a focus on teaching to a focus on learning

- From one-way communication in the classroom to interactive communication

- From a predesigned sequence of course content to student-sequenced learning

- From live settings to virtual settings

- From learning during a certain span of the life cycle to lifelong learning

- From standardized assessment to outcomes and performance assessment

- From competition to collaboration

What do these directions suggest for preparing graduate students to teach? To begin with, if totally new ways of conceiving of higher education come about, there may be a need for significantly fewer teachers; thus, other ways of supporting graduate education might need to be pursued. For example, Tate (1995) speculates that production, delivery, and certification organizations (PDCs) may begin to deliver education commercially. Boundaries between place of employment and place of learning, or between place of learning and home might blur. In this scenario, residential instruction would be more the exception than the norm. Residential instruction would largely be for the socialization of traditional-age undergraduates and would take place in equivalents of today's liberal arts or community colleges. Universities, much reduced in size without their residential undergraduate population, would focus on basic research and the training of new subject matter experts and researchers. Graduate students, in this arrangement, conceivably might be employed not by the graduate institutions themselves but by PDCs that would employ them as tutors, subject matter suppliers, instructional designers, or testers. They might also work as assistants in the liberal arts or community colleges, where undergraduates would be studying.

But the change goes beyond the graduate years and new kinds of graduate assistantships. If excellent, flexible-use instructional units on almost every range of subject matter are available commercially, and courses are no longer individually designed and delivered by faculty developing their own version of courses such as Sociology 101, the role of future faculty will also change. Fewer lecturers and course designers would be needed, and more people who can facilitate information processing, assess learning, and coach and motivate learners would be employed, often outside university settings. These changes would have ramifications for professionals in teaching roles outside academia as well because there would be a similar impact on the role of trainers and others who are routinely in information-presentation roles. A case in point are the videotaped instructions that are increasingly replacing personal delivery in such common venues as airplanes and hospitals.

Even if, as is quite possible, a less dramatic future is in store, the skills and knowledge base of graduate student teachers and of future teachers in higher education and professional settings generally will likely need to include the following:

- *Deep understanding of one discipline along with an appreciation for interdisciplinary connections.* The traditional focus on teachers as content matter experts is not likely to change, but as information shifts and proliferates rapidly, the ability to know how to access and evaluate information in a given field and to relate ideas and approaches of other fields will continue to grow in importance.

- *Skill in interactive pedagogy.* If the emphasis changes from "teaching as telling" to a focus on helping others learn, the task of the teacher changes from the notion of information transfer to facilitating "learning to learn." Working with students to help them learn how to access and use information is quite different from presenting information: It requires interaction with the learner and coaching skills. These teaching skills are not learned implicitly as a graduate student masters a discipline, but only through explicit concept-building, observation, practice, and reflection.

- *Understanding of student learning.* In order to be a learning coach, a teacher must have some model of the variety of ways in which students learn and how to facilitate these. Again, explicit attention to exploring the nature of learning would be a part of graduate education (see Chapter 5).

- *Knowledge of instructional design.* Those graduate students or faculty who are designing instructional units (and there will probably be fewer of these people needed if there comes a time when courses are not continually reinvented) will need to have a sophisticated knowledge of design principles. Rather than developing materials in idiosyncratic fashion, they will need to understand principles of sequencing, screen design and effective visual presentation, redundancy, the use of examples, and such conventions as hypertext glosses and branching options.

- *Teamwork.* While basic technical knowledge and computer competencies will likely be required in tomorrow's postsecondary teacher, the ability to work with a team in designing and delivering instruction is perhaps even more important. Graphic artists, videographers, programmers, systems analysts, and others—along with subject matter experts—will likely be involved in developing instructional units.

- *Links with experience.* Materials, whether for the course as it has been traditionally delivered, or in one of the future scenarios, will need to be linked more closely to the workplace and everyday life settings. Already a shift from lock-step education to stop-in/stop-out learning is occurring. Faculty in traditional settings are observing that they have more nontraditional-age learners and that traditional-age students are in the workplace as they study. Accordingly, graduate students in present or future teaching roles will need to learn how to engage students in the application and evaluation of knowledge.

- *Appreciation for difference.* Similarly, as the student population increases in diversity, college teachers in the future will more frequently be called upon to know how to build on life experience, cultural background, learning style, and other dimensions of difference to help students relate their prior experience to new information and to use their strengths to influence the development of new knowledge. This will continue to be true for those teaching in workplace settings.

- *Assessment techniques.* As assessment strategies focus on certification of performance rather than short-term recall or "seat time" at an institution, future postsecondary teachers will need to understand principles of assessment, including delineating outcomes, devising authentic tests, and developing scoring rubrics and other strategies for assessing learning effects. Once again, this knowledge is not ordinarily offered in a Ph.D. program nor readily discovered intuitively, so explicit attention during the graduate program will have to be devoted to these issues.

- *An understanding and facility with human relations.* As teaching professionals work with teams on instructional development projects, skills in dealing with the interpersonal dynamics of these teams will be important. Additionally, as facilitators of both individual and collaborative student learning, teaching professionals in the future will undoubtedly be called upon more frequently than their counterparts today to intervene, motivate, help resolve conflict, and build teamwork. While these skills are often assumed in new Ph.D.s, specific preparation would help to ensure that they have solid background in this vital area.

A look at this list reveals that though the context might be different, the skills and knowledge base of future teaching professionals will likely differ more in emphasis and degree than in type. Historically, the expectation has been that seasoned teachers will develop these attributes through experience and that, if this development does not happen, students will learn even without skilled teachers. The privacy of the classroom and distorted notions of academic freedom have permitted one-way presentations, done well or poorly, to substitute for teaching. Future realities quite possibly will eliminate this approach. It is thus more urgent than ever to focus on effective preparation of future postsecondary teaching professionals.

In a visionary speech launching the Teaching Initiative of the American Association for Higher Education, then-President Russell Edgerton (1990) pictured a future setting in which respect for the importance of learning to teach pervades graduate student education, from the chair who emphasizes that all professionals will be teachers in some way, to qualifying exams that test students on their ability to communicate their discipline, to teaching apprenticeships and residencies as part of the graduate experience. That vision fits well with the needs of higher education today but is even more crucial to its needs in the future.

REFERENCES

Barr, R. B., & Tagg, J. (1995). From teaching to learning: A new paradigm for undergraduate education. *Change, 27* (6), 13-25.

Border, L. (Ed.). (1998). *The professional apprenticeship: TAs in the 21st century.* Stillwater, OK: New Forums.

Brown, F. (1993, November). An institutional response to state legislative and regional accreditation mandates regarding teaching assistants. Program description from the conference, *Teaching graduate students to teach: Engaging the disciplines,* p. 26, Chicago, IL.

Buerkel-Rothfuss, N. L., & Gray, P. L. (1991). Teaching assistant training: The view from the top. In J. D. Nyquist, R. D. Abbott, D. H. Wulff, & J. Sprague (Eds.), *Preparing the professoriate of tomorrow to teach.* Dubuque, IA: Kendall/Hunt.

Carroll, J. G. (1980). Effects of training programs for university teaching assistants. *Journal of Higher Education, 51* (2), 167-83.

Chism, N. V. N. (Ed.). (1987). *Institutional responsibilities and responses in the employment and education of teaching assistants.* Columbus, OH: The Ohio State University, Center for Teaching Excellence.

Cox, M. D., & Richlin, L. (1993). Emerging trends in college teaching for the 21st century. *Journal on Excellence in College Teaching, 4,* 1-7.

Darling, A. L. (1987). TA socialization: A communication perspective. In N. V. N. Chism (Ed.), *Institutional responses and responsibilities in the employment and education of teaching assistants.* Columbus, OH: The Ohio State University, Center for Teaching Excellence.

Dolence, M., & Norris, D. (1995). *Transforming higher education: A vision for learning in the 21st century.* Ann Arbor, MI: Society for College and University Planning.

Eble, K. (1987). Defending the indefensible. In N. V. N. Chism (Ed.), *Institutional responses and responsibilities in the employment and education of teaching assistants.* Columbus, OH: The Ohio State University, Center for Teaching Excellence.

Edgerton, R. (1990). The teaching initiative. *AAHE Bulletin, 42* (6), 15-18.

Ervin, G., & Muyskens, J. A. (1982). On training TAs: Do we know what they want and need? *Foreign Language Annals, 15* (5), 335-44.

Gaff, J. G., & Lambert, L. M. (1996). Socializing future faculty to the values of the undergraduate education. *Change, 28* (4), 38-43.

Heenan, T. A., & Jerich, K. F. (Eds.). (1995.) *Teaching graduate students to teach: Engaging the disciplines.* Urbana-Champaign, IL: University of Illinois at Urbana-Champaign, Office of Conferences and Institutes.

Lambert, L. M., & Tice, S. L. (1993). *Preparing graduate students to teach: A guide to programs that improve undergraduate education and develop tomorrow's faculty.* Washington, DC: American Association for Higher Education.

Lambert, L. M., Tice, S. L., & Featherstone, P. H. (Eds.). (1996). *University teaching: A guide for graduate students.* Syracuse, NY: Syracuse University Press.

Lewis, K. G. (1993). *The TA experience: Preparing for multiple roles.* Stillwater, OK: New Forums Press.

Lewis, K. G. (1997, May). *Training focused on postgraduate teaching assistants: The North American model.* Invited paper presentation for a series of joint research seminars held by the Society for Research into Higher Education and the Committee of Vice-Chancellors and Principals of the Universities of the United Kingdom, London University, London, England.

MacAllister, A. (1966). The preparation of college teachers of modern foreign language. *The Modern Language Journal, 50* (6), 402.

Minkel, C. W. (1987). A graduate dean's perspective. In N. V. N. Chism (Ed.), *Institutional responses and responsibilities in the employment and education of teaching assistants.* Columbus, OH: The Ohio State University, Center for Teaching Excellence.

Nyquist, J. D., & Wulff, D. H. (1996). *Working effectively with graduate assistants.* Thousand Oaks, CA: Sage.

Nyquist, J. D., Abbott, R. D., & Wulff, D. H. (1989a). The challenge of TA training in the 1990s. In J. D. Nyquist, R. D. Abbott, & D. H. Wulff (Eds.), *Teaching assistant training in the 1990s.* New Directions for Teaching and Learning, No. 39. San Francisco, CA: Jossey-Bass.

Nyquist, J. D., Abbott, R. D., & Wulff, D. H. (Eds.). (1989b). *Teaching assistant training in the 1990s.* New Directions for Teaching and Learning, No. 39. San Francisco, CA: Jossey-Bass.

Nyquist, J. D., Abbott, R. D., Wulff, D. H., & Sprague, J. (Eds.). (1991). *Preparing the professoriate of tomorrow to teach: Selected readings in TA training.* Dubuque, IA: Kendall/Hunt.

Oblinger, D. G., & Rush, S. C. (1997). The learning revolution. In D. G. Oblinger & S. C. Rush (Eds.), *The learning revolution: The challenge of information technology in the academy.* Bolton, MA: Anker.

Parrett, J. (1987). A ten-year review of TA training programs. In N. V. N. Chism (Ed.), *Institutional responses and responsibilities in the employment and education of teaching assistants.* Columbus, OH: The Ohio State University, Center for Teaching Excellence.

Richlin, L. (1995). Preparing the faculty of the future to teach. In W. A. Wright (Ed.), *Teaching improvement practices.* Bolton, MA: Anker.

Rudolph, F. (1977). *Curriculum: A history of the American undergraduate course of study since 1636.* San Francisco, CA: Jossey-Bass.

Ruiz, H. (1987). The role of technique in teacher training. In N. V. N. Chism (Ed.), *Institutional responses and responsibilities in the employment and education of teaching assistants.* Columbus, OH: The Ohio State University, Center for Teaching Excellence.

Schultz, R. (1980). TA training, supervision, and evaluation. *Association of the Department of Foreign Languages Bulletin, 12* (1), 1-8.

Smith, K. A., & Waller, A. A. (1997). Afterward: New paradigms for college teaching. In W. E. Campbell & K. A. Smith (Eds.), *New paradigms for college teaching.* Edina, MN: Interaction Book Company.

Sprague, J., & Nyquist, J. D. (1991). A developmental perspective on the TA role. In J. D. Nyquist, R. D. Abbott, D. H. Wulff, & J. Sprague (Eds.), *Preparing the professoriate of tomorrow to teach.* Dubuque, IA: Kendall/Hunt.

Tate, R. (1995). At the crossroad: Higher ed and technology development. *Technos, 4* (4), 26-30.

vom Saal, D. R. (1987). The undergraduate experience and international teaching assistants. In N. V. N. Chism (Ed.), *Institutional responses and responsibilities in the employment and education of teaching assistants.* Columbus, OH: The Ohio State University, Center for Teaching Excellence.

Yoder, D. D., & Hugenberg, L. W. (1982). A survey of in-service teacher training programs for graduate teaching assistants. *Association for Communication Administration Bulletin, 39,* 59-63.

2

The Role of Centralized Programs in Preparing Graduate Students to Teach

Jacqueline A. Mintz

Although the professional development of graduate students as teachers has often required working against resistance or helping to create a culturally conducive climate, centralized programs currently abound in North America (Lambert & Tice, 1993). As the demand for higher education has increased and the size of undergraduate student bodies grown, so has the need for graduate student instructors to teach the discussion and laboratory sections of lecture courses. In large research institutions, graduate students also function as primary instructors in teaching foreign language and English composition courses. Institution-wide programs dedicated to integrating policy and services for teaching assistant preparation have proven advantageous to all the constituencies involved, from undergraduates, graduate students, and faculty, to departments, colleges, and administrators. The current plethora of centralized programs—their scope and accomplishments—attests to a new institutional awareness and commitment to this endeavor.

This chapter examines the role and issues surrounding centralized programs in the professional development of teaching assistants. It describes the essential aspects of centralized programs, the needs which must be met in order for the programs to function effectively within their institutions, the advantages and disadvantages of centralized programs, and, finally, possible future directions for centralized programs.

INFRASTRUCTURE AND INSTITUTIONAL PLACEMENT

Centralized programs are generally directed by a professional who holds a Ph.D. and may range from a staff of one to many. When funds are available, there is usually a combination of one or more professionals, graduate students experienced in teaching, and clerical support staff. In some institutions, departmental faculty may also become part of the staff, in a hands-on—or an advisory—capacity, on a rotating basis, part- or full-time. By far the majority of centralized programs are responsible for work with both faculty and teaching assistants. However, a small number of programs, such as the University of California, Berkeley, the University of Colorado at Boulder, and Syracuse University, have centers dedicated exclusively to working with teaching assistants. Though the goal is the professional development of teaching assistants, campus faculty may attend or give presentations as a part of centralized office programming.

The reporting lines and placement of centralized programs reflect their institutional charge and their relationship to the campus. While not as varied as the types of support provided for TAs, there is significant diversity in the reporting lines of centralized programs. In some schools they report to the highest academic officer, while in others they report to the provost for undergraduate affairs, to college deans, or to directors. They can even share reporting lines to senior graduate and undergraduate student academic officers. Nor do these examples exhaust the options.

While it may be optimal to consider the mission, needs, resources, and support within the institution in an integrated fashion before creating a centralized teaching assistant program, current reporting lines and locations of TA programs evidence a continuum from hasty additions to existing instructional development programs (Gappa, 1991) to more deliberate planning. Given the uniqueness of institutions, even with careful forethought, decisions would undoubtedly diverge. For instance, if one of a school's priorities is to focus on the needs of graduate student instructors as developing professionals in addition to the improvement of undergraduate education, placing a centralized program in the graduate school may facilitate the creation and implementation of policy. Another institution may opt to combine faculty and graduate student programs, on the other hand, precisely because of a strong belief that all teaching faculty belong on a single professional development track.

PROGRAM SUPPORT AND ACCOUNTABILITY

Though programs are variously situated in terms of their reporting lines, there is no dispute about the need to garner strong administrative and faculty support in order to secure the legitimacy, credibility, visibility, and resources to enable programs to thrive (Lambert & Tice, 1993; Smith, Byrd, Constantinides, & Barrett, 1991). For those getting started, Hiiemae, Lambert, and Hayes (1991) suggest that the program's outlines be worked out by a task force of planners drawn broadly from the campus, who in turn consult the community, in order to ensure "ownership and allegiance to the program" (p. 128). "Gaining that understanding and support is a complicated assignment for those who direct centralized TA programs, because each academic department has a unique culture, with traditions that must be respected; at most major research institutions, this means interacting with well over 50 departments on TA issues" (Lambert & Tice, 1993, p. 13).

Most centralized programs work with a campus-wide advisory committee consisting of the crucial constituencies affected by the program's outreach. These normally include central administrators, faculty from across the disciplines, and graduate students. These advisory committees suggest and sometimes set policy for the entire campus. Their various tasks might include advocating for specific teaching assistant issues on campus, helping to secure funding and publicity, advising the centralized program on current and prospective services, setting program priorities, acting as liaison with other related committees, supporting centralized program services, awarding departmental grants to faculty for teaching assistant preparation, choosing award winners among teaching assistants, and attending and sometimes speaking at functions which recognize teaching excellence among graduate student instructors.

Given the major roles of the advisory committee, program staff need to pay attention to continuity in the membership and the education of new members. A committee of primarily new members, uneducated in the history, mission, and approach of the centralized program, can detract from or even derail hard-won program-building efforts. Program directors need to work closely with the advisory committee chair to maintain a balance between experienced and new members, to educate new members about the committee history and program mission, and to set a clear and continuously updated agenda for each academic year. Most important is to bring members onto the committee who wish to work in support of teaching on campus in general and within their own departments. Obtaining participation of those faculty who have been recognized for both research and distinguished teaching sends a message to the community that teaching, along with research, is an institutional priority.

Centralized programs need to communicate and coordinate with all campus-wide units which provide services to teaching assistants in order to maximize the effectiveness of these services. Sending a calendar of tentatively scheduled events to campus colleagues promotes cooperation and prevents both redundant and conflicting scheduling for teaching assistants. This is particularly important in planning the fall orientation and teaching conference, a seminal event which could overlap with departmental orientations, receptions for new graduate students, and sundry responsibilities confronting new teaching assistants. Of utmost importance is the need to establish and maintain open and productive communication with administrative assistants and secretaries who work with teaching assistants in the departments. While policy decisions and implementation involve the chairs and other departmental faculty, the success of the central office programming often depends directly on the willingness of departmental staff to act as a conduit of information and even as advocates for its goals.

An adequate and dependable budget is essential to building a credible and effective program. Financial support for centralized programs comes from a variety of sources, the institution itself being primary among them. Funding also comes from "alumni associations, state governments, federal grants, language institutes" (Lambert & Tice, 1993, pp. 7–8) and donors. In order to maintain funding, centralized programs need to develop a philosophy and services whose goals reflect the values of the institution, its culture, and the subcultures within the departments. Loeher (1987) puts it this way: "I would argue that no program that openly violates or conflicts with the cultural norms and values of the institution will last for very long nor have much impact while it endures" (p. 106). Conversely, the institution creating a teaching assistant program must demonstrate a "deep-rooted and continuing commitment to the program's goals and objectives. . . . Without that commitment, and without its regular public affirmation at the highest levels, the program will not get the initial or continuing attention it deserves, and its long-term vitality will be impaired" (Hiiemae, Lambert, & Hayes, 1991, p. 129).

Support and accountability go hand-in-hand. Reporting lines generally determine the extent and nature of accountability within the institution. Some directors are asked for a yearly report describing their programming and evaluating its success; others must submit more detailed and frequent accounting. Orientations, workshops, and most one-time offerings are usually evaluated by a participant questionnaire at the conclusion of the event. Long-term events, like seminars and credential programs, are evaluated both short- and long-term to determine the lasting value or extent of change which has taken place during and following these events. Other means of determining programming effectiveness are to solicit feedback from program instructors, departments, and undergraduates. While it is difficult to assess the actual effect that working with TAs has on student learning, there is a great deal of interest in improving research methods for determining the effectiveness of all teaching assistant programming.

As a means to plan and create new programs, many directors collect more data and conduct more evaluations than is required by their academic officers. Research into their own programs helps the staff and advisory committee to learn what is having a desired impact and what is not. It also reveals outcomes which may not have been envisioned at the start. An evaluation and research unit on campus may suggest and help to conduct additional assessment activities of value to administrators and program staff (Hiiemae, Lambert, & Hayes, 1991). Some centralized programs have begun to take advantage of the opportunity to invite outside reviewers to evaluate their work and to make recommendations for future directions. These reviews may be requested by the centralized program staff, the advisory committee, senior administrators, or all three. Similar to a departmental review, professionals from other schools, together with faculty from the program's own campus, appraise the current program, interview program staff and impacted constituencies, and deliver an oral or written report for the centralized program and the administrators involved. Such reviews can provide a valuable perspective and help campus administrators and faculty to educate themselves about their own campus, the field of professional development for teaching assistants, and work being done on other campuses.

PROGRAM VALUES AND IMAGE

Centralized programs work more effectively if they have a clearly stated philosophy and mission. The philosophy manifests the beliefs and operating principles of the program and its staff while the mission delineates the ends toward which the program strives. A philosophy that informs daily practice, as defined in the mission statement, can be conveyed readily to new staff, advisory committee members, and to the communities with which the program works. For example, if one philosophical tenet of a centralized program is that individual teaching assistants are best served by maintaining confidentiality concerning one-on-one consultations, one goal of the program's mission might be to enhance the quality of undergraduate education by improving graduate teaching through confidential consultation. The philosophy and mission statements generally derive from program staff in consultation with the advisory committee. They reflect the assessed needs of the institution, including the constituencies impacted by the program. In this way, the campus community can put its support behind the program.

Centralized programs—because they exist apart from but work in conjunction with the departments—have an overview of their campuses, enabling them to see both the complex realities and the potential for improving the environment for valuing teaching. Allegiance to philosophy and mission does not mean maintaining the status quo. On the contrary, a fundamental responsibility of centralized programs is to stimulate change, to take risks, and to elicit new ways of thinking about how to achieve desired ends. Through working with their administrators and advisory committee and by having staff members placed on high-level committees, many centralized programs play a significant role in shaping policy determining the nature and extent of teaching assistant preparation on campus. A reputation on campus for integrity and quality work over time lends centralized programs, as agents of change, the authority to bring a healthy dissonance into their institutions.

In addition to integrity and quality work, centralized programs need to be aware of the differences in culture, style, interests, and values among the departments and individuals with whom they engage. Disciplines, faculty, and TAs are all comprised of different backgrounds, orientations, and world views, and they present a wide variety of approaches to teaching and learning. "The strongest programs are apt to develop when central unit staff can communicate appropriate educational principles in the language and style of each academic area. Such programs avoid inappropriate, reductionist, skill-based approaches" (Smock & Menges, 1985, p. 32). Professionalism and flexibility—grounded in knowledge, expertise, and experience—are essential to the profile of central program staff.

A positive and professional image is important for gaining access to the various communities on campus. While word of mouth is the most important recommendation for establishing a clientele, program communications need to reflect high standards in both form and content. Exposure to centralized programs for most of the campus population usually occurs through official correspondence, a handbook, newsletters, flyers, posters, news releases, videos, brochures, event-related materials, evaluations and surveys, sundry publications, email, and the World Wide Web. All of these warrant careful attention.

Many centralized programs work to maintain a high profile on campus, in their regions and states, across the country, and even in international educational development efforts. Staff members teach, present their work at conferences, sit on association boards and work on committees, referee journal articles and conference presentations, consult for other institutions, carry on their own research and writing, serve as editors for publications, and participate in national and international projects. Exposure to others' programs and conference attendance have been reported as the two most significant factors in preparing professionals for their work in educational development (Graf & Wheeler, 1996). Keeping up with the literature, together with actively engaging with colleagues in the field through various enterprises, contributes to the vision and practice of centralized programming on individual campuses.

ELEMENTS OF CENTRALIZED PROGRAMS

In attempting to highlight exemplary types of programs, many writers have noted the diversity among them, asserting "there are almost as many varieties in the types of support provided to teaching assistants as there are institutions offering them" (Diamond & Wilbur, 1990, p. 204). Though it is necessary and appropriate to examine similarities among programs, it is equally important to appreciate the differences in types of institutions, resources available, administrative and departmental support, size of the faculty and student body, and the institutional and subgroup cultures on each campus. While components of programs may be borrowed and adapted to new settings, owing to the realities of each particular context, no two programs will look exactly alike.

Graduate student teaching is at the heart of the centralized program. Understanding the stages of teacher—specifically TA—development and the different challenges required at each stage (Nyquist & Sprague, 1992; Ronkowski, 1993) is essential to designing programs to meet real needs. Some programs focus exclusively on teaching while others incorporate issues such as time management, preparing to be a faculty member, and courses on American higher education. On most campuses, domestic and international teaching assistants (ITAs) alike partake in all regular programming and services. In addition, most programs work with English as a Second Language or comparable campus units to assess and improve oral English language skills of the ITAs and to provide them with cultural and pedagogical preparation for teaching in the North American classroom. Some universities, such as the University of California, Berkeley, provide assessment and academic coursework within their own centers for prospective and current ITAs.

Beginning with orientations and teaching conferences, centralized programs have matured to provide an extraordinary array of services to individual teaching assistants, often in collaboration with departments or other service units on campus. For instance, some centralized programs provide free videotaping and consultation services in-house. Others contract with the campus office of media services to videotape the TA's section, but program staff provide the consultation. Still others train faculty or experienced teaching assistants in the departments to videotape and consult with TAs as a part of the departmental training program.

Centralized programs today stress the importance of comprehensive, ongoing preparation that combines centralized with departmental resources and expertise. Just as programs have moved from one-time orientations to integrated and developmental learning about teaching and the contemporary classroom, so they have shifted from skill-based to more reflective, theory-based approaches.

Most of the following services are found in centralized programs:

- Campus-wide orientation and teaching conference once or twice a year

- General or special interest workshops/seminars
- Consultation with individual TAs and faculty who teach with and prepare TAs in the departments
- Custom-designed workshops delivered within departments
- Microteaching
- Videotaping
- Classroom observation
- Small Group Instructional Diagnosis (SGID) (See Chapter 12)
- Grants to departments for programs to prepare TAs
- Library of resources: print, audio, video
- Awards/receptions in recognition of excellent teaching by TAs
- Preparing TAs to work as apprentices in educational development
- Program publications: handbook, newsletters, brochures, flyers, event- and subject-specific materials
- A World Wide Web page

Additional services may include:

- In-house English-language screening and courses for prospective and current ITAs
- A course in college teaching (see Chapter 8)
- Programs for departmental TA supervisors
- A seminar for faculty teaching with TAs
- Regular meetings with designated faculty representatives and/or TAs from departments
- Grants to TAs to improve teaching/learning in their labs, sections, or courses
- Certificate/diploma programs
- A listserv/computer bulletin board for TAs campus-wide
- Files of discipline-specific teaching materials

- Computer hardware and software for use in teaching

- Facilities to videotape and edit instructional videotapes

Over the last decade, many centralized programs have become partners with outside associations and granting agencies to offer new initiatives for preparing teaching assistants for future faculty positions. These projects (described in Chapter 16) are funded on special or continuing funds and address a specific group or aspect of teaching in higher education. Centralized programs provide a natural home for these initiatives, which involve graduate students in study and experience on and off their campuses.

OPPORTUNITIES AFFORDED BY CENTRALIZED PROGRAMS

Undergraduates are generally the first beneficiaries considered when discussing the benefits of programs to improve the preparation of teaching assistants. However, there are advantages to centralized programs for everyone involved with TAs. Within the institution, the central placement of the program allows for fluid communication with administration and departments. For the institution at large, the high visibility of the program assures students, parents, legislatures, funding agencies, potential donors, and the public that quality teaching is valued on campus.

From the Centralized Program Perspective

"The strength of a centralized program is its campus-wide perspective and concern for a professional instruction climate" (Gappa, 1991, p. 87). Working from a pedagogical orientation, centralized programs have the ability to assess needs throughout the institution and to work with an expert staff within and beyond traditional departmental or unit boundaries to find appropriate responses. This flexibility permits a flow of ideas and resources which enriches the overall teaching environment. As one program director (Andrews, 1987) wrote:

> We are a link to the body of research and writing on instructional methods and can often suggest fresh teaching ideas. We can be expert on the skills involved in eliciting participation, fostering learning, enhancing student self-esteem, and many other functions that cut across all disciplines...I have found that, with increasing experi-

ence, I have learned how to translate general teaching approaches into discipline-specific terms—to use brainstorming to analyze a literary work or to foster mathematical problem solving skills... (p. 109).

Most centralized programs help initiate and support departmental programs for teaching assistants. In so doing, they are able to bring research, resources, experience, experts, and often grants to advance departmental efforts. Familiarity with programs across campus and across the country enables centralized program staff to recommend particular strategies or a variety of options and materials. Data about the effectiveness of certain practices may even be available to help in making decisions about which alternatives to choose. For example, workshops on teaching and learning styles and developing teaching portfolios have become a staple of many centralized programs. Centralized program staff can help maximize the benefits of the portfolio for each student by helping to design a portfolio component into discipline-specific departmental teaching seminars.

Sharing materials and expertise among departments is only one way in which centralized programs work to build community in support of improving teaching. Over the course of each year, the advisory committee, special interest groups, TA or faculty focus groups, and staff programs bring together disparate members of the campus population to improve teaching assistant preparation. These programs provide opportunities for faculty and TAs to work closely with colleagues from other departments. At the University of California, Los Angeles, and Florida State University, teaching assistant consultants (TACs) and members of the Teaching Associate Program (Gappa, 1992, 1993; Gappa, Gaddis, Rogers, & Wholey, 1993) respectively carry out responsibilities to their departments and to the centralized programs. At UCLA these teaching assistants are funded entirely through the centralized program for the quarters they are jointly appointed. At Stanford University, the Center for Teaching and Learning runs a volunteer program of peer training and consultation that provides much of the center's individualized services to TAs (Marincovich & Gordon, 1991). Several schools have faculty and TAs mandated as official liaisons between the centralized program and the department. With responsibilities varying according to school, faculty representatives may be asked to attend biannual meetings with advisory committee members and the centralized program staff and to be the departmental contact regarding information and policy on teaching assistant issues.

Faculty and TAs from across the campus working together outside the department over common concerns creates a safe and neutral atmosphere to share thoughts and ideas. Teaching assistants claim that they can talk openly about their interest in teaching more readily in these contexts than in discussions with their departmental advisers or even with the course instructor. Similarly, outside the department it is easier to work on generic issues of mentoring or how to maximize the faculty-teaching assistant working relationship. To this end, the University of California, Berkeley's Graduate Student Instructor (GSI) Teaching and Resource Center designs and runs a nine-hour seminar over three weeks each spring for faculty teaching with graduate student instructors.

Among all the teaching assistant support units on campus, centralized programs—together with their advisory committees—are best poised to see and integrate particular concerns within the big picture. Informed about national and even international issues involving teaching assistants and continually responsive to administrative, departmental, teaching assistant, and even undergraduate concerns on campus, the centralized program is positioned to make considered and thoughtful recommendations on policy. When a policy has been mandated, on the other hand, the program has the resources and know-how to facilitate implementation. Course 398T is a faculty-taught, department-based, semester-long class on teaching that evolved as a result of a mandate at the University of Texas, Austin. To assist those responsible for such courses, the university's centralized program, the Center for Teaching Effectiveness, offers a seminar for faculty teaching the course, provides materials, a handbook (Lewis, 1992), and special request workshops, in addition to a full panoply of center services for TAs. Also in response to a campus mandate, the Center for Instructional Development and Research at the University of Washington provides a year-long program for international teaching assistants, beginning with a preautumn workshop and continuing with consultations throughout the year.

From the Departmental Perspective

Despite the fact that in most institutions the chief responsibility for TA preparation rests with the departments, that the origin of TA preparation began in the departments, and that numerous departmental faculty may support this work in theory, many departments fail to take the initiative to start comprehensive programs. Those that do start programs—with the notable exception of language departments—generally have responded to limited and specific needs such as safety in chemistry laboratories or orienting teaching assistants to how the department conducts the mechanics of teaching: the location and use of the copy machine, issuing keys, filling out forms to ensure timely paychecks, and so on.

The rise of the centralized program has occasioned a partnership and collaboration of a win-win nature. With support of department-based efforts as a primary part of its mission, centralized programs have, together with departmental faculty, spawned a myriad of custom-designed programs throughout their campuses. Faculty, as well as teaching assistants, have available to them extensive support for their efforts. Many centralized programs also provide grants to accompany their services. These grants may cover the cost of assembling a reader for a graduate-level course on teaching, paying a stipend to an experienced graduate student working with the faculty instructor to design the course or research the reader articles, creating a videotaping and consultant program for teaching assistants in the department, supporting a video about pedagogy specific to teaching in a discipline, or creating an archive of departmental syllabi and materials on pedagogy for current and future TAs and faculty mentors.

Many centralized programs celebrate the accomplishments of the departments, providing rewards and recognition. Program and campus-wide publications share departmental achievements with the community, while distinguished or remarkable undertakings may become the subject of journal articles or monographs. Awards for teaching assistant and even faculty efforts on behalf of teaching assistants are the impetus for annual outstanding teaching receptions. The centralized program, graduate school, or administration may separately or together acknowledge a smaller group of distinguished teacher-scholars for exceptional accomplishments in teaching. Such is the Teaching Effectiveness Award at the University of California, Berkeley, that singles out a limited number of previously acknowledged excellent TAs for defining and responding to a problem in teaching or learning in their sections or laboratories. The award consists of a stipend and the publication of the winning entries, which are then distributed campus-wide. All these awards bring credit to the individuals and to their departments as well.

From the Teaching Assistant and Graduate Student Perspective

There is no question that graduate student allegiance, TA or not, belongs first to the department or discipline. Nevertheless, centralized programs are designed to meet needs that often extend beyond the individual department's expertise or resources. Campus-wide orientations, confidential consultation or video consulting services, teaching portfolio development, and a multitude of programs provide a foundation of knowledge and practice which crosses all disciplines and serves the individual and specialized needs of teaching assistants.

The recognition of teaching excellence through campus-wide awards, certificates, and diplomas adds a dimension to the job résumé beyond acknowledgement of the department alone. In addition to campus-wide recognition for awards, centralized programs offer numerous opportunities for experienced teaching assistants to join professional staff in the development and delivery of programs. Many teaching assistants teach generic and discipline-specific workshops as part of the fall and spring orientation and teaching conferences. Throughout the year, there are workshops and colloquia, seminars, and consultations which offer additional experience and professional development. In their study, Lambert and Tice (1993) found that it is a "hallmark of many programs" to put graduate students in "roles of key responsibility to TA-program leadership" (p. 14). Participation in centralized programs exposes teaching assistants to colleagues and students from every discipline and a variety of backgrounds. It broadens skills and provides a deeper knowledge and appreciation of teaching from an enlarged perspective.

Unexpected advantages which centralized programs have produced include the hands-on preparation of scores of advanced and experienced graduate students who have become professional, part-time, staff members. These students receive a high degree of preparation and perform functions including and beyond the responsibilities of departmental teaching assistants who conduct occasional campus-wide programs. Hired for their superior teaching and interpersonal communication skills, these staff members may work with faculty and teaching assistants from across campus in designing and implementing departmental programs, interpreting midterm teaching evaluation forms, observing classroom teaching, performing guided videotape consultation, sitting on campus-wide committees of faculty and administrators, interviewing orientation workshops leaders, writing or editing program materials or articles for the newsletter, and more. The view of higher education glimpsed from this new vantage point broadens the TA's thinking to encompass issues beyond the scope of a traditional graduate school disciplinary education. The experience that these professionals gain gives them further advantage in their future job searches. In today's tight job market, the skills gained from an instructional development program are highly valued.

SOME ISSUES SURROUNDING CENTRALIZED PROGRAMS

On balance, centralized programs are flourishing in North America. However, the integration of new ideas and change in higher education can be a slow process. No coming-of-age story would be complete without reflecting on the problems and struggles yet to be resolved.

On most campuses today, teaching assistant preparation is considered to be both a right and duty belonging to the departments. In Lambert and Tice's (1993) words, "... the reality is that the quality of the graduate teaching assistantship experience depends directly on how willing faculty in the disciplines are to commit themselves as mentors and guides" (p. 17). Nevertheless, departmental and faculty support for TAs is highly variable. "Some departments devote much time and energy to TAs' preparation; others devote virtually none" (Weimer, Svinicki, & Bauer, 1989, p. 60). Given that few faculty have been prepared for this responsibility, the finding is not surprising.

Whether by mandate or not, centralized programs often find themselves in the position of coordinating university efforts and stepping in when departmental mentoring is lacking. On occasion, sheer presence seems to invite opposition. Some faculty believe that good teaching cannot be taught and that teaching efforts are a waste of time. Others describe all centralized teaching improvement programs as one-size-fits-all: "... teaching is seen as general, generic, and technical, merely a matter of performance ... something outside of what we really do as scholars in our disciplines" (Smith, 1997, p. 5). Very likely it is those with no firsthand knowledge who fault centralized TA programs for being remedial rather than developmental. Most problematic is the faculty member who has no connection to the centralized program but actively discourages teaching assistants from participating in programs that can aid their teaching and raise their self-confidence. For example, international TAs who express interest in improving their English proficiency through centralized program offerings often are advised by faculty not to take these courses because they intrude on the TAs' degree programs.

On the other hand, some centralized program supporters believe that these programs can be all things for all people. Well-meaning recommenders ask staff to take on new responsibilities without added resources or personnel. Many centralized programs have been asked to afford all graduate students, not only teaching assistants, the opportunity to access their offerings. Even if resources are available and staff are hired, the learning curve is steep. Bringing on graduate students—a longtime practice and commitment of many program directors—takes increased time and dedication of experienced staff. Often it takes a year or more for new staff to become prepared in the range of services offered by programs. In an area where continuity and expertise are crucial, teaching assistants ideally should be available to work with the programs for at least two years.

Center directors and assistant directors often teach in their disciplines in addition to carrying out full-time center responsibilities. Most often these professionals do not have tenure or security of employment. Frequently they are not eligible for other privileges enjoyed by more traditional faculty such as priority access to campus technology or the ability to be nominated for outstanding teaching awards. Though many duties come to them by default, precisely because they are in the "center," they are marginalized by comparison to their discipline-identified colleagues in terms of status and pay.

Advocates for broad cultural change in higher education point out that many members of the academy would benefit from a reexamination and readjustment of institutional priorities. Columbia's David Damrosch (1995) identifies individualism, specialization, and isolation among faculty as distinctive of the academy. Products of the star system, these values stand in opposition to the emphasis on collaboration, teamwork, and inclusiveness which are hallmarks of centralized programs. Even when, at the highest level, teaching and mentoring are applauded as desirable achievements and though some faculty may "see themselves as developers of people" (Walker & Quinn, 1996, p. 321), contradictory values continue to undermine the enterprise.

In spite of these unresolved difficulties, most centralized program staff eagerly rise to the challenges presented in their work and embrace the opportunity to be creative and to make a difference. They find their profession fulfilling and are enthusiastic about continuing to improve at what they do. Not unexpectedly, many report an ongoing struggle for more time for reading and research for their own professional development and for the good of their programs (Chism & Szabo, 1996). As educational development becomes more established as a field, it is necessary that institutions explore new ways to support and recognize developers and their significant contributions to teaching and learning in higher education.

FUTURE DIRECTIONS OF CENTRALIZED PROGRAMS

Philip Candy (1996), professor of higher education and director of the Academic Staff Development Unit at the Queensland University of Technology, writes and lectures on faculty and educational developers as knowledge workers in the academy. He draws from the work of K. E. Sveiby (1992), who defines this work as nonstandardized, creative, highly dependent on the work of individuals, and involving complex problem-solving. These qualities, which echo those that developers single out as the most satisfying about their work, are the ones that Candy believes will equip the university for the challenges it faces in the new century.

Most centralized programs, having laid a firm foundation, are primed for meeting new challenges. With reputations for professional expertise and flexibility in working with myriad situations and diverse populations, the staffs of these programs are suited to developing and furthering educational initiatives on their campuses. Primary to fulfilling this role will be the continued education of the whole community about the importance of the centralized program mission in preparing TAs and the value of this mission to the campus. Program personnel who have relied on the good will of volunteer faculty mentors and the support of like-minded administrators will need to focus attention and energy on setting and implementing campus-wide policy. At the University of California, Berkeley, culminating years of preparatory planning, the Graduate Council—the Academic Senate Committee advisory to the Graduate Division which oversees the centralized TA program—has passed a far-reaching policy on the mentoring of teaching assistants and the responsibilities of departments, faculty members, and teaching assistants. It lays the groundwork for both departmental and individual faculty accountability by taking the first steps to include mentoring in individual promotion and tenure and in departmental reviews. As the policy is implemented, the role of the centralized program will be to work even more closely with departments, faculty, and teaching assistants to prepare them for their responsibilities in this collaborative effort. In particular, program staff will endeavor to support individual faculty interested in creating mentoring portfolios and will offer information and expertise to departmental review teams and the university promotion and tenure committee.

Like teaching assistants, whose roles have grown to encompass nontraditional tasks and settings, especially in light of changes in technology, centralized programs will need to continue to initiate creative collaborations beyond traditional boundaries. For example, centralized programs can maximize the strengths and resources of small, related departments by helping them to collaborate in developing a comprehensive TA program to meet the needs of all their respective teaching assistants. They can contribute to collaborative efforts by other teaching support units and teaching assistants themselves. The centralized TA program at UC Berkeley works closely with the Professional Development Program teaching assistants, drawn from several academic departments, whose mission is to design curriculum, create problem sets, and facilitate nontraditional sections for gateway science and math courses.

Additionally, centralized programs will need to continue to work with departments and administrators to urge all responsible parties within the academy to fully prepare both teaching assistants and all graduate students in general for a wide variety of career options. Departments can expand their graduate programs to include serious academic courses on teaching and learning in their discipline. The department of computer sciences and electrical engineering at the University of California, Berkeley, is proposing a minor in teaching for its Ph.D. students. Taking teaching seriously helps candidates gain multiple skills and makes them clear and effective communicators for any future profession. Centralized programs, for their part, are able to work on planning boards, at conferences, and throughout the year with disciplinary, research, and advocacy associations in higher education to ensure their active roles in providing for the future of today's graduate students. Program staffs should continue to collaborate with local colleges, community organizations, and national programs to provide their teaching assistants with a full range of experiences in and related to their fields in order to make them better prepared and more attractive applicants for a variety of roles.

Enthusiasm for contemporary concerns and interests sometimes substitutes for careful needs assessment, planning, and collaboration. This enthusiasm, as in the case of technology advances, can lead to precipitous decision-making within institutions. Centralized programs can—and need to—ask the hard questions: What is the pedagogical value of the proposed changes? How will student learning be enhanced? What are the implications for TAs? Will there be increased responsibility or additional skills required for their positions? How will these skills be acquired? Looking closer to home, as the pressure for more accountability shifts the emphasis from requirements fulfilled to verified outcomes, it is essential that centralized programs revisit their philosophies and mission statements to make certain that their actions and programs are consonant with what they preach. Some centralized programs are currently redefining their mission statements in light of demands to release information about what was formerly considered confidential work with TAs. It is difficult to predict whether external and internal pressures eventually will undermine or reconfigure fundamental tenets of professional practice or what the broad implications of these changes might be. However, it is particularly important to strive for sufficient independence to exercise informed professional judgment whenever the welfare of clients is concerned.

Millenial fervor has taken hold in the academy as it has in society at large. Predictions of doom and delivery mix with the realities of evolving change which, by and large, describe the work of centralized programs from day to day and year to year. Looking at our campuses, we can see for the first time a substantial number of mostly newer faculty who have been swept up in the wave of commitment to teaching with a genuine appreciation for its complexities and the awareness of the need to prepare the next generations of professors for a changing and challenging future. Centralized programs have contributed substantively to the education of this new generation of teacher/scholars. But there is much left to be done. Without question, program staff will need to bring the lessons of history, their own personal experiences, the collaborative wisdom of colleagues, and the mounting research in the field to bear on the continuing and new challenges ahead.

REFERENCES

Andrews, J. D. W. (1987). Department-based and centralized TA training programs. In N. V. N. Chism (Ed.), *Institutional responsibilities and responses in the employment and education of teaching assistants.* Columbus, OH: The Ohio State University, Center for Teaching Excellence.

Candy, P. C. (1996). Promoting lifelong learning: Academic developers and the university as a learning organization. *The International Journal for Academic Development, 1* (1), 1-18.

Chism, N. V. N., & Szabo, B. (1996). Development issues of professional development practitioners. Pilot Study. Ames, IA: POD Network.

Damrosch, D. (1995). *We scholars: Changing the culture of the university.* Cambridge, MA: Harvard University Press.

Diamond, R. M., & Wilbur, F. P. (1990). Developing teaching skills during graduate education. *To Improve the Academy, 9,* 199-207.

Gappa, L. (1991). A professional teaching assistant program: Custom designing for your institution. *The Journal of Staff, Program, & Organization Development, 9* (2), 83-92.

Gappa, L. (1992). Effective programming for TA development. *To Improve the Academy, 9,* 207-216.

Gappa, L. (1993). TA programs which provide a bridge to professorial careers. In T. A. Heenan & K. F. Jerich (Eds.), *Teaching graduate students to teach: Engaging the disciplines.* Champaign, IL: Office of Conferences and Institutes.

Gappa, L., Gaddis, B. K., Rogers, E., & Wholey, D. (1993). Teaching associate program: Fusing disciplinary knowledge and university-wide teaching improvement tools. In T. A. Heenan & K. F. Jerich (Eds.), *Teaching graduate students to teach: Engaging the disciplines.* Champaign, IL: Office of Conferences and Institutes.

Graf, D. L., & Wheeler, D. (1996). *Defining the field: The POD membership survey.* Ames, IA: POD Network.

Hiiemae, K., Lambert, L., & Hayes, D. (1991). How to establish and run a comprehensive teaching assistant training program. In J. D. Nyquist, R. D. Abbott, D. H. Wulff, & J. Sprague (Eds.), *Preparing the professoriate of tomorrow to teach: Selected readings in TA training.* Dubuque, IA: Kendall/Hunt.

Lambert, L., & Tice, S. (1993). *Preparing graduate students to teach: A guide to programs that improve undergraduate education and develop tomorrow's faculty.* Washington, DC: American Association for Higher Education.

Lewis, K. G. (1992). *Teaching pedagogy to teaching assistants: A handbook for 398T instructors.* Austin, TX: The University of Texas, Center for Teaching Effectiveness.

Loeher, L. (1987). Factors in locating a program within the university organization. In N. V. N. Chism (Ed.), *Institutional responsibilities and responses in the employment and education of teaching assistants.* Columbus, OH: The Ohio State University, Center for Teaching Excellence.

Marincovich, M., & Gordon, H. (1991). A program of peer consultation: The consultants' experience. In J. D. Nyquist, R. D. Abbott, D. H. Wulff, & J. Sprague (Eds.), *Preparing the professoriate of tomorrow to teach: Selected readings in TA training.* Dubuque, IA: Kendall/Hunt.

Nyquist, J. D., & Sprague, J. (1992). Developmental stages of TAs. In J. D. Nyquist & D. H. Wulff (Eds.), *Preparing teaching assistants for instructional roles: Supervising TAs in communication.* Annandale, VA: Speech Communication Association.

Ronkowski, S. A. (1993). Scholarly teaching: Developmental stages of pedagogical scholarship. In L. Richlin (Ed.), *Preparing faculty for the new conceptions of scholarship.* New Directions for Teaching and Learning, No. 54. San Francisco, CA: Jossey-Bass.

Smith, R. (1997). Making teaching count in Canadian higher education: Developing a national agenda. *Teaching and Learning in Higher Education, 21,* 1, 3-10.

Smith, R., Byrd, P., Constantinides, J., & Barrett, R. P. (1991). Instructional development programs for international TAs: A systems analysis. *To Improve the Academy, 10,* 151-168.

Smock, R., & Menges, R. (1985). Programs for TAs in the context of campus policies and priorities. In J. D. W. Andrews (Ed.), *Strengthening the teaching assistant faculty.* New Directions for Teaching and Learning, No. 22. San Francisco, CA: Jossey-Bass.

Sveiby, K. E. (1992). The knowhow company: Strategy formulation in knowledge-intensive industries. In D. E. Hussey (Ed.), *International review of strategic management.* New York, NY: John Wiley.

Walker, C. J., & Quinn, J. W. (1996). Fostering instructional vitality and motivation. In R. J. Menges, M. Weimer, & Associates (Eds.), *Teaching on solid ground: Using scholarship to improve practice.* San Francisco, CA: Jossey-Bass.

Weimer, M., Svinicki, M. D., & Bauer, G. (1989). Designing programs to prepare TAs to teach. In J. D. Nyquist, R. D. Abbott, & D. H. Wulff (Eds.), *Teaching assistant training in the 1990s.* New Directions for Teaching and Learning, No. 39. San Francisco, CA: Jossey-Bass.

3

The Disciplinary/Departmental Context of TA Training

Shirley A. Ronkowski

Discipline-based training for teaching assistants (TAs) is a primary means for preparing graduate students as college and university professors. Long before there were formal or identifiable TA training and development programs, faculty mentored and modeled for their graduate students the role of university teacher as well as that of researcher.

University interest in TA training and development has been steadily growing since the 1970s when campus-wide TA training programs were formalized as part of the movement that created instructional development and teaching excellence centers across the country. In the 1980s, when national attention turned more specifically to TA training—apart from faculty and instructional development—emphasis was placed on campus-wide training programs. It was not until the 1990s that instructional development practitioners focused national attention on departmental TA training programs (Heenan & Jerich, 1995; Ronkowski, 1995). There are at least four reasons that come to mind for this delay in clearly focusing on departmental TA training.

First, as large numbers of campus-wide TA training programs matured, campus-wide TA trainers acquired the expertise, and, in some cases, the funding, to assist departmental training. Second, increasing university emphasis on effective teaching put pressure on academic departments to emphasize teaching skills for both faculty and graduate students. Third, the increasingly competitive academic job market has required departments to place greater emphasis on TA development opportunities in order to give graduate students an edge when seeking faculty positions. Finally, although campus-wide programs can and do offer many quality TA training activities, general teaching skills must be accompanied by teaching strategies specific to the academic discipline. In discussing the scholarly content of TA training, this chapter will argue that the very nature of teaching as a scholarly endeavor demands that a certain portion of TA training and development be done from a discipline base.

TWO TYPES OF DISCIPLINARY TA TRAINING

Discipline-based training encompasses two types that should be differentiated: course-specific and department-specific. Faculty who teach a course for which one or more TAs are assigned have a responsibility for course-specific TA training. The form this responsibility takes will vary with the philosophy of the individual faculty member and with each TA, depending on factors such as, but not limited to, the TA's stage of professional development (Nyquist, Skow, Sprague, & Wulff, 1991), the type of course responsibilities the TA will be given, and whether the TA is international or American. With each TA, the faculty member needs to assess the type of supervisory role he or she should assume: manager, educator, or mentor (Nyquist & Wulff, 1996).

Departmental TA training refers to discipline-specific teacher training that takes place within the academic department and is designed for TAs who are assigned to a variety of different courses. Most commonly, this type of training consists of a departmental teaching orientation that lasts from a few hours to a few days and of ongoing training activities that may be as formal as a course or as informal as occasional seminars or workshops. Activities often focus on first-time TAs. In addition, some departments have extensive training for more experienced TAs and special courses in professional development that prepare graduate students in skills not needed just for their role as teaching assistants, but essential for their future role as faculty members (e.g., course design and syllabi writing).

This chapter focuses on departmental TA training programs: their activities, content, creation, and continuation.

DEPARTMENTAL TA TRAINING ACTIVITIES

Departmental TA training programs vary widely among disciplines. A major source for what we know empirically about departmental TA training comes from descriptions of exemplary programs taken from a survey in the early 1990s (Lambert & Tice, 1993). From the results of that survey, a number of broad programmatic generalizations can be made about departmental TA training within various disciplinary clusters.

Programs in the physical sciences usually require TAs to run laboratory sections. Exemplary TA training programs in such departments as biological sciences provide training that typically includes a wide variety of activities: microteaching; videotaping; in-classroom critiques; lab safety training; international TA training seminars; teaching portfolio development; workshops on grading, tutoring, and questioning skills; information on learning styles; and discussion of typical teaching situations stimulated by videotape vignettes of classrooms and labs (Herreid, 1993).

Departments such as English, in its writing and composition programs, and foreign language typically require TAs to teach more than assist. TAs are often responsible for the day-to-day operation of the class, for choosing subject matter, assigning and responding to student writing, developing quizzes and tests, and grading students. TAs in these departments are given extensive orientations, frequent seminars or semester-long courses, team-teaching experience, and year-long intensive mentoring by faculty. TAs are familiarized with teaching issues and the philosophy of teaching within their discipline through extensive reading of journal articles, lectures by faculty, and seminar discussions (Jolliffe, 1993; Rava, 1993).

Some academic disciplines, such as mathematics, have developed multicampus TA training programs through national grants. In these programs, TAs are exposed to the use of small groups, instructional computing, strategies for teaching problem solving, and methods for evaluating student work. In at least one university, TAs who become teaching associates (i.e., faculty of record) can earn a certificate in university teaching by working with a faculty mentor, developing a teaching portfolio, and taking courses on such topics as the history of higher education, the philosophy of mathematics, and the teaching of college science (Case & Huneke, 1993).

In the social sciences, TA training commonly consists of 1) formal or informal presemester discussions with follow up during the semester and/or 2) regularly scheduled credit or noncredit seminars throughout the year. It is reported that in some departments, new faculty go through the training along with the TAs. Graduate students who are assigned as faculty of record for a course—who may be referred to as teaching associates, teaching fellows, or associate instructors—are given advanced training for their course responsibilities (Saunders, 1993).

Each departmental TA training program, regardless of discipline or university campus, is an often unique combination of commonly employed training activities. Departments can benefit from knowing about one another's training programs and exchanging ideas and materials. Campus-wide programs can assist departments by gathering and distributing information about departmental TA training requirements, orientations, courses, workshops, and seminars. Such a list can provide departments with concrete ideas that they may want to incorporate into existing programs and can be of even greater help to departments that are creating new programs.

CONTENT OF DEPARTMENTAL TA TRAINING

Scholarship, as it has been broadly defined, includes four aspects: discovery, integration, application, and teaching (Rice, 1991; Boyer, 1990). Scholarly teaching has three main elements: academic content knowledge, pedagogical content knowledge, and knowledge about how students learn. Each of these elements is appropriate and necessary for inclusion in TA training programs.

- Academic content knowledge requires the teacher-scholar to draw together various areas of an academic discipline, explain how they relate, and place concepts in the larger context of the discipline.

- Pedagogical content knowledge refers to the interaction between learning processes and academic content, that is, expertise in designing examples, analogies, metaphors, and simulations that help students integrate new knowledge into their existing schema.

- Knowledge about how students learn refers to such topics as learning styles and preferences, student motivation, general learning principles, modes of information processing, and stages of student cognitive development.

This third aspect of scholarly teaching, that of how students learn, is one of the areas in which campus-wide programs provide extensive TA training. Academic content knowledge and pedagogical content knowledge must necessarily be based in a specific discipline.

Academic Content Knowledge

It is easy to see that the first of these three elements of scholarly teaching—content knowledge—is within the domain of the academic discipline. It is also easy for departmental TA training programs to overlook this most basic aspect of TA training because departmental training involves TAs who will be teaching a variety of different courses. Dealing with content is therefore left to the individual faculty for whom the TA assists. But what is at issue here is not just the facts and concepts of course subject matter. Departmental TA training needs to also focus on the relationships among the major concepts of the various areas within the discipline in general. It can concentrate on how those areas relate historically, conceptually, and analytically. Understanding these relationships can give TAs a better handle on the discipline and allow them more intellectual mobility. When a student asks a question in section, TAs who might not be able to give a detailed answer could instead give an answer based on their overall knowledge of conceptual relationships. This ability could help free those new TAs who are overly concerned about knowing every detail of every fact covered in the course.

Pedagogical Content Knowledge

Pedagogical content knowledge refers to knowing why particular content is taught, the teaching strategies specific to that subject matter, issues related to student understanding of that field, and the reasoning behind curricular structures (Grossman, 1990). These understandings can only come from within academic disciplines because of the uniqueness of each discipline. Three major types of variation contribute to this uniqueness: 1) the extent to which the discipline is composed of an agreed upon and well-defined body of knowledge and skills, 2) how rapidly knowledge in the subject area is changing, and 3) the extent to which those within the discipline think knowledge in the subject is ordered with respect to the presentation of topics. These variations contribute to the structure of knowledge and have been found to affect how the discipline is taught (Stodolsky & Grossman, 1995).

The structure of knowledge within each discipline is also unique. Even though all disciplines may agree upon important elements of judging what is knowledge, each discipline places differing emphasis on the importance of each element. For example, while consistency is a criterion used by most disciplines to judge truth, disciplines also rely to varying degrees on precision and coherence as criteria and on processes such as empirical evidence, reproducibility, conflicting evidence, and peer review. Other factors that vary among disciplines include conceptual framework, model design, comprehensiveness, techniques, and innovations. The unique combination of these aspects of knowledge contributes to the structure of the discipline and underlies what is taught and how it is taught (Donald, 1995). Graduate students who become teaching assistants must learn not only the scholarly structure of their discipline but also how to convey that structure to their students.

Differences among disciplines have also been found to exist with regard to teaching behaviors. In a study conducted by Murray and Renaud (1995), trained observers visited classrooms of 401 faculty in various disciplines. One hundred teaching behaviors were grouped into ten categories, six of which were found to vary by disciplinary cluster. For example, arts and humanities faculty were found to use more behaviors in the categories of interaction (e.g., addressing students by name) and rapport (e.g., showing concern for student progress) than faculty in the social and physical sciences. Social and natural sciences faculty were observed using more behaviors favoring organization (e.g., putting a lecture outline on the board) and pacing (e.g., sticking to the point in answering questions). For those working in TA training and development, these findings suggest that there are specific teaching behaviors that may tend to be neglected by TAs, and these behaviors can be predicted by discipline. There is also evidence to suggest that faculty within particular sets of disciplines favor specific teaching styles (Grasha, 1996). TA training programs can encourage TAs to explore the less favored as well as the commonly used styles within their discipline. Having a choice of teaching style and facility with a variety of teaching techniques allows the TA greater flexibility in reaching a variety of students with varying instructional needs.

Knowing which effective behaviors tend to be associated with a particular discipline gives a road map for improving teaching in that discipline.

Departmental training programs can use this type of comparative research to encourage TAs to reflect on their teaching, the teaching they have experienced as students, and on the strengths and weakness to which they and their disciplines are prone.

How Students Learn

The research on college student learning (see Chapter 5) offers a vast array of knowledge that can be applied to teaching. Familiarity with the stages of student cognitive development (Baxter-Magolda, 1992; Belenky, Clinchy, Goldberger, & Tarule, 1986; Perry, 1970) is particularly useful when teaching the humanities and social sciences. Understanding the stages helps in creating assignments that facilitate students' ability to think in nondualistic ways, entertain a variety of perspectives, and learn ways of evaluating and choosing from among those perspectives. Models of student perceived efficacy (Perry, 1997a) and student motivation (Covington, 1997; McMillan & Forsyth, 1991; Lucas, 1990) point to ways of designing instruction to improve student achievement (Perry, 1997b).

Sheila Tobias' (1990) qualitative study of how students learn science provides a great deal of insight for TAs in the physical sciences, particularly for TAs teaching nonscience majors. Tobias (1992a) offers specific approaches to teaching physics, biology, chemistry, mathematics, and problem solving in general. She also addresses problems with how science is currently taught, discusses a multidisciplinary approach, and suggests specific reform (Tobias, 1992b).

Models of student learning styles can help instructors understand a variety of student needs and preferences (Sims & Sims, 1995; Johnson, 1992; Claxton & Smith, 1984; Kolb, 1984; Entwistle & Ramsden, 1983; Keirsey & Bates, 1978). TAs and faculty can design instruction that takes into account the strengths and weaknesses of various styles (Anderson & Adams, 1992; Svinicki & Dixon, 1987; Kolb, 1985). Also of interest to departmental programs for first-time TAs is information on teaching styles (Grasha, 1996; Reinsmith, 1994; Elbe, 1980) and models that integrate teaching and learning styles (Grasha, 1996; Andrews, 1981).

Communication technology is making continual changes in the ways students are able to access information and the courses they take. TAs, as future faculty, must be prepared to deal with the diversity among students and for the continual changes in how courses are taught and how education, in general, is delivered. In future years, TAs and faculty will be called upon to reconceptualize teaching and learning in their disciplines to meet the demands of different kinds of students in a very different kind of university. To do this, they will need to be expert teacher-scholars. They will need to rethink how to teach and how they want their students to learn, given the vast possibilities that instructional and communication technologies continually make possible. This, too, is a subject for TA training and one that presents challenges for both TAs and faculty (see Chapter 11).

TA TRAINING VERSUS TA DEVELOPMENT

To be most effective, TA training activities need to be matched to the various developmental stages through which TAs, and all professionals, tend to pass as they gain experience and expertise (Nyquist, Skow, Sprague, & Wulff, 1991; Ronkowski, 1993). For those new TAs with little or no classroom experience, it is appropriate to provide training in presentation skills, authority issues in the classroom, principles of student learning, and basic teaching strategies and styles. At this level, the term "TA training" may be appropriate. Once TAs feel ready to move on, it is more appropriate to refer to "TA development." The purpose is, after all, to assist TAs in their professional development as college and university professors.

After TAs are comfortable with assuming authority, are confident in their subject matter, and skilled at basic presentation skills, they need to begin closely examining student learning and ways that instruction can facilitate that learning. They can benefit from discussing academic and pedagogical content on a deeper level than was possible during their first year of TAing. With each TAship, TAs are ready to understand scholarly teaching at deeper levels—both theoretical and practical.

In terms of general teaching strategies, experienced TAs should become skilled in at least one or two active learning techniques such as the case approach, computer-assisted instruction, and cooperative or collaborative learning groups. They should also be able to apply these methods of active learning to discipline-specific content.

CREATING DEPARTMENTAL TA TRAINING PROGRAMS

The most effective way to organize a departmental TA training program varies with the culture of the academic discipline and that of the campus. In this author's experience and observations, physical science and engineering departments can effectively use very rule-based, top-down structures for TA training. Humanities and social science departments usually prefer to use more TA input and TA participation in both the planning and implementation of the training program. In these latter two kinds of departments, TA feedback is crucial.

In general, when considering the creation of a new program or the revitalizing or restructuring of an existing program, the most important considerations include support, participation, input, quality, and funding.

Support and Participation

Ideally, the department's entire faculty and graduate student body would be involved enthusiastically in the creation of a departmental TA training program. In reality, it may be only one faculty member or one graduate student who puts forth the ideas, enthusiasm, and energy needed to create a TA training program. Or it may be the result of a bit of arm twisting by the department chair or graduate division. However the program is initiated, it needs the support of the department chair, the approval of the department faculty, and the input of graduate students.

When creating new TA training and development programs, particularly in the humanities and social sciences, seeking graduate student input and participation in the planning process is key to success. Without this input, current graduate students can take a negative attitude toward the training, and this attitude can quickly spread to incoming graduate students. The effect may be continual questioning of and complaining about each activity or requirement, halfhearted participation, subtle subterfuge, or even outright lack of cooperation by some. After the program has been in existence for a few years, assuming that it provides worthwhile activities and information, TAs and graduate students in general usually come to accept the training as part of their graduate studies. But the first few years can be troublesome without input and some degree of support from current and past TAs, even when the program solely targets new TAs.

Faculty are also key to a successful program. Unless faculty are supportive of the training, TAs may not take the program seriously. In order for faculty to approve of the program, it is essential to provide them with its rationale, the opportunity to discuss proposed training requirements in faculty meetings, and a means to offer both general and specific suggestions about the program.

At many universities, TAs take on the major planning and implementation of departmental TA training under varying degrees of supervision by faculty. These TAs are given various titles such as TA consultants, master TAs, TA facilitators, and lead TAs. On most campuses, they work under the auspices of or in cooperation with the campus-wide TA training program. These experienced TAs make important contributions to departmental programs. The proceedings of the national conferences on TA training are filled with TA contributions to TA training programs as well as graduate student research on teaching and TAing, TA applications of general teaching theories to specific disciplines, and TA-designed teaching strategies (Heenan & Jerich, 1995; Lewis, 1993; Nyquist, Abbott, Wulff, & Sprague, 1991; Chism, 1987). *The Journal of Graduate Teaching Assistant Development* provides further evidence of the ongoing contributions TAs make to their own and their peers' training and development.

Departmental office personnel may also be significant participants in the program. They are often called upon, or take it upon themselves, to distribute the department's TA training literature, publicize TA training events, plan event catering, and, in some cases, even keep track of who completes the training requirements. In terms of organization and planning, they can offer a practical perspective and make suggestions that will make the program easier to administer.

Program Quality

In order to get widespread support within the department, the program will, of course, need to be well thought out and provide worthwhile experiences for TAs. Otherwise, TAs and the department's entire graduate student body may view the training as just more time-consuming work and more hoops through which graduate students must jump.

A scholarly approach to teaching helps ensure program quality. The academic faculty and staff of campus-wide teaching centers and campus-wide TA training programs are excellent sources for information on theoretical frameworks of particular teaching approaches, recent research on college teaching, and the academic literature on learning theory. On many campuses, they can provide teaching skills workshops, brown bag discussion groups, confidential consultations, feedback on teaching, and teaching resource libraries. There are a variety of ways they can provide support for both traditional and innovative approaches to teaching in higher education.

Another aspect of designing and maintaining a quality program is to ensure that TAs are treated fairly. There should be a firm and regular date by which TA assignments are given. Last-minute changes in assignments should be done on only the rarest of occasions. Since some courses require a heavier TA workload than others, TAships should be assigned in such a manner as to ensure equity over time. It should also be taken into account that some faculty are more demanding of TAs than others. Departments should have a tracking system of such variations so that over the period of a year or two the workload assigned to TAs is equitable. Of course, this requires a system whereby TAs can report the amount of time and types of duties required for each course they TA. This reporting system might initially be seen as a burden, but when TAs know the reason for the reporting, they will no doubt want to participate in or even conduct the record keeping.

Funding

Ample funding is certainly desirable, but most departments will find it difficult to acquire. If the departmental budget cannot carve out modest funds for TA training, the graduate division and the campus teaching excellence center may be sources of funding for specific purposes. Extramural funding is sometimes possible for innovative programs with specific goals, such as international TA training, TA training consortia, or future faculty development.

On some campuses, TA training funds provide honoraria for faculty and TAs to plan, implement, and evaluate departmental programs. On other campuses, faculty are given course-load credit to conduct TA training seminars and courses. This latter compensation is only effective when the course credit is part of the faculty load and not overload credits that are looked upon as unimportant and peripheral to graduate education. Emeriti faculty are sometimes willing to take over TA training for small honoraria. Experienced TAs who assist with the leadership of TA training can be compensated with stipends or given a TAship with fewer class sessions in recognition of their leadership activities.

Rarely, if ever, are TAs compensated for time spent in training. The TAship compensates them for their teaching while they gain classroom experience, but training activities are usually considered part of the graduate studies curriculum. Departments generally give course credit for both TAing and for TA training courses.

The faculty and TAs who participate in the leadership of TA training programs usually learn a great deal about teaching and learning as well as about TA training. Unfortunately, their valuable knowledge and insights can be lost when they move on to other projects or universities. There are, however, ways to create programs, or reconstruct existing programs, that will increase their longevity.

PROGRAM LONGEVITY

The life expectancy of departmental TA training programs has varied depending on the burnout rate of the TAs or faculty members who create them. When an interested faculty member or TA takes charge, the program thrives. When that interest wanes or the leading member of the program leaves the university, the program dies. Restarting a program after it has been inactive or nonexistent for a few years usually requires all the time and effort of creating a completely new program. The resources, requirements, and materials of the original program have vanished, and the department must start anew. This section will discuss some of the ways departments have been able to increase the longevity of their programs (Ronkowski, Conway, & Wilde, 1995).

Program Leadership

The composition of a TA training leadership team may vary between the two extremes of being an all-faculty team to being an all-TA team. Logically, a leadership team including both TAs and faculty members appears most favorable to promoting program longevity. Each brings unique strengths to the task of TA training. TAs, by virtue of their recent experience, may be more closely attuned to the training needs of current TAs, while faculty tend to be more experienced and less transient. However, the exact formulation of a leadership team may be heavily influenced by a department's character and the disciplinary culture.

For example, a department may have a system in which a committee of experienced TAs works with a single faculty member to lead the department's training program. Each year one member of the TA committee serves as master TA or lead TA and, along with faculty, carries the main burden of responsibility for the program. The mantle of leadership is passed on to one of the other committee members each year. A committee of at least three ensures that at least one person who has been involved in the training is likely to be available to head the program each year.

This same system can protect against faculty burnout. A partnership or committee of two or three faculty can serve as a TA training committee, with one person taking on the major responsibility for the program each year. These faculty members can also learn from one another and create more involvement by other faculty members.

Institutional Memory

There are many ways that campus-wide TA training programs, graduate divisions, teaching centers, and departments can support the existence of departmental TA training. In addition to providing funding, they can help create institutional memory. Graduate divisions can require departments to submit general TA training objectives and plans. When department chairs change or faculty move to other campuses, the training plans remain and can be referred to by the graduate division, the faculty, and TAs. The more public and detailed the plans, the better the chance that they will be ongoing.

For those campuses that are able to provide funding for departmental TA training programs, that funding can be designed to be renewed each year. When funding renewal is not automatic, the chance that the department will reconsider, reevaluate, and otherwise attend to the training program each year is greater.

Campus-wide TA training programs that work closely with departments can also assist by collecting departmental TA training materials. These materials can then be exchanged among departments through campus training activities or the Internet. Departments will find it easier to create, build, or rebuild programs when training materials are readily available as models.

Departmental TA Training Requirements

Creating documentation of TA training requirements can be critical to program longevity. Loss of program continuity is less likely to occur if the department has written TA training requirements and if there are training structures in place such as TA training courses, required activities conducted by the campus-wide TA training program, and a standardized departmental orientation for new TAs on the same day each year (e.g., second day of registration week each fall semester).

Ongoing Needs Assessment and TA Feedback

The content of TA training should vary with the needs of the TAs, and the best way to assess the needs of TAs is to ask them. TAs who have just gone through the training are the best source of feedback about the training activities. The more senior TAs can give another perspective. Faculty can provide a third view on the essential elements that should be covered in TA training. Departments with ongoing assessments have a constant feedback loop so that the program does not become stale or outdated. Sometimes a simple thing like changing the sequence of seminar topics can make a big difference to the satisfaction of TAs.

Rewarding Teaching

Rewarding and otherwise encouraging faculty and TAs in the professional development of their teaching can help to create interest in teaching, alleviate faculty burnout, and increase TA training program longevity. Departments can work with graduate divisions, campus-wide TA training programs, and campus teaching centers to increase the attention paid to teaching. Ongoing programs support activities that include speakers from off campus, seminars by distinguished on-campus faculty, workshops on specific teaching strategies, campus conferences on teaching, and opportunities for faculty and TAs to attend professional conferences on teaching and TAing.

ON THE IMPORTANCE OF DEPARTMENTAL PROGRAMS

Faculty as well as TAs gain from ensuring excellence in the TA training program. TAs who become faculty at other universities represent their faculty mentors and their former universities in terms of their teaching as well as their research. According to a qualitative study by Boice (1992), the most successful first-year faculty are those who are able to quickly adapt to their new role by competently and efficiently carrying out their teaching responsibilities and integrating their teaching with their other scholarly activities.

New faculty in this study who did not quickly adapt to their positions were hesitant to go beyond the "facts-and-principles" approach to their teaching, even when their student ratings were lower than they anticipated. They seemed to need greater encouragement to learn new teaching approaches and respond to student needs and feedback. It is unfortunate that these new faculty did not learn a variety of teaching approaches during their graduate student years. It would seem less risky to try new approaches as a graduate student TA than in the midst of tenure pressures. Faculty in the departments are ideally situated to encourage TAs to take these risks and develop a variety of approaches in the early, less pressured stages of their careers.

Departments have an obligation to prepare graduate students as teacher-scholars as well as research scholars. As future faculty members, they will need both these skills as they seek to advance in their careers.

REFERENCES

Allen, R. R., & Rueter, T. (1990). *Teaching assistant strategies: An introduction to college teaching.* Dubuque, IA: Kendall/Hunt.

Anderson, J. A., & Adams, M. (1992). Acknowledging the learning styles of diverse student populations: Implications for instructional design. In L. L. Border & N. V. N. Chism (Eds.), *Teaching for diversity.* New Directions for Teaching and Learning, No. 49. San Francisco, CA: Jossey-Bass.

Andrews, J. A. (1981). Teaching format and student style: Their interactive effects on learning. *Research in Higher Education, 14* (2), 161-178.

Baxter-Magolda, M. (1992). *Knowing and reasoning in college: Gender-related patterns in student development.* San Francisco, CA: Jossey-Bass.

Belenky, M. F., Clinchy, B. M., Goldberger, N. R., & Tarule, J. M. (1986). *Women's ways of knowing: The development of self, voices, and mind.* New York, NY: Basic Books.

Boice, R. (1992). *The new faculty member.* San Francisco, CA: Jossey-Bass.

Boyer, E. L. (1990). *Scholarship reconsidered: Priorities of the professoriate.* Princeton, NJ: The Carnegie Foundation for the Advancement of Teaching.

Case, B. A., & Huneke, J. P. (1993). Discipline-based TA programs and practices: Programs of note in mathematics. In L. M. Lambert & S. L. Tice (Eds.), *Preparing graduate students to teach: A guide to programs that improve undergraduate education and develop tomorrow's faculty.* Washington, DC: American Association for Higher Education.

Chism, N. V. N. (Ed.). (1987). *Institutional responsibilities and responses in the employment and education of teaching assistants.* Columbus, OH: The Ohio State University, Center for Teaching Excellence.

Claxton, C. S., & Smith, W. F. (1984). *Learning styles: Implications for improving educational practices.* ASHE-ERIC Higher Education Report No. 4. Washington, DC: George Washington University, School of Education and Human Development.

Covington, M. V. (1997). A motivational analysis of academic life in college. In R. P. Perry & J. C. Smart (Eds.), *Effective teaching in higher education: Research and practice.* New York, NY: Agathon.

Donald, J. (1995). Disciplinary differences in knowledge validation. In N. Hativa & M. Marincovich (Eds.), *Disciplinary differences in teaching and learning: Implications for practice.* New Directions for Teaching and Learning, No. 64. San Francisco, CA: Jossey-Bass.

Elbe, K. E. (1980). Teaching styles and faculty behavior. In K. E. Elbe (Ed.), *Improving teaching styles.* San Francisco, CA: Jossey-Bass.

Entwistle, N., & Ramsden, P. (1983). *Understanding student learning.* New York, NY: Nichols.

Grasha, A. F. (1996). *Teaching with style: A practical guide to enhancing learning by understanding teaching and learning styles.* Pittsburgh, PA: Alliance Press.

Grossman, P. L. (1990). *The making of a teacher: Teacher knowledge and teacher education.* New York, NY: Teachers College Press.

Herreid, C. F. (Ed.). (1993). Discipline-based TA programs and practices: Programs of note in the biological sciences. In L.M. Lambert & S. L. Tice (Eds.), *Preparing graduate students to teach: A guide to programs that improve undergraduate education and develop tomorrow's faculty.* Washington, DC: American Association for Higher Education.

Heenan, T. A., & Jerich, K. F. (Eds.). (1995). *Teaching graduate students to teach: Engaging the disciplines.* Proceedings of the 4th National Conference on the Training and Employment of Graduate Teaching Assistants. Chicago, IL.

Johnson, J. L. (1992). *A manual of learning styles: Scales for use with college students.* Portland, ME: University of Maine Testing and Assessment Center.

Jolliffe, D. A. (1993). Discipline-based TA programs and practices: Programs of note in English and composition. In L. M. Lambert & S. L. Tice (Eds.), *Preparing graduate students to teach: A guide to programs that improve undergraduate education and develop tomorrow's faculty.* Washington, DC: American Association for Higher Education.

Keirsey, D. A., & Bates, M. (1978). *Please understand me: An essay on temperament styles.* Del Mar, CA: Prometheus Nemesis Books.

Kolb, D. A. (1984). *Experiential learning.* Englewood Cliffs, NJ: Prentice-Hall.

Kolb, D. A. (1985). *Learning style inventory* (rev. ed.). Boston, MA: McBer.

Lambert, L. M., & Tice, S. L. (Eds.). (1993). *Preparing graduate students to teach: A guide to programs that improve undergraduate education and develop tomorrow's faculty.* Washington, DC: American Association for Higher Education.

Lewis, K. G. (Ed.). (1993). *The TA experience: Preparing for multiple roles.* Stillwater, OK: New Forums Press.

Lewis, K. G. (Ed.). (1996-97). *The Journal of Graduate Teaching Assistant Development.* Stillwater, OK: New Forums Press.

Lucas, A. F. (1990). Using psychological models to understand student motivation. In M. D. Svinicki (Ed.), *The changing face of college teaching.* New Directions for Teaching and Learning, No. 42. San Francisco, CA: Jossey-Bass.

McMillan, J. H., & Forsyth, D. R. (1991). What theories of motivation say about why learners learn. In R. J. Menges & M. D. Svinicki (Eds.), *College teaching: From theory to practice.* New Directions for Teaching and Learning, No. 45. San Francisco, CA: Jossey-Bass.

Murray, H. G., & Renaud, R. D. (1995). Disciplinary differences in classroom teaching behaviors. In N. Hativa & M. Marincovich (Eds.), *Disciplinary differences in teaching and learning: Implications for practice.* New Directions for Teaching and Learning, No. 64. San Francisco, CA: Jossey-Bass.

Nyquist, J. D., Abbott, R. D., Wulff, D. H., & Sprague, J. (1991). *Preparing the professoriate of tomorrow to teach: Selected readings in TA training.* Dubuque, IA: Kendall/Hunt.

Nyquist, J. D., Skow, L., Sprague, J., & Wulff, D. (1991, November). *Research on stages of teaching assistant development.* Paper presented at the 3rd National Conference on the Training and Employment of Graduate Teaching Assistants. Austin, TX.

Nyquist, J. D., & Wulff, D. H. (1996). *Working effectively with graduate assistants.* Thousand Oaks, CA: Sage.

Perry, R. P. (1997a). Perceived control in college students: Implications for instruction in higher education. In R. P. Perry & J. C. Smart (Eds.), *Effective teaching in higher education: Research and practice.* New York, NY: Agathon Press.

Perry, R. P. (1997b). Teaching effectively: Which students? What methods? In R. P. Perry & J. C. Smart (Eds.), *Effective teaching in higher education: Research and practice.* New York, NY: Agathon Press.

Perry, W. (1970). *Forms of intellectual and ethical development in the college years: A scheme.* New York, NY: Holt, Rinehart, & Winston.

Rava, S. (Ed.). (1993). Discipline-based TA programs and practices: Programs of note in the foreign languages. In L. M. Lambert & S. L. Tice (Eds.), *Preparing graduate students to teach: A guide to programs that improve undergraduate education and develop tomorrow's faculty.* Washington, DC: American Association for Higher Education.

Reinsmith, W. A. (1994). Archetypal forms in teaching. *College Teaching, 42* (4), 131-136.

Rice, R. E. (1991). The new American scholar: Scholarship and the purposes of the university. *Metropolitan Universities: An International Forum, 1* (4), 7-18.

Ronkowski, S. A. (1993). Scholarly teaching: Developmental stages of pedagogical scholarship. In L. Richlin (Ed.), *Preparing faculty for the new conceptions of scholarship.* New Directions for Teaching and Learning, No. 54. San Francisco, CA: Jossey-Bass.

Ronkowski, S. A. (1995). Trends in TA training: An analysis of national conferences on TA-ing from 1986 to 1993. In T. A. Heenan & K. F. Jerich (Eds.), *Teaching graduate students to teach: Engaging the disciplines.* Chicago, IL: University of Illinois.

Ronkowski, S. A., Conway, C. M., & Wilde, P. D. (1995). Longevity issues for departmental TA training programs. In T. A. Heenan & K. F. Jerich (Eds.), *Teaching graduate students to teach: Engaging the disciplines.* Chicago, IL: University of Illinois.

Saunders, P. (Ed.). (1993). Discipline-based TA programs and practices: Programs of note in the social sciences. In L. M. Lambert & S. L. Tice (Eds.), *Preparing graduate students to teach: A guide to programs that improve undergraduate education and develop tomorrow's faculty.* Washington, DC: American Association for Higher Education.

Schoenfeld, A. C., & Magnan, R. (1994). *Mentor in a manual: Climbing the academic ladder to tenure* (2nd ed.). Madison, WI: Magna.

Sims, R. R., & Sims, S. J. (Eds.). (1995). *The importance of learning styles: Understanding the implications for learning, course design, and education.* London, England: Greenwood Press.

Sprague, J., & Nyquist, J. D. (1989). TA supervision. In J. D. Nyquist, R. D. Abbott, & D. H. Wulff (Eds.), *Teaching assistant training in the 1990s.* New Directions for Teaching and Learning, No. 39. San Francisco, CA: Jossey-Bass.

Stodolsky, S. S., & Grossman, P. L. (1995). Subject-matter differences in secondary schools: Connections to higher education. In N. Hativa & M. Marincovich (Eds.), *Disciplinary differences in teaching and learning: Implications for practice.* New Directions for Teaching and Learning, No. 64. San Francisco, CA: Jossey-Bass.

Svinicki, M. D., & Dixon, N. M. (1987). The Kolb model modified for classroom activities. *College Teaching, 35* (4), 141-146.

Tobias, S. (1990). *They're not dumb, they're different: Stalking the second tier.* Tucson, AZ: Research Corporation.

Tobias, S. (1992a). *Revitalizing undergraduate science: Why some things work and most don't.* Tucson, AZ: Research Corporation.

Tobias, S., & Tomizuka, C. T. (1992b). *Breaking the science barrier: How to explore and understand the sciences.* Tucson, AZ: Research Corporation.

4

THINKING DEVELOPMENTALLY ABOUT TAs

Jody D. Nyquist and Jo Sprague

Anyone who works with a large group of TAs over any period of time—and we have worked with hundreds over many years—soon realizes that no single model of TA training comes close to fitting all situations. Disciplines differ, as do individuals and their teaching assignments. Underneath the differences, however, are some similarities, which we began to tentatively chart in the late 1980s. It appeared that as TAs moved through their programs, there seemed to be some underlying stages or phases they went through in their development.

We were drawn to stage approaches to human behavior because they offset some of the problems of the various styles approaches that were so much in vogue at the time. Completing inventories such as the Myers-Briggs or classifying oneself into the quadrants of any number of quite heuristic grids runs the risk of freezing individuals prematurely and/or permanently. We were bothered by the tendency of TAs to sidestep reflection on the impact of their teaching with the all-purpose comment, "Well, that's just my teaching style."

The developmental perspective we adopted at the time (Sprague & Nyquist, 1989, 1991; Nyquist & Sprague, 1992) is not the only, or even the best, way to think about TA training. Imperfect as our initial model has turned out to be, though, the approach has offered a way of thinking that has directly influenced the design and presentation of many TA programs in the last decade. When we see TAs as professionals in a constant state of development, we must think of them, ourselves, and our programs as mutable and contingent. The full complexity of the process by which people move from being students toward being professors mitigates against programs designed around teaching tips or a series of quick workshops. Thus, the developmental way of thinking turned out to fit well with a number of other movements that were taking place in the scholarly literature and in the broader arenas of academia. It allowed us to organize our and others' observations and experiences with TAs, and offered insights as to why working with graduate students as they aspire to become effective teachers is so challenging and complex, yet at the same time, meaningful and rewarding as well as intellectually stimulating. Thus, we have continued to pursue the developmental approach in our quest to better understand how graduate students become effective teachers and how to assist them in that process.

CONTEXT FOR THE STUDY OF THE TEACHING DEVELOPMENT OF GRADUATE TAs

Obviously, even when we think developmentally about graduate teaching assistants, we must do so within a context. TAs are surrounded by influences, pressures, tensions, and expectations of those to whom they report, their own aspirations, motivations, and individual issues. So, as we attempt to identify where TAs are developmentally and how best to assist them, we need to contextualize our thinking within at least three frames of reference: what is already known about the development of graduate teaching assistants, the broader trends affecting higher education, and factors related to the individual TA.

The Context of the Scholarly Literature on TA Development

Although there was no prior research on TAs' development, our work did not begin from scratch. We were able to draw reasonable inferences about how TAs develop as teachers by looking at several related bodies of literature. Learning to be a professor is similar to other forms of professional development. Schön's important work (1987) gave insight into the rich apprenticeships of practice that lead to professional competence as architects, doctors, and designers. Other scholars were studying the phases in the professional development of teachers, counselors, and junior faculty members (Connolly & Bruner, 1974; Hunt, 1971; Kagan, 1988; Perry, 1970; Sprinthall & Theis-Sprinthall, 1983). All of this work provided parallels to observations about how TAs seem to evolve in their skills and judgment.

The Context of the Academy

Outside the scholarly literature, educational policymakers were engaging in a national conversation about preparing the professoriate of the future. There has been no lack of critics of the traditional assumption that knowledge of subject matter is a necessary and sufficient condition for knowing how to be a university faculty member. Yet, despite a few reform attempts such as the doctor of arts degree in the 1970s, the supremacy of the doctoral-granting universities as gatekeepers of quality and credentialers of faculty members has not been seriously challenged. However, leaders in graduate education began to recognize that their students were being hired into faculty positions in institutions very different from their own. In addition to wanting assistant professors who were superbly qualified to launch a research program, these institutions were looking for colleagues who could teach a wide range of courses, develop curriculum, advise students, serve on faculty committees, and work collaboratively as colleagues. An important national movement, Preparing Future Faculty (PFF),[1] provided incentives for research universities to form partnerships with other types of institutions and to design learning experiences for graduate students that would prepare them to choose the academic context in which they could make their best contribution.

At the same time, there has been renewed attention paid to the quality of undergraduate teaching at research universities. In response to pressures from parents and taxpayers, institutions have moved away from viewing the TA appointment as primarily a low-cost way to provide instruction while funding graduate students' education. In the short term, this has led to much greater investment in the design of quality TA training experiences. In the longer term, it has meant that rewards and resources, even in the most prestigious research departments, have become linked to some extent to stewardship of undergraduate instruction. Graduate students began to observe that no matter how brilliant a researcher a faculty member is, a certain level of teaching effectiveness is expected.

These factors inside and outside the academy were all driving a move away from treating work with TAs as a matter of only providing training for introductory courses. Such training, though still important, is now being seen as embedded in broader visions of graduate education and the powerful ways that early teaching experiences set the stage for later professional development as faculty members.

The Context of an Individual's Experience

The development of the instructional competence of graduate teaching assistants is individual and influenced by many factors. In our current work on a national research project on TA development, we have begun to realize how factors outside of the developmental models we had examined, as well as our own framework, affect TA development.[2] Three of these factors may be difficult to influence, but should be considered when trying to understand the process of assisting graduate students to develop into college/university teachers: TAs' prior understandings of effective teaching, messages TAs receive about teaching and how they process them, and the influence of other graduate students on a TA's development.

Private theories/personal visions about teaching. Graduate students enter graduate school with their own private theories about what makes an effective teacher. They have sat in classrooms for at least 16 years, been taught rigorously and continuously by parents, relatives, and friends, and can describe—in interviews—what attributes they want in their teachers. This is all based, of course, on what worked for them as learners, on what teachers and professors did that helped them personally. TAs refer to their fourth grade teacher, their eighth grade science instructor, and their Girl Scout counselor. These personal visions (Brookfield, 1990; Wulff, 1993; Nyquist, 1993) are deeply rooted. TAs can tell us what those instructors did that assisted them to learn. They want to do the same. Unfortunately, however, their models may work only for students like themselves. In addition, we find there is a tendency for graduate students to hold tightly to those ideas, distorting information about teaching to fit their personal visions of effective teachers. Learning theory, studies in higher education teaching and learning, or even the wisdom of practice can be deflected or modified if they do not fit the graduate student's private theory or personal vision of effective teaching.

Messages TAs receive about teaching. Although institutions and most departments believe that they send strong, clear messages about the importance of teaching, graduate students in our current study report that those messages are very mixed:

> *Everyone tells you that a research assistantship is to be prized over a teaching assistantship.*
>
> *My advisor worked diligently to assist me to win a Fulbright but never discussed with me or supported me in my teaching, even though I was a teaching assistant for him for three years.*
>
> *If this department cared about teaching, it would give you your assignment earlier than the Friday before the Monday that you start to teach.*
>
> *I don't feel in the slightest bit that my advisors could give less of a crap about what kind of a TA I am. First of all, the professors don't care how good a TA I am. All they care is that the work gets done.*
>
> *The president and the provost and the department chair all tell us how teaching assistants are critical to the instructional programs of the university, how the undergraduate programs depend heavily on our effective performance, how this opportunity, if performed effectively, will affect the rest of our professional lives. It sounds good, and the messages seem believable and accurate. Soon, however, you begin to receive messages that are in contradiction: Your advisor says not to spend too much time on teaching, not to let it get in the way of your course and lab work.*

Not only do the messages about teaching appear to be contradictory, but TAs process them in different ways. Determining how to assign meaning to those messages often brings graduate students to sharing their perceptions with their peers and attempting to assess their own responses relative to others.

Peers/other graduate students. As TAs in Darling's study (1986) reported, they ask their peers for advice when the issues are of significance. Staton and Darling (1989) described this phenomenon in the following way:

> When TAs needed information that was highly salient, risky, and unobtainable through observation, they typically consulted a reliable third party (for example, they

asked an experienced TA how a particular professor would be likely to respond to a challenge). Only when the information concerned something of low risk (for example, how to approach a particular topic in class, or whether there would be changes in the schedule) were new TAs likely to consult professors directly (p. 19).

Darling (1986) found that experienced TAs become the primary informants for new TAs and provide critical sources of information regarding teaching assignments in departments, including expectations, policies, accepted procedures, and innovative ideas. This reliance on peers as the ultimate authority on teaching can create difficulties, as we will see when we look more closely at our developmental framework.

ONE CONCEPTUALIZATION OF THE DEVELOPMENT OF GRADUATE TEACHING ASSISTANTS

As mentioned previously, to help us better understand what was going on with our graduate teaching assistants developmentally, we posited a framework that seems to be a useful way of thinking through how graduate students develop into teachers. In our model, we propose three stages that TAs seem to move through and label these with the general role descriptors of senior learner, colleague-in-training, and junior colleague. As the titles suggest, senior learners still identify strongly with students, but they function as experts who are capable of providing assistance; colleagues-in-training have begun to shift their identification to the role of teacher and recognize the need to master the skills of that role; and junior colleagues have reached a level of confident functioning in many parts of the role and may lack only the formal credentials, the length of experience, and the seasoned judgments that are required of those who are considered full members of the profession of higher education faculty.

Research findings from our current national study underscore the very different levels at which graduate students enter these roles as TAs. In the same cohort of doctoral students, for example, might be some who are complete novices as teachers, some who have taught secondary school, some with community college teaching experience, and some from excellent TA training programs in M.A.-granting institutions. Not only do TAs enter at different levels, but, obviously, they grow at different rates in many different dimensions.

TABLE 4.1
Indicators of TA Development

SENIOR LEARNER	COLLEAGUE-IN-TRAINING	JUNIOR COLLEAGUE
Concerns		
Self/survival	Skills	Outcomes
How will students like me?	*How do I lecture, discuss?*	*Are students getting it?*
Discourse Level		
Presocialized	Socialized	Postsocialized
Give simplistic explanations	*Talk like insiders, use technical language*	*Make complex ideas clear without use of jargon*
Approach to Authority		
Dependent	Independent or Counterdependent	Interdependent/collegial
Rely on supervisor	*Stand on own ideas— defiant at times*	*Begin to relate to faculty as partners in meeting instructional challenges*
Approach to Students		
Engaged/vulnerable; student as friend, victim, or enemy	Detached; student as experimental subject	Engaged/professional; student as client
"Love" students, want to be friends, expect admiration, or are hurt, angry in response, and personalize interactions	*Disengage or distance themselves from students— becoming analytical about learning relationships*	*Understand student/ instructor relationships & the collaborative effort required for student learning to occur*

Adapted from: Sprague, J., & Nyquist, J. D. (1991). A developmental perspective on the TA role. In J. D. Nyquist, R. D. Abbott, D. H. Wulff, & J. Sprague (Eds.), *Preparing the professoriate of tomorrow to teach: Selected readings in TA training* (pp. 295-312). Dubuque, IA: Kendall /Hunt.

So how can supervisors determine where TAs are in their development in order to meet their individual needs? In trying to analyze developmental levels, we have naturally turned to the academic discipline in which we have our roots, communication. We believe that the way TAs talk is a revealing indicator of their levels of development. The underlying assumption is that speech is a reflection of attitudes, beliefs, and values. We know that the phenomenon is much more complex and interesting than that, however. Communication theorists no longer indulge in chicken-and-egg arguments about whether speech reflects thought or vice versa. The relationships among language, culture, identity, consciousness, and action are infinitely recursive. The way TAs talk tells us about their beliefs, but it also tells us a great deal about the communities in which they are embedded. In our research about the messages TAs receive, we are beginning to see the applications of Bakhtin's (1981) statement that we do not just speak our language, but our language speaks us. From the perspective of Vygotsky (1986), this means that "individual development" is inherently and profoundly social. Growth is not a matter of unfolding according to some preprogrammed plan; it occurs with other people in conversation and joint action. We borrow each other's words and phrases. In time they become our own, and with them ideas and beliefs from the social world become internalized, and then become part of our action and identity. Knowing this, then, we began to listen to how TAs talk about themselves in their instructional roles. As Table 4.1 shows, we believe that changes in TA development can be charted along four dimensions revealed in their talk about their concerns, their discipline, their relationships to students, and their relationship to authority.

TA Concerns

A substantial body of literature is available, some of which has directly involved teaching assistants (Book & Eisenberg, 1979; Fuller, 1969; Staton-Spicer & Bassett, 1979), reporting the ways that teachers describe their professional concerns. At the earliest stage, concerns center on self and survival. TAs worry about what to wear, how their students will address them, whether they will look and sound enough like an instructor to gain respect, and whether they will please their students and employers. After initial experiences, TAs' concerns tend to center on issues related to mastering the skills of teaching such as lecturing, leading discussion, grading, and constructing exams. Only at a somewhat advanced point, when there is a reasonable comfort level in the instructional role and some degree of proficiency in teaching, do TAs' concerns turn to the impact of instruction. It is then that they worry most about whether their students are learning, and if not, how best to assist them. What follows are typical comments taken from transcripts of interviews with the TAs in our current study that illustrate these stages.

- **Senior Learner**

  "I hope that there aren't enough gaps in my knowledge to make them doubt me as a competent teacher." (male/math)

  "I think I was nervous. Just being effective and if my students like me and stuff like that." (female/zoology)

  "Whether I gave a good impression to my students—of, number one, me, and number two, the subject that I study. That's always something you want to do." (male/math)

- **Colleague-in-Training**

  "I've come to like it [lecturing] a lot. Still for me, I don't know how the students feel about these things, but still for me, it's kind of exciting to really sit and plan and think about things and how I would present them. It's kind of strange that I'm new at this a little bit, and so I don't know the effectiveness of my presentation. They generally aren't going to tell you very much or give you much feedback." (male/math)

  "Part of it is a scheduling thing, I think, that figuring out how much, of not giving them too big of a task to do in their group so that the task fits the amount of time that they have, and then making sure that there's time to pull everybody back together and see that they feel that they've gained some main points out of that." (female/history)

- **Junior Colleague**

  "I think I cared less at the end [about whether students liked me]. I cared more about if they are getting it, and not do they like me." (female/zoology)

  "As the quarter progressed what I started to notice was that the one man in the class did all the talking. So then I started to think this is a gender thing. How am I going to negotiate this? I think it's really important that I facilitate my students' confidence in their right to speak. Especially the women. But I'm also very protective of quiet students. Their comfort zone. So I had a really difficult time with that." (female/English)

TA Discourse

A second dimension along which development can be traced is the way TAs talk about their disciplines. Typically, entry-level TAs combine rather rudimentary technical vocabulary with extremely informal and colloquial speech. A colleague reports walking by a classroom where a novice instructor of introductory broadcasting was saying something like this: "So the FCC is all, 'You guys have to comply with this rating thing.' And the networks are all, 'No waaaay!'"

The colleague reports that the students seemed enthralled. This kind of discourse is classified as presocialized (Williams, 1986), because it reveals that its user has not yet been socialized into the academic discourse community. She was not using specialized terms with precision nor modeling the rhetorical conventions that scholars in her field use to build arguments.

As TAs move further along in their own graduate studies, they become more deeply immersed in their discipline and thoroughly steeped in specialized ways of talking about knowledge. In this socialized discourse stage, they are much more fluent, precise, and confident. Unfortunately, this development is a double-edged sword. With this greater mastery comes a tendency to display the new vocabulary, practice on their students, hold forth on unimportant distinctions, and indulge in scholarly digressions. The teaching effectiveness of TAs may temporarily seem to regress during this time as they lose sight of what will be meaningful to beginning students.

At the third developmental level, instructional talk becomes postsocialized. That is, the speaker connects the language of the new community with the language of the broader community. A teacher can be precise without being pedantic, simple without being simplistic. Often explanations are shorter and crisper than at the previous two stages, leaving more time for providing connections through aptly chosen stories, metaphors, and examples. TA comments from our interviews which reflect the levels of their discourse include:

- **Senior Learner**

  "There are some things in the business algebra course, like the section on linear algebra. There are good things, there are interesting questions in that field. Not so much anymore. There are interesting aspects of that field. It ties into a lot of meaty subjects in mathematics. So, you know that particular part of the class. There is a lot of neat stuff that you can do with that." (female/math)

"That's one thing that I think is cool about math. Generally, people break it into algebra, which doesn't require calculus in effect and an analysis which is basically things that start from calculus and go from there. Generalize it in some way to higher dimensions or strange surfaces or whatever. There are some other subfields that are harder to classify. Different people lump them in different ways, topology." (male/math)

- **Colleague-in-Training**

"It's definitely that I am thinking a lot more through the intellectual job that I am doing as opposed to sort of the skills-oriented job." (female/zoology)

"I guess (the course) is just to keep a broad-based knowledge of chemistry and so that you are familiar with all the concepts and the terms. It's a lot of hand waving. A lot of like okay, so this happens but it really doesn't ever happen. They will tell you things that happen that really don't happen. Just because it's too complicated to explain what really does happen. A lot of steps get skipped in between and they will give you a lot of rules that get broken. Like they will say this is a rule in chemistry and then when you get into a class higher up, they will say, okay, this rule you learned in general chemistry isn't always true. Actually, it's not that true usually. It's kind of like that. It's a lot of like magic. A lot of formulas come out of the air and stuff like that. It's just a general overview and here are a bunch of formulas and here are how things, how heat and energy relate in all these things. So that if you need to know, if you are working in biology, you need to know these things, you need to know where to find them." (male/chemistry)

- **Junior Colleague**

"The whole idea of the feeding of this organism is actually really complicated... So what I did was I just told them that the room was, like we were inside the organism. And I kind of took them on this tour as if we'd just been eaten by the organism and everything in the room kind of took on significance as like the anatomy of the organism. And by us trying to escape, I kind of brought them into this feeling that they were eaten. And I said, if we went this way, how would we be caught? And I showed them like how effective a feeder is because that's kind of one of the main things about this organism. And they really were into it." (male/zoology)

Relationships with Students

A third developmental dimension is how TAs relate to their students. At first, the relationship is personal and intense. Students are friends or enemies, victims or bullies. TAs want very much to be liked, and often they are. The students of beginning TAs reciprocate their warmth with compliments, gifts, and, occasionally, inconvenient crushes. Many times, TAs extend themselves for their students in various ways, assuming that their generous efforts will be appreciated. When, as often happens, that is not the case, the TA feels hurt and personally betrayed. Other TAs feel threatened or intimidated by particular students or whole classes and suffer emotions ranging from rejection to outrage over conflicts that arise.

After a few experiences of these agonies and ecstasies, TAs generally move to a phase in which they become considerably more detached and analytical about students. (Some of them become downright cynical.) They are more interested in being respected by the majority of students than in being liked by every single one. In general, the emphasis moves away from the individual student to the group. For example, a TA who previously might have granted an exception to a rule would invoke the need to be consistent out of fairness to the class as a group. Instructional decisions are driven less by an intuitive identification with students and more by an intellectual rationale, perhaps grounded in learning theory or based on some teaching model. There can be great intellectual excitement at this stage, as TAs realize they can take control of curriculum and pedagogy. Given the time and support, they create elegant lectures and design elaborate learning activities, but sometimes they remind us more of generals strategically moving troops on the battlefield than of the passionate student advocates they were just a term before.

At the most advanced stage of development, TAs re-engage their students in a more complex relationship, one that takes on special features in the educational context. Though once again they relate to their students more as unique individuals, TAs no longer feel so personally vulnerable in those relationships. TAs approaching professional maturity are less likely to center on the conflict between wanting to be liked as a friend versus needing to be respected as a teacher. They let go of this false dichotomy, which in fact puts a focus on the needs of the instructor, and think about each student's educational needs. The interpersonal relationship becomes one important resource to draw on in working toward the underlying goal of supporting learning. At this level, the perception of students may best be captured by the word "client." This word calls up the connotation of a relationship involving a skilled professional who is guided by a code of ethics and unselfishly provides a valuable service. Almost paradoxically, at the same time that TAs increase their sense of professional obligation to students, they become less likely to take full responsibility for the outcomes of each interpersonal encounter, realizing that students, too, have obligations for the way a pedagogical relationship evolves. In our interviews, when we listen to TAs talk about their relationships with students, we can hear these rather dramatic shifts:

- **Senior Learner**

  "The most enjoyable interaction with students is more individual type interaction. I mean time-wise it would be hard to do something but I would have loved to have even more time when it was just office hours with the students. I really enjoyed that and I would do as much of it as I could fit in and it would be hard to fit that much more than whatever, eight hours a week or something like that. I would be happy to do more like that. That was the most rewarding interaction between students." (male/zoology)

  "They tell me I am the only teacher that really cares about them. One of them brought me a little card to thank me for all my help on the assignment. There is one guy in the morning section that is just laying for me every day. He thinks he is so smart and whenever he can, he gets his two buddies going along with him. I just want to kick him out. He is always testing me, and I hate it. They hate the theoretical part, but I just say, come on you guys, let's get through this together, and then we can do something more fun." (female/communication)

- **Colleague-in-Training**

  "You know, I am not their mother and they don't need me to be their mother. They need to learn to take care of themselves." (female/psychology)

  "I would say 'use this kind of tube,' and they would take a different tube. And it was just really hard to deal with that, you know. Having people not listen to you when you're teaching them. And I had a lot of trouble with that. You know, what do you do? I ended up being really mean, and

hard on the students. I think I became a lot less chummy over the course of the quarter. " (female/zoology)

- **Junior Colleague**

"I feel like as the quarters have gone on I think I feel maybe less emotionally invested in my students. I don't think that that's necessarily a bad thing. I mean I am still available, and I am definitely being much more careful about being there for my office hours and encouraging people to come in and doing that kind of thing but in terms of an emotional thing. I think that part of it is that when I first got here I really was clinging to my teaching as the thing that was sort of the only thing that was still the same from my old program here. I went from a real small department to a real big department. I knew that I could teach and this was sort of the thing that I was really getting a lot of my identity from. I feel like that's less true. That may be a really healthy thing but it may also not be, I'm not sure. The real rewarding thing was really being more individual and having students that really had problems understanding a concept come to me and hashing it over with them until they understood it. That's like the best feeling, that I really managed to pass along some information or some idea that they didn't get before. " (female/English)

"Um, I think it's a real balance because I have definitely moved away from trying to relate to them, to be their friend. I am in a position of authority over them, and I think it's a mistake to pretend that we're just peers engaging in some process together. At the same time, I really want them to feel comfortable with me. I see myself as trying to facilitate their success in college, and I want them to know that that's really important to me. " (female/English)

"It's a lot of work and [my students] are really rising to the challenge. I feel like that's what I am there to do. I don't, I kind of have a clashing view with some of the other TAs and some of the people running the [writing] program in that I feel like I'm there to push them as far as they can go. That means not necessarily having every assignment be like a closed assignment where I lay out 'here is exactly what I want, fill in these blanks . . .' I feel like that is not what I am about. I do feel like one of the most important things I can do is give [my students] the freedom to achieve as much as they can. " (female/English)

Relationship with Authority

Relationship with authority is the final dimension on which we have charted changes in TAs. At the point of entering TA assignments, TAs are usually very dependent on the faculty supervisor or other experienced instructors with whom they work. They want to know the "right way" to perform as a TA and require a great deal of support and feedback. When TA orientation programs become too philosophical, TAs make no secret of their need for prescriptive and practical advice on what to do in class or lab. A good supervisor is one who provides structure and guidelines and serves as a model of what to do.

Once some experience is gained, often in as little as one term, the TA's relationship with authority begins to change. Especially if there has been positive feedback from students, the TA is eager to become more autonomous. She or he may chafe at standardized course requirements or express philosophical differences with a supervisor. This stage is described as counterdependent because sometimes the motivation goes beyond establishing independence and reflects a need to break with authority.

The third stage of relating to authority is characterized by a more collegial connection between TAs and supervisors. Though the relationship may fall short of full egalitarianism, the TA is likely to be trusted with considerable autonomy and to play a collaborative role in important decisions. Neither hero worship nor resistance is present. Having taught a few terms and inevitably changed some of their own early ideas and practices, TAs gain a respect for the insights a supervisor may have based on years of experience. They can tolerate differences in philosophy and approach without needing to determine if the supervisor's way is right or wrong. There is a growing recognition that underneath the differences are shared goals and necessary, long-term connections to each other as members of the same profession. The changes in attitudes toward their supervisors and faculty members are reflected in these statements:

- **Senior Learner**

   "I would go to my supervisor and find out what she had to say about it. But a lot of times it's little things that can easily be cleared up by just saying 'What do you think of this situation? Does this sound like the right thing to do or is that out of line?'" (female/English)

"That time I had a cheating problem I went in to talk to him and he shuttles me into the chair and that was nice that he held my hand to go in and talk with the department chair and figure out how to handle it." (female/math)

"She didn't give me enough help, and I was just not ready to teach the course." (female/English)

"She's just great. She is the definition of supportive. She is just terrific. Even in the beginning when she came into my class for the very first time. In fact, it was the worst class I'd ever conducted because I changed my agenda to suit her visit. We were going to do some journal entries and a couple of things that the students would do on their own but I thought that she would want to see me teach, and so I went on and did something that I wasn't prepared to do and she saw it, and I'm sure the students saw it and I felt it. But through it all, she was so supportive." (female/English)

- **Colleague-in-Training**

"It's like he [the professor] tries to make it too simple. I guess my feeling— I'm not sure if I can give a good example just off the cuff—but my feeling is I want to give them [the students] the first chance to make some pretty, not extremely, but some relatively complicated links between things without having to explain them." (male/math)

"Another criticism, in terms of his teaching style... His teaching style, for my tastes, talks down to the students too much. You know, treats them as being less intelligent than they really are." (male/math)

"You can talk about it theoretically all you want. This is the biggest problem that I felt with the professor and the way that he taught. He didn't want to give examples because always you are going to give an example that doesn't quite fit. So he talked about it in terms of 'x' and 'y.' So, literally he used the phrase 'x' and 'y'. It was just going over their heads." (female/psychology)

- **Junior Colleague**

"I heard her once telling her class that... if you fall on your tailbone and break the tailbone, there is no way to correct it other than medication. I went down to the library, pulled out a chiropractic book, because I knew

exactly the technique that they did, copied it for her, brought it back, and slipped it to her… and she would go home and read it and just be absolutely entertained, where she would learn something new." (male/biology)

REFINEMENTS OF THE FRAMEWORK OF TA DEVELOPMENT

Now that it has been about a decade since we first offered this model of TA development, we have had opportunities to test it through research and to receive feedback from TAs and those who work with them on how well the model fits their experience. On the whole, we are gratified to learn that it is congruent with the experiences of teaching assistants in many disciplines and on many campuses. At the same time, any generic model runs the risk of oversimplifying and overgeneralizing. What follows are some ways that our thinking has been elaborated and amended as we have worked with the basic model.

Each Stage Has an Essential Role to Play in Development

A key assumption of developmental models—and of our framework—that sometimes gets lost is that movement through a series of steps or phases is a cumulative process. Even if it were possible, it would not be desirable to skip steps in a developmental process because each phase plays an essential role. The behaviors and attitudes of the novice phase are not to be shed, but transformed as growth continues.

Just as a well-adjusted adult retains a healthy component of the joyful and curious child, so do the very best seasoned professors we know somehow retain many of the traits of the senior learner. In our years of work with brand new TAs, we are still amazed at the idealism, openness, and zeal with which they enter our profession. Often their students give them astoundingly high ratings and describe them as the best teachers at the institution. It is easy to discount this as peer identification or "mere popularity," but there is a very important message in the student response to many new teachers: They are doing something right, something that must not be extinguished as they are trained and professionalized.

In the colleague-in-training stage, the TAs add a more analytical component to their teaching identity. This requires a level of detachment. They disengage from their students enough to think about group issues rather than a series of dyadic relationships. They step back from their subject matter to examine its structure and make decisions about curriculum. They see that their graduate faculty do not exhaust the pedagogical or curricular approaches they might adopt. There is an intellectual excitement about teaching issues at this stage that we hope will be internalized and not abandoned when a person becomes more comfortable and adept. It is certainly troubling to hear a TA say, "Now I know how to teach this course," or "I have figured out how to handle this student issue," because there is a sound of finality that may seal off the career-long journey we hope they will pursue.

The third stage of TA development, junior colleague, is intended to represent a synthesis of the important components of the two previous stages. The passion, engagement, and experience of risk-taking of the fledgling TA are brought back and now integrated with the intellectual frameworks, analytical distance, and sense of control that have evolved. Earlier experiences are reconceived and reintegrated. There is a danger that TAs and those who work with them will not see the importance of this final stage of development, so essential to the future professoriate. For the TA, especially if the early experiences of teaching were disenchanting, it is tempting to discard all the assumptions and impulses of the senior learner and hold firmly to the rational and technical insights of the colleague-in-training phase.

TAs' Development Is Neither Linear nor Smooth

Moving through the stages of TA development is not a tidy, step-by-step process. Although there are some dramatic turning points and breakthroughs, like most of life's developmental processes, the professional growth of TAs is frequently clear only in retrospect when some sort of pattern becomes visible out of a ragged "two-step forward, one-step back" process. Supervisors can signpost this growth that may not be evident to TAs themselves: "I know you are discouraged, but remember how only a couple of months ago you were struggling with..."

We have stressed from our earliest explorations of this topic that the path of TA development is best envisioned as a spiral. A vertical line or simple steps suggest that growth all moves in one direction, covering new ground at each phase, which does not capture TA development. Similarly, the popular image of the pendulum is not a completely acceptable alternative. It suggests that teachers cover the same ground over and over again, looking for the perfect spot to land. Most of the time they are wrong, for example, being too lenient, then overreacting by being too strict, and passing over the perfect middle ground along the way. The spiral image is a combination of a pendulum and an ascendant line. TAs are not usually wrong; they are usually right. They may revisit ideas and approaches they have used before, but they return to slightly modified perspectives because of where they have gone in the meantime. Instructors are always faced with issues of classroom management, explaining material that may be fairly new to them, meeting the needs of diverse students, designing courses and pedagogy that will actively engage students, and a myriad of other challenges. Each time we face those issues, as we spiral up, we face them on the basis of new experience and knowledge—at least we do if we are systematic and reflective about our teaching.

The growth and development are never finished. Completion of the formal TA experience does not mark a sharp transition from colleague-in-training to a fully prepared faculty member. The research on new faculty experience makes it clear that, for many, the quest for a teaching identity persists well into the early years of faculty life. Assistant professors, even those with graduate degrees from institutions with strong TA programs, continue through spirals of engagement and disengagement from students or collaboration and separation from their senior colleagues. In their new positions, their concerns change back to self concerns, and they struggle to find the right discourse level for various levels of instruction.

The Role of Affect Cannot Be Minimized in Understanding TA Development

The teaching/learning encounter is first and foremost an intense human activity. Anyone who moves into the role of teacher will make some profound personal changes. No model of stages completely captures the existential highs and lows that TAs live through. Each transformation is accompanied by some very painful realizations. In the move from senior learner to colleague-in-training, for example, TAs usually have to let go of a passionately held view of the teacher/student relationship. Dozens of TAs have reported feeling personally hurt when they first discovered that one of their students had cheated on an assignment. The experience of betrayal by a student or disillusionment with an admired mentor is not unlike the feelings a person has when spurned by a partner in a truly committed relationship. Sometimes the pain is so great that the individual never risks closeness again. So teachers, unless caringly supported through their early disappointments, may withdraw from ever making themselves vulnerable to students again, thus sealing off much that is precious in teaching.

A similar cynicism can ensue when a new TA spends hours working out a course design that backfires. That person may choose to heed the ubiquitous messages to "work smart" and never again make a major intellectual investment in teaching. Though appearing on the surface to be a competent teacher, he or she may treat instruction as a job, saving passion and risk-taking for research. The developmental model is not meant to present the journey from new TA to active professional as predictable and therefore safe. Each transition involves wrenching changes that require the support of a caring professional community.

Meaningful TA Development Entails Development of Reflectiveness

An important expansion of our thinking about TA development is the role of reflectiveness. For the majority of TAs there is not only a change in what they say about their concerns, their disciplines, their students, and their supervisors; there also are changes in how they talk and, presumably, how they think about their teaching assignments. In general, they become more reflective and more articulate. The comments they make about teaching and learning become richer and more differentiated and better capture the complexity of these activities and their observations.

These changes in reflectiveness raise some questions for us. At a theoretical level, perhaps our model should include a dimension that shows low reflectiveness for senior learners and moves toward high reflectiveness at the junior colleague level. Certainly one cannot reflect until there are some experiences to reflect upon. A teacher cannot think comparatively about groups of students before teaching a few different classes, or see the pros and cons of different teaching approaches until a few have been tried. But beyond these rather obvious changes, our observations suggest that growth in reflection is far from automatic. In fact, new TAs spend a great deal of time reflecting on their teaching experiences. They relive their classes, retell their stories in great detail, and speculate at length about what might have been different. At the same time, many more advanced TAs actually reflect less as they master the basic skills of teaching and their work becomes routinized. Why do some TAs become more reflective while others resist introspection and remain relatively

TABLE 4.2

Responses Indicating Minimal Reflection
Math, Male TA

	STRENGTHS	AREAS FOR IMPROVEMENT
1ST INTERVIEW (first year—halfway through)	*At this point in your teaching, what would you say are some of your primary skills and abilities in teaching math, as the course you are teaching?* I don't know. *No idea at all?* No. *I mean have you heard, could you say anything, have you gotten feedback from the students? Like when someone says, "oh that explanation you gave us was really helpful" or something like that?* No, not really.	*What about things that you feel like you might want to develop, have you identified anything yet that you think you might want to work on or might want to be a hallmark of the way that you teach?* I don't know. Not...I mean, no. I haven't analyzed to that degree. *What do you think a student would say if I asked a student? What does this guy do the best in this classroom?* That, I honestly couldn't say.
2ND INTERVIEW (first year—at end)	My strengths. Well, I guess like if asked, I can usually get across what I am trying to say. I can explain something if people have questions about it, so that is a good thing.	Well, I think that I occasionally get bogged down in notation and things like that. Just using symbols for things. Occasionally sometimes...It's if you haven't seen a subject before and somebody is writing down a string of Greek letters then it looks imposing.
3RD INTERVIEW (second year—halfway through)	*We've talked about your strengths before. Let's do this both as a graduate student and as a TA. What do you think are your strengths?* (Pause) *Is it more in the content, is it more of the way you relate to me as a student, is it the way you can work with supervisors?* I don't know. (Pause) I think I've been pretty relaxed about things. That can be good. *You mean from the stress standpoint? You don't get too much stress about "I've got to do this...?"* Well, I don't know. Sometimes. But, you know. Just do it.	*In your TAing are there areas that you'd like to be better at, or you think "I gotta work on that more before next quarter"?* Sometimes, yeah. I don't know, sometimes...It's more like a specific example thing. Like, you know, like I have two sections, one right after the other, and I'll do the same thing in each section. Like I'll cover the same material. But sometimes I'll go to the second section...I'll say it differently because I'll say it the first time and for some reason it just seems better to say, at the time at least, see it's better to say it the other way. *So you learned something from that? Doing it twice?* Yeah. But I don't know if there's a general principle I can extract from that.

inarticulate about their teaching experience? Table 4.2 details the responses by the same individual over a period of 14 months in three different interviews.

This TA seems to actively resist reflection, even when the interviewers first invite, and then even prod, him to think about his teaching. He is consistently unwilling to stretch for words to describe his experience. Moreover, he appears to be holding on to a prior model of education that is deeply ingrained and somewhat magical: "I just do it."

It is possible that this TA has "developed" on some of the dimensions of our model, but any development will hit a ceiling of "mere competence" if it is not accompanied with increasingly sophisticated reflection on teaching. At the level of personal career fulfillment, the unreflective university instructor will not be intellectually challenged by the unending puzzles that present themselves in our classrooms. From the perspective of our universities' requirements for a well-prepared future professoriate, there is an urgent need for colleagues who are willing to tackle the complex intersection of ethical, practical, and philosophical issues facing higher education. Reflection is essential.

TAs' voices are composites of significant people who have influenced them, replete with contradictions and tensions. The TA who could not talk in any detail about his own strengths and weaknesses, even in the third interview, was probably not a member of a group that participated in guided reflection. He probably did not have a supervisor who supported his reflective development by engaging him in discussions of the richness of his early teaching experiences.

Returning to the communication perspective introduced earlier, we believe that a careful attention to nuance of language is useful for purposes beyond identifying the TAs' development level. Knowing the many messages that TAs are already receiving from some of their professors and peers, TA supervisors can decide to add other voices to the mix by actively modeling the forms of discourse that characterize reflective practitioners. Though we do not want graduate students to imitate us, we admit to being flattered when junior colleagues with whom we have worked closely pick up some of our trademark phrases such as Jo's "it's a balancing act between x and y" or Jody's "help me think about this." How can a person regularly use such phrases in talking about teaching without starting to think and act as if it were a complex and collaborative activity?

Besides choosing vocabularies that neither trivialize nor privatize teaching, supervisors can use discourse to structure even more active interventions that aid TA development. The kind of speech communities created in TA meetings and individual conferences can be carefully calibrated to elicit TAs' inner struggles to assist them in their thinking through difficult issues. In Vygotskian terms, a teacher or mentor "scaffolds" learning by offering verbal props and prods to help crystallize new insights. Assistance to a learner only works if it falls within a realistic zone; the learner needs to be challenged yet cannot be pushed too far beyond the current developmental level. Effective scaffolding is a delicate blend of recognizing and affirming where the learner is and inviting him or her to flex just a little. If a group of brand new TAs is expressing self concerns and demanding advice on classroom management, the supervisor will not refuse to give them tips and suggestions. But instead of offering definitive prescriptions, perhaps that supervisor can gently nudge them toward reflecting a bit on alternatives. If a TA is engaged in what sounds like student bashing, the supervisor should resist the temptation to reject the feelings of anger or disappointment that gave rise to the expression. After expressing empathy, it can be helpful to ask a question like "What could your students possibly be thinking that would make so many of them interpret the assignment that way?" At moments of developmental transitions, conversations with peers and supervisors have special salience. In these moments a new kind of discourse can be established and internalized, perhaps to become the basis for future action and thinking about teaching.

CONCLUDING THOUGHTS

Obviously, given the perspectives we have just outlined, TA supervision is not a routine management job. If we are really thinking developmentally about the teaching preparation of the future generation of college/university faculty or the teaching preparation needed in other professional careers, we who supervise TAs must think systematically and developmentally about what we are doing and how we are doing it. TAs are continuously developing, and we must adapt our strategies, our expectations, and our relationships with them to meet the needs of growing professionals. What does all this mean for a TA supervisor faced with a group of graduate students with varied experiences as teachers who must in a short space of time become qualified, competent interpreters of a discipline to undergraduates? And what does this all mean for TA supervisors who are responsible for assisting graduate students to grow into thoughtful professionals who will be equipped to teach in higher education or in positions in business, industry, and government? The challenge itself is daunting.

We have suggested elsewhere (Nyquist & Wulff, 1996) how the supervisor's role might change across a number of dimensions: relationships with TAs, teaching assignments, teacher training activities, and evaluation processes which are appropriate at various developmental stages. As graduate students change and develop, they will need supervisors who can model the values, behaviors, and characteristics of a professional in their field. TAs will benefit from supervisors who adapt as the TAs change, providing close supervision in the beginning but progressing to a role as consultant and colleague. For this to happen, the supervisor must incrementally and appropriately transfer responsibility for instructional decisions to the TA. In the ideal situation, the assignments for TAs should show a similar progression from specified duties or an assisting role to assuming responsibility for class sessions or even a whole course. TA preparation activities would also need to move from directed supervision to reflective practicums where approaches, results, and new ideas would be shared among colleagues. And, finally, assessment practices of TA performance should move from direct, daily/weekly assessment to providing collegial feedback helping the TA to develop a personal teaching style.

TA supervisors need not face alone the challenges we have identified. They can form partnerships with TAs, even going so far as explaining to TAs how one approaches supervisory challenges. Some supervisors we know share the framework described above with their TAs and find that TAs can relate to the stages and can even place themselves on the four dimensions of their concerns, their discourse, and their relationships with students and with authority. The supervisors report that such an experience is supportive for TAs and allows them to better understand their own needs and ways of getting them met.

Other supervisors use the framework to guide their own assessment and planning for TAs and to introduce the insights of the developmental process incrementally. When they deal with concerns, they assure novices that intense concerns about themselves are natural—that soon they will be able to move to concerns about the impact of instruction on student learning. When TAs report their first anxieties about students, the supervisor takes time to talk about the natural progression from a personalized relationship to a collaborator/client relationship with students through detachment and objectivity. And many supervisors report that it is helpful to understand the middle stage that TAs go through, where they can almost seem to be regressing on some dimensions. Can this TA who acts as if you cannot do anything that is acceptable be the same person who used to cling to your every word? Parents live through the terrible twos and the horrors of adolescence more comfortably when they see the defiant acts of those periods as essential steps of growth. So, too, when supervisors are able to reframe TA "resistance" as temporary, they will let go more easily, encourage TAs to explore other models of teaching and to find several mentors. They do not abandon leadership but find ways to foster growth with a lighter touch.

But thinking developmentally goes beyond the preliminary model we posed for our colleagues who work with TAs. Surely our three-stage diagram is only a starting point, modified by the many contextual factors and individual differences we have mentioned, and under continued revision as we conduct our current study. What is most important about this way of thinking, we argue, is the opportunity it provides for us to listen carefully to TAs, to seek to capture some part of the dynamic and complex nature of their experience, and to consider more creative and comprehensive ways of working with them.

ENDNOTES

[1] For information on the original project, contact the Council of Graduate Schools in Washington, DC, or see Gaff and Lambert (1996). See also Chapter 16 of this volume.

[2] Due to the generous support of the Pew Charitable Trusts and the Spencer Foundation, we have now completed three years of a four-year, multisite study entitled "The Development of Graduate Students as Prospective Teaching Scholars: A Longitudinal Research Project." Other coprincipal investigators are Ann Austin, Michigan State University, and Donald Wulff, University of Washington. The team includes research assistants: Bettina Woodford, University of Washington; Patti Fraser, Michigan State University; Claire Calcagno, San Jose State University;

and Laura Manning, University of Washington. Unless otherwise indicated, quotations in this chapter are from this study.

REFERENCES

Bakhtin, M. M. (1981). *The dialogic imagination: Four essays* (C. Emerson & M. Holquist, Trans.). Austin, TX: University of Texas.

Book, C., & Eisenberg, E. M. (1979, November). *Communication concerns of graduate and undergraduate teaching assistants.* Paper presented at the convention of the Speech Communication Association, San Antonio, TX.

Brookfield, S. D. (1990). *The skillful teacher: On technique, trust, and responsiveness in the classroom.* San Francisco, CA: Jossey-Bass.

Connolly, K. J., & Bruner, J. S. (1974). *The growth of competence.* New York, NY: Academic Press.

Darling, A. L. (1986). *On becoming a graduate student: An examination of communication in the socialization process.* Paper presented at the annual meeting of the Speech Communication Association, Chicago, IL.

Fuller, F. F. (1969). Concerns of teachers: A developmental perspective. *American Educational Research Journal, 2,* 207-226.

Gaff, J. G., & Lambert, L. M. (1996). Socializing future faculty to the values of undergraduate education. *Change, 28* (4), 38-45.

Hunt, D. (1971). *Matching models in education.* Toronto, ONT: Ontario Institute for Studies in Education.

Kagan, D. M. (1988). Research on the supervision of counselors and teachers-in-training: Linking two bodies of literature. *Review of Educational Research, 58,* 1-24.

Nyquist, J. D. (1993). The development of faculty as teachers. In M. Weimer (Ed.), *Faculty as teachers: Taking stock of what we know.* University Park, PA: National Center on Postsecondary Teaching, Learning, and Assessment (NCTLA).

Nyquist, J. D., Abbott, R. A., Wulff, D. H., & Sprague, J. (Eds.). (1991). *Preparing the professoriate of tomorrow to teach: Selected readings in TA training.* Dubuque, IA: Kendall/Hunt.

Nyquist, J. D., & Sprague, J. (1992). Developmental stages of TAs. In J. D. Nyquist & D. H. Wulff (Eds.), *Preparing teaching assistants for instructional roles: Supervising TAs in communication.* Washington, DC: Speech Communication Association.

Nyquist, J. D., & Wulff, D. H. (1996). *Working effectively with graduate assistants.* Thousand Oaks, CA: Sage.

Perry, W. G. (1970). *Form of intellectual and ethical development in the college years.* New York, NY: Holt, Rinehart, and Winston.

Schön, D. A. (1987). *Educating the reflective practitioner: Toward a new design for teaching and learning in the professions.* San Francisco, CA: Jossey-Bass.

Sprague, J., & Nyquist, J. D. (1989). TA supervision. In J. D. Nyquist, R. D. Abbott, & D. H. Wulff (Eds.), *Teaching assistant training in the 1990s.* New Directions for Teaching and Learning, No. 39. San Francisco, CA: Jossey-Bass.

Sprague, J., & Nyquist, J. D. (1991). A developmental perspective on the TA role. In J. D. Nyquist, R. D. Abbott, D. H. Wulff, & J. Sprague (Eds.), *Preparing the professoriate of tomorrow to teach: Selected readings in TA training.* Dubuque, IA: Kendall/Hunt.

Sprinthall, N. A., & Theis-Sprinthall, L. (1983). The need for theoretical frameworks in educating teachers: A cognitive developmental perspective. In K. R. Howey & W. E. Gardner (Eds.), *The education of teachers: A look ahead.* New York, NY: Longman.

Staton, A. Q., & Darling, A. L. (1989). Socialization of teaching assistants. In J. D. Nyquist, R. D. Abbott, & D. H. Wulff (Eds.), *Teaching assistant training in the 1990s.* New Directions for Teaching and Learning, No. 39. San Francisco, CA: Jossey-Bass.

Staton-Spicer, A. Q., & Bassett, R. E. (1979). Communication concerns of preservice and inservice elementary school teachers. *Human Communication Research, 5,* 138-146.

Vygotsky, L. (1986). *Thought and language* (A. Kozulin, Trans.). Cambridge, MA: MIT Press. (Originally published 1962).

Williams, J. M. (1986, November). *Hidden meanings: Critical thinking and acculturation.* Paper presented at the University of Chicago Conference on Cognition and Writing in Discourse Communities, Chicago, IL.

Wulff, D. H. (1993). Tales of transformation: Applying a teaching effectiveness perspective to stories about teaching. *Communication Education, 42* (4), 377-397.

5

CREATING A FOUNDATION FOR INSTRUCTIONAL DECISIONS

Marilla D. Svinicki

Surely there must be something in the research that could tell me how to teach my students!"

Many a TA has had the experience of not knowing how to decide on the best way to reach students or even what alternatives are possible. In the past, there was not much that could be gleaned from the literature on learning theory because the field was in its infancy with regard to the practical applications. Now, however, psychological research has come a long way, and there are effective strategies for maximizing student learning.

The goal of this chapter is to condense the theory and research on learning into a succinct and pragmatic discussion of how a TA can help students learn. Five areas of study in psychology showing the most promise for instructional design are highlighted. They focus on the following student learning tasks: the learning of basic content, the development of application and intellectual skills, the development of attitudes and values, the recognition of individual differences in learning, and the development of motivational and emotional control.

In what follows, I will describe each of these areas in brief, explain several key ideas from that area, and provide examples of practice. The discussion only brushes the surface of each of these areas, but it should help TA trainers decide what material on learning theory is important for TAs to know.

HELPING STUDENTS LEARN BASIC CONTENT

The underlying learning process: In learning basic content, the students are attempting to connect the new content to what already makes up their personal understanding of the world.

Key word: Connections.

How This Process Affects Instruction

1) What the students already know or believe about a topic (prior knowledge) will influence how they learn new information about that topic. We all interpret new information in light of our current world view (our prior knowledge). For example, if we already think a certain politician is a liberal, we will "hear" those things he or she says that are consistent with our beliefs about liberal politics and either "not hear" or reinterpret comments he or she makes that have a conservative flavor.

Sometimes our prior knowledge affects what we are able to see in a situation. For example, individuals with prior knowledge about baseball will get much more out of watching a baseball game than those with no knowledge of baseball. They will understand the nuances behind the action, why a particular pitch is made at a particular time, why some runners are out while others are not, what it means to be "3 and 2." The same is true in classes: Students who already know something about the topic get more out of a learning episode than those who are brand new to it, which is one reason why it seems easier to teach majors than non-majors.

In another example of the influence of prior knowledge, one of the most difficult tasks for a learner is to unlearn a well-established bad habit, whether it is something physical like an idiosyncratic backhand in tennis or something intellectual like a prejudice against a given subpopulation. In each case we are dealing with faulty prior knowledge. But faulty or not, the fact that the knowledge, belief, or skill is already a part of the long-term memory makes it hard to dislodge.

These examples mean that teaching assistants must be aware of what prior knowledge students bring to the situation and how it can influence student learning. That way misconceptions can be countered, and helpful prior knowledge can be used as the basis for connections with new information students are learning.

Examples of ways to use this idea to structure teaching:

- At the start of a session, remind students of what they already know about the topic as a way of activating their prior knowledge and using it as a base for new information.

- If there are commonly held misconceptions about information in your field, confront them directly if you want to change them. Create a survey of those misconceptions and use it as the basis for bringing beliefs to the surface for discussion.

- Use examples from the students' own background to capitalize on their prior knowledge. Invite students to give you examples of content from their own perspectives so they will see how what they are learning connects with their experience.

2) Perhaps the most important part of learning for long-term retention of content is making connections between ideas, old and new. Long-term memory is conceived of as a vast network of connections between old and new information, processes, and beliefs. If new information can be connected to that network, it will be available in the future. The more connections that can be made, the easier the information is to resurrect.

Examples of ways to use this idea to structure teaching:

- Highlight connections between new information and the students' past experiences inside and outside the class.

- Provide multiple concrete examples to which the students can relate. Concrete examples often are more visual in nature, and visual images are a very good source of connections because they are so rich in information.

- Have the students expand on the basic information by thinking up examples from their own experience and by speculating on how they could use it. Have them create analogies to other information they already understand.

3) An important component of learning content is the development of an understanding of the underlying structure of a topic, including what the superordinate categories are and what other information is subsumed under them, what relates to what, and how ideas and procedures intersect. Understanding the deep, interrelated structure of a content area allows a learner to take in new information more easily because he or she already has a place to put it. It is not necessary to remember every detail of new information as long as the learner can place the information in the overall structure of the subject and from that reconstruct the original information. For example, if I know that there are four foods—breads and cereals, fruit and vegetables, meats and dairy products, and fats—it is not necessary to memorize where bananas belong; by understanding the categories, I can place bananas into the appropriate category fairly readily.

Examples of ways to use this idea to structure teaching:

- Provide or have students create outlines or concept maps of a topic to illustrate the underlying structure of the content.

- Ask questions in class and on exams that require students to make use of their structural knowledge about the content. For example, asking "why" or "how" questions is more likely to elicit deep processing of ideas than asking "what" questions.

- In presenting information, use comparison charts and tables that illustrate structural divisions, such as pros and cons, categories of objects (such as a table of the four food groups having one row for each group), or have students construct such organizers themselves.

4) Concrete examples are one of the first ways in which new information is processed. In learning concepts, especially abstract concepts, students will initially focus on one or more examples that the instructor uses as illustrations. Those examples then become the standards against which other examples are tested. Any example not matching these prototypes will be discarded as not correct. Therefore it is important to have carefully crafted concrete examples early in learning, followed with clear yet contrasting concrete examples that highlight key differences between examples and nonexamples of the concept.

Examples of ways to use this idea to structure teaching:

- Give more than one example of a concept in order to ensure that the students have at least one that is meaningful to them.

- Give concrete examples of abstract concepts if at all possible to provide an anchor for the students' initial understanding.

- Give both positive and negative examples of a concept to help students identify the key features.

HELPING STUDENTS LEARN TO APPLY PROCEDURES OR SKILLS

The underlying learning process: In learning procedures or skills of all types (including intellectual skills such as analysis or critical thinking), the learner creates a mental model of how to perform that skill and uses that model to guide his or her own performance, similar to the way an apprentice learns by observing and assisting a master craftsman.

Key words: Apprenticeship, coaching, demonstration (modeling).

How This Process Affects Instruction

1) An effective demonstration or model of a skill is one in which the key skill characteristics are easy to identify. In order for a learner to be able to create a good mental representation of the skill being learned, he or she has to be able to recognize its key behaviors. Experts forget what it is like to be a novice at a particular skill and often blur the distinctions between steps or skip steps entirely because they seem so obvious. For example, think of the number of steps you would have to list in order to describe how to tie a bow. What seems like a very easy skill is actually quite complex and often difficult for an expert to describe and a novice to understand.

The same thing happens in the classroom. For example, if an instructor is demonstrating how to solve a particular type of problem on the board, and he or she goes through the process really quickly, skipping or collapsing some steps and giving only the barest details of others, it will be very difficult for the students to reproduce that problem solving process on their own later.

In order to provide an effective model of a skill, an expert must analyze its component skills and decide which components to highlight during the demonstration. Then when demonstrating, the expert must go more slowly and deliberately, with more emphasis of the key steps, and, if at all possible, a running narrative that explains the how and why of each component.

Examples of ways to use this idea to structure teaching:

- Allow students to bring problems to class so you can attempt to solve them in class. Throughout the problem solving process, talk aloud about what is happening and why so that students can follow.

- Work out the steps of a process you will be demonstrating before the actual demonstration in order to be sure that all the key components are presented and highlighted.

- Give the learners a preview of the steps of a skill before actually doing the demonstration so that they will know what to look for while it is performed.

2) A learner needs to remember the key components of the skill in order to guide his or her own performance. Often when we are first learning a skill—physical or intellectual—we need a crutch to help us remember what comes first, what comes next, and what to be sure to include. For example, children are taught the phrase "Stop, drop, and roll" to help them remember what to do if their clothes catch on fire. Each word represents an action, "Stop" (don't run), "drop" (lie down), and "roll" (roll over and over to put out the flames). On a more advanced level, journalists use the five W's in writing a story: "Who, what, when, where, and why?" Such phrases or mnemonics help the learner remember the components of the skill and then serve as a guide for performance. Sometimes the mnemonic will be a visual image that can guide a response. For example, tennis coaches often tell their students to make the service motion as if they were throwing a ball. For the analytical skill of understanding structure, students can visualize the process of a flow chart in which each branch highlights a different step in the procedure.

Examples of ways to use this idea to structure teaching:

- Create a mnemonic for students to talk themselves through the performance of a skill or process, and share it with them from the very beginning so they get a firm grasp on the sequence or components.

- Encourage the students to talk themselves through the process initially until the steps in the procedure become second nature.

- Use visual metaphors to help students remember components or sequences of a skill.

3) An important step in learning any skill is the opportunity to practice it and receive timely feedback on one's performance. We would never consider going out after only one tennis lesson and challenging the first person we meet to a match. Simply knowing how to hit the ball is not enough to produce proficiency. A skill, whether physical or intellectual, needs to be practiced, preferably under the guidance of a coach who will give corrective as well as supportive feedback.

In the same manner, learners need opportunities to practice application of intellectual skills under the guidance of a coach, either the instructor or another more proficient student. For example, in guiding the learning of argumentation the coach might prompt students with the key questions: "Was the argument that was presented in an analytical critique a good one? Did the argument include sufficient supporting material? Were the thoughts chosen the most persuasive?"

Examples of ways to use this idea to structure teaching:

- After demonstrating how to perform a problem analysis or critical thinking task, give the students an opportunity to apply the process themselves, while you are still available to provide feedback and offer guidance.

- As students become more skilled, they can act as coaches for one another by observing a peer's performance and providing a critique. This has the added advantage that the coach is sharpening his or her skills at the same time.

4) Learners need to learn to observe and modify their own learning. Eventually, of course, every apprentice must learn to monitor and critique his or her own work. The same is true for cognitive apprentices: They must learn to recognize when they do or do not understand, to select a strategy for learning that is most appropriate for the situation, and to modify that strategy according to its results.

Examples of ways to use this idea to structure teaching:

- Encourage or require students to keep a journal of their problem solving processes so that they can review and critique what they did and how they got where they are. This will support the development of their self-observation skills.

- Pause occasionally during lecture or discussion and invite students to review what they understood about what just happened in class. This review can be done individually or in groups; it can be written or just described. Then provide feedback on the accuracy of their understanding by giving a short summary of your own.

HELPING STUDENTS DEVELOP ATTITUDES AND VALUES

The underlying learning process: Learners develop attitudes and values by challenging their beliefs and observing others who represent the target attitudes and values.

Key words: Challenge and support; role models.

How This Process Affects Instruction

1) A student's beliefs about how we know what is true influences how he or she will go about learning. Much has been written in recent years about students' epistemological beliefs and their impact on learning (Baxter-Magolda, 1992; Perry, 1970; Gilligan, 1982; Belenky, Clinchy, Goldberger, & Tarule, 1986). In a very general way, all these theories say that students begin their educational journey with a very fixed view of truth: There is a right and a wrong answer, and the authorities will be testing you on how well you can repeat those absolutes. As a result of these beliefs, beginning students will exhibit an overdependence on the instructor, the textbook, or any other source perceived as speaking with authority. Students will be unwilling to challenge ideas because they will not believe in the possibility that they might be correct if they challenge an authority. Papers from students at this stage will be summaries or paraphrases rather than true critiques, their preferred teaching mode will be lecture, and their most common study strategy memorization.

As students become more comfortable with the lack of certainty that comes with greater understanding, they will be more willing to engage in a true dialogue with the instructor and with one another as a means of learning. They will be more likely to tackle topics that are not as "safe." They will question authority and seek a fuller explanation for events. Papers from students at this stage will be more dialectic in nature; they will enjoy discussions and problem solving classes more, and they will be more open to looking at the subject in an integrative way. Their study strategies will become more varied and appropriate to the situation.

Examples of ways to use this idea to structure teaching:

- Even in beginning classes, make an effort to model scholarly questioning of ideas so that students develop a more complex model for thinking by observing you.

- Make assignments that encourage students to look at an idea from many perspectives and to make choices among competing beliefs on the basis of understanding rather than unquestioned acceptance.

2) Progress toward more complex epistemologies requires practice in making and responding to challenges of one's beliefs, but it also requires a safe environment in which the learner can feel free to fail. The goal of higher education is to move students toward a more contextual understanding of truth or a reasoned commitment to a given perspective, toward the belief that the situation affects what might be true, and that the learner has a responsibility to resist an unquestioned acceptance of authority and develop his or her own analysis of the truth. Even though TAs are still students themselves, they are further along in developing the kind of scholarly thinking this goal entails. One difficulty TAs may have with this issue is doubts about their own understanding of the material and a fear of being asked a question they cannot answer. They often worry that any appearance of uncertainty will undermine their authority. While this is a very common and understandable concern, we should be aware that students are in need of good role models who can be comfortable with uncertainty and change.

Examples of ways to use this idea to structure teaching:

- Respond in a positive, nondefensive way to students' initial attempts at questioning authority. Help them view their attempts from the perspective of the questioning process by asking probing questions about evidence, clarification of positions, and implications of their question.

- During discussions of issues, talk aloud about the process of challenge, articulating the steps one takes to determine the value of an argument. For very new students, provide an algorithm that will help them remember what to ask and why. With repeated practice, the students will eventually internalize the process.

- Recognize the value of demonstrating how to deal emotionally with uncertainty by discussing your own experiences of doubt and how you deal with them.

RECOGNIZING AND RESPONDING
TO INDIVIDUAL DIFFERENCES IN LEARNING

The underlying learning process: There are some individual preference and skill differences among learners in how they go about learning.
Key word: Variety.

How This Process Affects Instruction

1) The concept of learning styles is useful for recognizing that in the same situation learners make different choices based on preferences, skills, aptitudes, and past successes, but learning styles should not be taken as a classification system with which to stereotype individuals. Each individual will have one or more preferred ways to go about learning new information or skills. It would be premature, however, to believe that we know enough about human learning to put learners into neat categories intended to explain everything they do. In reality, all learners have multiple strategies that are appropriate for different situations. Good learners are adept at manipulating these strategies to maximize their learning, but all learners can be encouraged to expand their repertoire and learn to use strategies more effectively.

Patterns of differences in learning are more well established in some areas than in others. For example, one individual difference that has been investigated is the degree to which a learner prefers either to get a big picture before the details are introduced or to let the big picture emerge out of the sequential presentation of the details. In the literature this is known respectively as holistic versus serial processing of information (Pask, 1988), or global versus analytic processing (Kirby, 1988). It is easy to see how this preference can translate into instructional sequence design: Holistic processors would prefer that a class begin with an overview, while serial processors would prefer to move step by step and build to a climax.

Another individual difference that is often mentioned is the idea that learners prefer different channels of content presentation. The three most commonly cited modes are visual, auditory, and kinesthetic. Visual learners look for images and create graphs or maps of information as a way of understanding its structure. Auditory learners are most comfortable with an oral presentation of ideas, as is the case in lectures. Kinesthetic learners prefer to get involved directly with the manipulation of the concepts, especially where performance of the skill is the goal.

Quite a bit of research has concentrated on the concepts of field independence versus field sensitivity in learning (Witkin, Moore, Goodenough, & Cox, 1977). Individuals demonstrating field independence can more readily extract from a situation the key ideas or variables and consider them separately from the surround, while field-sensitive individuals are more adept at looking at an idea in context and responding relative to that context. Therefore, disciplines in which there is a great deal of abstraction required, such as math, would be more attractive to field-independent learners and more troublesome for those exhibiting a preference for field sensitivity, whereas disciplines such as the social sciences, where situational cues are extremely important, would be easier for field-sensitive learners.

Another much studied area of individual difference is extroversion versus introversion. Since these concepts are fairly well understood by the general public, I will only say here that they have implications for the degree to which students are comfortable in collaborative learning environments and active learning situations that involve public performance.

However, one possibly related characteristic that has a more direct impact on learning is risk-taking. Some students are more willing to take risks, and some situations lend themselves more readily to risk-taking. One theory supporting this difference focuses on student goal orientation (Eison, 1981; Ames, 1992). In the literature, students are characterized as having either a mastery orientation or a performance orientation, a learning versus a grade orientation, deep achieving versus surface achieving, and other descriptors. Students exhibiting a mastery orientation have as their goal mastery of the content or skill, no matter what it takes. These students are more willing to take risks if they believe that they can learn from the experience. Students exhibiting a performance orientation have as their goal the demonstration of their competence at a particular task. These students are not interested in taking risks because risks could lead to failure, which could in turn imply low levels of competence. Therefore, they will do their learning in private and only go public when they are convinced that they have reached an acceptable level of performance.

Examples of ways to use this idea to structure teaching:

- Because we tend to teach in a way consistent with our own learning preferences, an instructor should be aware that a student's failure to understand may not be an indication of a lack of intelligence but simply a temporary incompatibility between conflicting learning preferences. Therefore, inviting a student to describe how he or she went about learning or understanding rather than simply repeating our own version would be more likely to help us support that learning.

- As instructors, we should develop multiple ways of representing ideas so that students will be able to choose one that is most meaningful to them or best fits their preferences. Offering multiple examples, multiple modes of input, and multiple ways of accomplishing the same objectives allows students to tailor the instruction to their needs.

- If possible, we should help students develop alternative learning strategies under a variety of conditions so that they will not be tied to only one. This can be done by modeling multiple strategies and pointing out the processes that underlie them. Students can also learn strategies from other students through the process of collaborative learning.

HELPING STUDENTS DEVELOP THE MOTIVATIONAL ASPECTS OF LEARNING

The underlying learning process: Learning is influenced by the learner's motivational and emotional state as well as his or her intellectual state.

Key words: Value of the task; estimates for success; self-efficacy.

How This Process Affects Instruction

1) Motivation is a function of the value of the task, intrinsic or extrinsic. Not all learning is of equal value to all learners. However, the greater the value of the learning to a given learner, the higher the motivation to complete it and the higher the likelihood of success. This is especially true if the motivation is intrinsic, that is, if it derives from within the learner rather than being imposed from the outside. There are many ways to help learners see the value of a task. For example, if the goals of the task are consistent with those of the learner, it will have higher task value. Helping learners see that relationship is a way of enhancing their motivation to learn. Another way of increasing the task value is to schedule the learning just before there is a real need for the skills the task represents. I personally never learned much statistics until I had to use it on my dissertation, when I could see a real need for it.

Aside from the utility value of tasks, there are some qualities inherent in the task itself or the situation that enhance its value. For example, some content is simply more attractively packaged or inherently interesting. We hardly ever have to assign the chapters on deviant sexual behavior when we are teaching introductory psychology; those chapters were just more interesting to our students than perception or cognition. Sometimes it is the way the material is presented, for example, with graphics and elaborations, that appeals to different types of learners.

In the area of research on intrinsic motivation, two factors are particularly salient: challenge and control. In research on the concept of "flow," which represents the ultimate experience of intrinsic motivation (Csikszentmihalyi, 1975), researchers have found that individuals who are working at a task that is just at the upper edge of their skill level (so that it is a challenge) but who still feel in control of the situation report very high levels of motivation. They attribute the high motivation to the value of being able to face and succeed at a challenging task.

A second intrinsic source of motivation is the feeling of having control over your world (Deci & Ryan, 1985). Learners who are given choices as to how they will accomplish a given objective experience a higher level of motivation than those who are working in a prescribed way at required tasks.

Examples of ways to use this idea to structure teaching:

- Create assignments for which the goals are clearly related to areas of learner interest or future requirements and make that relationship clear.

- Give students a choice in the ways in which to fulfill course requirements.

- Make the learning tasks challenging enough that students will feel a pride in having accomplished them.

- If possible, use motivation sources that are intrinsic to the learner rather than imposed from the outside.

2) Motivation is a function of the learner's expectancy for success. Although the task value is an important component of motivation, equally important is the perceived likelihood of success at the task. If students feel that they have no chance of ever learning the material well enough to succeed in its use, their motivation will be low and their tolerance for frustration and setbacks almost nonexistent.

Learners base their estimates for success on several factors. There is, of course, the difficulty of the task itself. Some tasks, like learning quantum physics, are very difficult, individual differences aside. The extent to which the learner possesses skills that match the demands of the task also affects estimates for success. For example, much as I would like to be able to dunk a basketball like Michael Jordan, my height (5'2") is simply not matched to the demands of that task. I could practice all day every day and still not come even close.

Of course, a student's perceived skill level, or sense of self-efficacy, and his or her actual skill level may not be consistent, which will cause other problems in motivation down the line. In addition to self-efficacy, there may be some overall self-evaluation that increases or decreases a learner's estimates for the probability of success. One student may think of himself or herself as a good student, and, therefore, have higher estimates for success than another student who is convinced that he or she is a poor student in general.

Learners also base their success estimates on past experience. If this task is something at which they have been successful in the past, they are likely to predict success in the future as well.

Examples of ways to use this idea to structure teaching:

- To help students raise their estimates of success, it is helpful to start them out on the learning task with some early successes. Since they base their estimates on past performance, this would increase their feelings of optimism with regard to the task.

- It is also helpful to have the students compare their current skills with those required of the task in order to get a good estimate of success. Sometimes students overlook their own skills or deficits, either of which could lead to an erroneous interpretation of the situation.

3) How a learner interprets the outcome influences motivation. Regardless of the realities of a situation, an important influence on students' motivation is their belief about what caused their success or failure. If they believe that they are in control of the situation, their motivation to put forth effort will be higher than if they see themselves as tossed about by fate or outside malevolent forces. This concept of "locus of control" is an important determiner of student motivation and is one of the first to be worked on with at-risk learners (Weiner, 1979).

What we would really strive for in this situation is not necessarily a totally internal interpretation of cause and effect relationships. Sometimes it really is not the learner's fault that he or she failed, and it is just as important to recognize that as to take responsibility when it is his or her fault. Similarly, it is important for a learner to recognize when his or her own behavior has resulted in success and when it was really just a matter of luck. Our goal should be to help students develop a realistic assessment of the causes of success and failure.

Examples of ways to use this idea to structure teaching:

- Keep real data on student study efforts and success rates. If the instructor can demonstrate that there is a relationship between effort and success, students will be more likely to accept the fact that they can contribute to their own success.

- When a student fails, help the student diagnose what behavior patterns might be responsible for the failure so that he or she can make adjustments in future situations.

SUMMARY

We began this chapter with a plea for information based on research and theory. We end with the recognition that much more work needs to be done. Human learning is a complex task that is difficult to study. Nevertheless, psychology has been able to identify some useful generalizations that can be made and used while we continue to search for more refinements in our understanding of learning.

In TA training, the inclusion of information on these generalizations gives the TAs a better idea of how to structure their teaching to capitalize on student learning patterns. They will be able to help students who stumble and boost those who want to become better students as well as learning the content. They will feel less helpless in the face of student difficulties or even in the face of the daily design of instruction.

TAs will also find that the information is as helpful to them in their own lives as students. Since most of them will not have had direct instruction on many of the areas of learning that have been discussed, they will discover new strategies for learning, explanations for failures or successes, and a better intellectual understanding of the learning process.

REFERENCES

Ames, C. (1992). Classrooms: Goals, structures, and student motivation. *Journal of Educational Psychology, 84* (3), 261-271.

Baxter-Magolda, M. (1992). *Knowing and reasoning in college: Gender-related patterns in students' intellectual development.* San Francisco, CA: Jossey-Bass.

Belenky, M., Clinchy, B., Goldberger, N., & Tarule, J. M. (1986). *Women's ways of knowing: The development of self, voice, and mind.* New York, NY: Basic Books.

Csikszentmihalyi, M. (1975). *Beyond boredom and anxiety: The experience of play in work and games.* San Francisco, CA: Jossey-Bass.

Deci, E., & Ryan, R. M. (1985). *Intrinsic motivation and self-determination in human behavior.* New York, NY: Plenum.

Eison, J. (1981). A new instrument of assessing students' orientations toward grades and learning. *Psychological Reports, 48* (3), 919-924.

Gilligan, C. (1982). *In a different voice: Psychological theory and women's development.* Cambridge, MA: Harvard University Press.

Kirby, J. (1988). Style, strategy, and skill in reading. In R. Schmeck (Ed.), *Learning strategies and learning styles.* New York, NY: Plenum.

Pask, G. (1988). Learning strategies, teaching strategies, and conceptual or learning style. In R. Schmeck (Ed.), *Learning strategies and learning styles.* New York, NY: Plenum.

Perry, W. G. (1970). *Forms of intellectual and ethical development in the college years.* New York, NY: Holt, Rinehart, and Winston.

Weiner, B. (1979). A theory of motivation for some classroom experiences. *Journal of Educational Psychology, 71* (1), 3-25.

Witkin, H. A., Moore, C. A., Goodenough, D. R., & Cox, P. W. (1977). Field-dependent and field-independent cognitive styles and their educational implications. *Review of Educational Research, 47* (1), 1-64.

6

TA Training: Strategies for Responding to Diversity in the Classroom

Mathew L. Ouellett and Mary Deane Sorcinelli

Traditionally, discussions of diversity in TA training programs have focused on variations in student learning styles and preferences. More recently, the focus has turned to consideration of social diversities such as race, ethnicity, and gender. Student diversity is important in TA training because of the changing texture of the student population and the evolving nature of the relationship between TAs and students.

Changes in both the demographics of the applicant pool and college admission policies are creating greater diversity among traditional college-age students (Ouellett & Sorcinelli, 1995). Women now make up half or more of the total population at many institutions; more students of diverse racial and ethnic backgrounds are college-bound; more students with learning and physical disabilities enter college; and gay, lesbian, and bisexual students are making us more keenly aware of their presence. These changes, in turn, have presented TAs, faculty, and faculty developers with a variety of instructional and institutional challenges as they work together to make the classroom an effective and inclusive learning environment for all students.

In addition, on many campuses the roles of graduate students and faculty are more interdependent than ever before. At our university, TAs serve as primary instructors for some 13% of all courses (primarily in introductory and general education courses), and they teach about 83% of discussion sections and laboratories. Efforts to help TAs recognize and respond effectively to increasing diversity in the classroom mean that they will be able to teach more effectively. Many TAs will begin their teaching careers at campuses with more diversity than in the research universities in which they trained. As the future professoriate, these teachers will take with them into their academic careers the habits of thought and practice they learned as TAs. To help them learn to make their classrooms inclusive thus serves a dual purpose.

Student diversity and TA training interconnect around another issue of recent and considerable interest to institutions: student retention. Research on what encourages students to persist beyond the first year in college has identified faculty and peer contact, both in and outside of the classroom, as critical variables (Astin, 1993). Many TAs are on the front line in terms of their responsibility for the kinds of positive teacher-student relationships that can help students overcome barriers and achieve academic success.

Finally, attention to classroom diversity and TA training may also create a more supportive environment for new faculty of color. There is ample documentation on the shortage of ethnic minority faculty. As colleges and universities strive to diversify their faculty, an increasingly popular strategy is to recruit and mentor into the disciplines a more diverse population of graduate students. In many instances, issues of diversity in the classroom can arise when TAs of color, as well as students of color, represent the "diversity." Thoughtful attention to teaching and learning environments can increase the likelihood that TAs of color will enjoy successful careers in academe. Ultimately, this creates a healthier climate for all—students, teachers, and institutions.

This chapter highlights TA programs that link teaching and diversity development. We identify some of the challenges of program development, describe models that have proven successful, and summarize what we have learned about program development from both research and practice.

CHALLENGES TO CREATING TA PROGRAMS ON ISSUES OF DIVERSITY

Few recent issues in higher education have been the subject of such heated and ongoing debate as the dialogue on the meaning and appropriate place of diversity issues on the college and university campus (Musil, Garcia, Moses, & Smith, 1995). Accusations of covert ideological agendas, sloppy or self-serving scholarship, and indulgence in special interest group politics have been rife. These and other tensions can hinder efforts to address diversity in TA development programs.

We suggest that, for many TA development programs, resistance emerges from at least three basic sources. The first is unresolved issues arising from unskilled prior efforts. The second is a tendency to overemphasize the role of students and, consequently, to underrate the importance of faculty and TAs in changing intergroup relations. The last common source is confusion regarding how racism (and other forms of social oppression) manifests itself on college and university campuses today.

Unskilled Prior Efforts

Discussions of diversity on many campuses have been clouded by the lingering damage from unskillful or inadequate prior efforts. Change initiatives built solely on an advocacy-based model may have afforded some gains in the short run but have left long-term misunderstandings among groups. On many campuses, diversity goals have been misapplied in such extreme ways that communication has become paralyzed (e.g., over insistence on the use of particular words without clear definitions or an overwhelming demand for pseudoconsensus rather than a meaningful exchange of ideas). In the most unfortunate examples, these efforts have degenerated into the assignment of shorthand labels (e.g., "politically correct" or "racist") at any sign that full agreement may not be immediate. Even well-intentioned programs have relied too heavily on disconnected, one-shot interventions (often in response to a crisis situation) which may have left a lingering doubt in the affected communities about the degree of genuine commitment to institutional change.

Programs seeking to assess both the nature and quality of diversity training will find that Banks (1995) offers a useful model for understanding curricular reform. He suggests four approaches to reform: the contributions, the ethnic additive, the transformation, and the decision-making and social action. The contributions approach represents the least intrusive intervention since acknowledgment of individuals or singular events are added to the existing curriculum in order to celebrate diversity (e.g., holidays, ethnic foods, cultural performances). At the other end of the curricular reform continuum, the decision-making and social action approach requires critical analysis, integration of multiple viewpoints, and action for greater social equity. While this model was developed with curricular reform in mind, it provides a standard by which TA development programs can gauge their progress.

Limited Focus on Faculty Versus Student Development

To date, most institutions have focused diversity awareness efforts on students and peer relationships with little sustained attention given to TAs or faculty. This has likely been a result of two key factors. The first is the traditional perspective that diversity concerns are a student issue. Many student service offices, already striving to provide comprehensive responses to the needs of students, have shifted staffing and program infrastructures to facilitate diversity awareness. This has tended to bind diversity issues on many campuses to a student development perspective and to suggest extracurricular social support is all that is needed. It is sometimes clearer to see how to respond to the needs and concerns of an individual student, to whom one can add a face, a personal story, and a context, than it is to challenge the culture of an institution.

The second factor has been the relative reticence of many TAs and faculty members (especially whites) to become involved in addressing issues of diversity in the classroom. It is of course risky to make too broad a generalization about the roots of this ambivalence other than to say it is a hydra-headed creature. On one hand, research demonstrates that faculty members tend to report more liberal attitudes and egalitarian values than found in the broader society (Sax, Astin, Arredondo, & Korn, 1996). However, on many campuses, all but a select group of faculty members (e.g., those with direct research interests, altruistic motivations, or who teach diversity-related courses) seem to be detached from the diversity dialogue. Some TAs and faculty also note concerns about what they perceive to be the erosion of high academic standards by the abandonment of the traditional "canon." Some remain unconvinced that these issues genuinely belong to the teacher-student relationship, and still others believe that their discipline is by nature neutral or bias free. In many respects, these responses mirror those found across society when, for example, national policies like affirmative action initiatives come up for debate.

While the academy may be as at sea about these issues as the broader public, to maintain a leadership role in society at large, it behooves us to address diversity and inclusion issues proactively and democratically. Without engagement in such dialogue, as current faculty inevitably grow older, many may find that they are increasingly "different" from their students in far more subtle and complex ways than age or academic experience. In fact, the intuitive understanding and shared cultural touchstones that historically have undergirded the student-faculty relationship may continue to evaporate.

Changing Views of Racism

Current manifestations of racial prejudice, an important impediment to the success of racial minority students on campus, have changed their nature and character (Dovidio & Gaertner, 1986). Today, we less often see the old style aggressive racism that has historically defined racist behaviors, values, and attitudes. Instead, there is a new racism more insidious and difficult to confront because of its subtle nature. Gaertner and Dovidio (1981) in their theory of "aversive racism" report that racism today manifests itself more typically as avoidance behaviors (e.g., avoiding contact with members of certain racial groups or withholding what is referred to as "helping behaviors").

In fact, on most campuses when we address issues of diversity in TA development, we rarely mean addressing old style, openly hostile, prejudice-based behavior. While clearly still present on campuses, it is not the norm in the classroom. Social prejudices in teaching situations are often subtle in nature, and this very subtlety can make it difficult for teachers and students alike to articulate what feels wrong. For example, a white instructor may feel personally confident that she is not an overt or consciously racist person. However, her good intention does not mean that students of color will necessarily perceive that teacher's behaviors and teaching methods as academically inclusive, socially supportive, or equitable. The good news is that we are not often asked to address grossly inappropriate teaching behaviors. The challenge is to ask TAs and faculty to change teaching behaviors that flow from good, or at least benign, intentions but result in students feeling marginalized, disrespected, or unwelcome. Conversations on these issues can quickly heighten everyone's feelings of defensiveness and vulnerability. And, unfortunately, even well-meaning attempts at greater representation and equity may have become so emotionally loaded, and communities so polarized, that for faculty to enter into the dialogue can feel like spiraling off the edge of a precipice.

Nevertheless, the struggle to clarify the values, goals, and practices of multicultural education can be found on many campuses and in the agendas of national and regional graduate student and faculty teaching development conferences. A significant, if different, bellwether of the importance of these goals can be seen in the trends of educational improvement grants. By directing substantial funds to multicultural education, the Pew Charitable Trusts, Hewlett Foundation, Ford Foundation, and Kellogg Foundation have drawn important attention to the development of inclusive teaching initiatives.

FOUR TA TRAINING ACTIVITIES: A CONTINUUM OF INTERVENTIONS

A better understanding of the diverse classroom often first requires building a forum for self-reflection and intergroup dialogues on the cultural values and meanings embedded in particular teaching methods and behaviors. This may mean development of a shared lexicon, new understandings of how to solicit and interpret feedback from students, and effective ways to maintain a sense of confidence while learning and implementing new practices. Despite the complexities, increasing numbers of TA development programs have begun to address inclusion issues in the classroom. Their primary goal is to increase TAs' skills in creating classroom relationships that are inclusive, equitable, and strongly grounded in the dimensions of good teaching (Chickering & Gamson, 1987). An important principle for good practice in undergraduate education is the encouragement of student-faculty contact. The guiding principle of many diversity initiatives is to cultivate in TAs the skill and comfort level necessary to develop meaningful relationships with all students, not just those that come from similar cultures and value systems.

These same principles of good teaching also suggest that attention to the diversity of students in the classroom can encourage respect for diverse talents and ways of learning. While beyond the scope of this chapter, excellent models have been developed that incorporate research on learning styles into teaching strategies that help to create more inclusive classroom environments (Baxter Magolda, 1992; Wlodkowski & Ginsberg, 1995). Familiarity with a range of these learning theories can help TAs to understand better the role that different teaching methods have for the individual students in their classrooms, departments, and institutions.

Perhaps most daunting in developing TA training programs on diversity is developing a plan for where to begin. Additionally, most programs have limited staffing, support, and funds, so decisions to include one set of goals inevitably exclude others. It is important to bring into the conversation on multiculturalism and diversity a range of program opportunities that offer multiple points of entry and require different degrees of sophistication. In general, programs line up along a continuum, from lower-risk activities that focus on the experience and needs of others (e.g., watching videos or responding to reading materials) to activities that ask participants to engage in higher-risk activities (e.g., workshops requiring self-reflection, personal disclosure, and dialogues). Because there is usefulness in each type of program, it is important to design a range of opportunities that requires different degrees of sophistication for participation.

When asked about their willingness to address diversity topics like racism in their classroom discussions, one of the biggest concerns instructors identify is the fear of managing the discussion successfully. This same concern often exists for faculty and TA developers. Whether in a workshop or intensive seminar, there are likely to be complex group dynamics. It is important to be as prepared as possible for the range of positions and contributions likely within any group of TAs.

In designing effective diversity programs for TA development, it is helpful to frame a series of discussions that break the overall goals into smaller, more specific steps. Naturally, by focusing the learning goals of sessions carefully, the developer can manage a more successful presentation and discussion. Marchesani and Adams (1992) have developed a model that defines four fields for exploring classroom diversity: 1) teaching methods and pedagogy, 2) course content, 3) teacher self-awareness, and 4) awareness of student diversity. Chesler (1993) has developed a similar model of the important factors affecting the diverse classroom, incorporating external influences like broader social movements and institutional values.

Bibliographies, Videotapes, and Print Materials

A safe place for TA training programs to get started is to develop an instructional resource library for TAs and faculty. A library offers an accessible, relatively low-threat means for TAs, either alone or in small groups, to learn about and improve their teaching in a diverse classroom.

Materials and resources offered might include useful definitions, anno-tated bibliographies, examples of concrete strategies or teaching behav-iors, exploration of key theoretical concepts, and concise descriptions of exemplary programs. The advantage of print and web-based materials is that TAs can enter into the dialogue on teaching improvement and diversity with a degree of comfort provided by the privacy of reflective reading. Many centers now make their print materials available via their web-based home pages, making it extremely easy to access and retrieve materials.

Several teaching centers have also made instructional videotapes. The University of Washington's *Teaching in the Diverse Classroom* and Har-vard University's *Race in the Classroom* provide realistic models of inclu-sive teaching methods and behaviors. Selected videotape collections offer self-contained modules that address specific aspects of diversity in the classroom. At their best, like the two mentioned above, videos offer rich opportunities for individuals or small groups of TAs to review and reflect on their own practices. An example of an annotated bibliography and a videography that highlight issues of teaching and learning in the diverse classroom can be found on the web site of the Center for Teaching, Uni-versity of Massachusetts, Amherst (http://www.umass.edu/cft/).

Campus-Wide Workshops

Diversity initiatives also can benefit from offering several tested, self-con-tained workshops such as social diversity and learning style issues in the classroom or understanding cross-cultural dimensions in teaching and learning. Presenters are often considered experts on the topic or have emerged as exemplars due to their teaching success. Workshops are usu-ally one-shot activities. They require little advance preparation on the part of participants and little specific follow-up or support afterwards. Depending on the topic and presenter, workshops strive for a low-risk atmosphere because of the range in experience of TAs and faculty who may choose to attend. These workshops may be offered at TA orienta-tions, departmental luncheons, or in a brown-bag series.

Workshops provide opportunities to hear from peers and to actively engage in an exchange of ideas. At their best, they can inspire and chal-lenge by example, interaction, or dialogue. Participants report that such sessions heighten awareness of diversity in the classroom and encourage collegiality and the teaching acumen of TAs. Because of time constraints, the content of these workshops often focuses on the cognitive realm (e.g., new information, statistics, or reports) with only secondary attention paid to the affective dynamic.

TA Development and Intensive Seminars

Seminars that extend across an academic year or even over a graduate career are most successful in helping TAs acquire new teaching skills, behaviors, and attitudes. However, they are also the costliest intervention in terms of institutional support and follow up. Two exemplars of this model are the Preparing Future Faculty program (see Chapter 16) and the Teaching and Learning in the Diverse Classroom project. Sponsored by the Association of American Colleges and Universities, the Council of Graduate Schools, and the Pew Charitable Trusts, Preparing Future Faculty educates graduate students for their role as the teachers of undergraduates today and the faculty of tomorrow. Selected participating institutions have developed materials and seminar sessions on the diverse classroom. For example, Emory University has offered sessions entitled Teaching in a Multicultural Setting and Teaching in a Multicultural Curriculum.

The University of Massachusetts, Amherst, has initiated an innovative seminar that brings issues of diversity to the forefront of teaching development. This pilot program provides a unique model for pairs of faculty and teaching assistants from across the disciplines engaged in a year-long seminar to improve their understanding of diversity and teaching issues. The seminar works with a group of approximately eight TAs and eight faculty members in a four-tier program. The tiers include 1) an intensive one-day immersion workshop at the outset of the year, 2) a monthly seminar on teaching and learning in the diverse classroom, 3) individual consultation on teaching and learning, and 4) a department-based teaching and learning project designed by each team. For details on the goals, criteria for selection, and elements of the program, see Ouellett and Sorcinelli (1995).

Individual and Departmental Consultation

Most faculty development centers have strong traditions of offering one-to-one teaching consultations. Successful strategies and methods (e.g., class visits, videotaping, student feedback) offer important models for working with TAs and other instructors on goals related to teaching improvement and diversity. Few services are as labor intensive or as substantial as classroom observation and feedback strategies. But this kind of relationship with an individual instructor can provide a terrific opportunity for coaching on strategies to seek out student feedback (anonymously, regularly, in brief writing exercises, etc.).

A linchpin in TA development for diversity is establishing a dialogue with students in class, either through formal measures (e.g., evaluations or structured questionnaires) or more informally (e.g., anonymous, brief writing assignments that assess perceptions of learning, climate, pacing of material, texts, etc.). How someone receives, defines, and interprets messages can, naturally, be somewhat culture-bound. Acknowledging and accommodating this can help TAs to seek out and interpret information from students in a manner that may not necessarily be an intuitive choice. However, students' perceptions of the classroom experience, if gathered early on, can assist TAs in refining a course effectively. It may require practice, but generally students will be forthcoming about whether or not individual behaviors or group dynamics in the classroom contribute to feelings of isolation, marginalization, or exclusion from the academic community (whether based on gender, race, ability, or other status).

One-to-one consultation may open the door to departmental consultations as well. They offer the opportunity to develop within existing, ongoing work groups the inspiration and skill required for sustained change efforts. This kind of consultation service allows faculty developers to tailor the content and materials to the particular needs of individuals and departments. We suggest that department or program-based consultations work best if sponsored by senior, well-respected members whose involvement underscores the importance of teaching and diversity issues. These consultations can offer an opportunity to help TAs (and their faculty) clarify the relationship between different course offerings, both in terms of content and sequences. Such training may also help them to articulate departmental goals and practices, especially as related to teaching development and diversity, and may aid both in the assessment of current curricular offerings and in the choice of future directions for bringing attention to diverse learners and learning styles. For example, participants may help determine the best use of field placements, internships, and related experiences to enhance and extend opportunities for academic excellence and achievement. Ultimately, it will take the good faith efforts of entire departments and action across the whole institution for traditionally underrepresented students to feel genuinely welcomed into the academy.

<h2 align="center">EARLY LESSONS LEARNED</h2>

Bringing together the two streams of teaching development and diversity education requires flexibility, responsive facilitation, and a range of program opportunities. It also requires the gathering of formative and summative evaluation throughout the process. Addressing diversity issues requires participants to consider not just their minds, but also their hearts, since changes are often predicated upon reminders of egalitarian values and positive self-images (Dovidio & Gaertner, 1986; Stassen, 1995). Having now piloted all four models of diversity initiatives, we offer some general lessons on this challenging, as well as inspiring, terrain.

Adopt a Systemic Change Orientation

Centers for teaching are often asked to lend leadership and guidance on diversity issues, because they are skilled in facilitating cross-disciplinary dialogues. Nonetheless, centers have moved slowly in tackling issues related to diversity. We suggest that this delay is partly a result of faculty developers having to do their own diversity awareness work first. Developers have then had to do extensive and time-intensive needs assessments in order to identify stakeholders, gather suggestions for the content and format of programming, and develop strategies for navigating the tides of campus politics. Focusing on diversity issues in the classroom quickly extends beyond the teacher-student relationship.

In fact, it is important to remember that issues of diversity are sensitive topics for the entire institution. The extent of collaboration and intergroup dialogue needed to successfully launch and then institutionalize meaningful change efforts is often underestimated. Systemic changes are often the prerequisites, however, if the culture and values of an institution are to genuinely support inclusive teaching practices. Our approach is to infuse diversity as an important value in all work we undertake. We try to perform our work as a teaching development center in a manner that models these behaviors, attitudes, and values. For example, before we implement any initiatives, create new print materials, or offer campus workshops (e.g., instructional technology, teaching portfolios, classroom methods, etc.), we review our objectives, content, and program design for inclusion. Additionally, we consult regularly with faculty and TAs across the campus that can provide us feedback on our progress.

Define "Diversity" Broadly

We define diversity in terms of all the elements of one's social identity where issues of power and prejudice come into play, including race, gender, economic class, sexual orientation, religion, and age. We also include issues that are specific to the classroom, such as academic preparation, ability, and learning styles. Our experience suggests that this broad, inclusive definition works most effectively in TA diversity training.

Be Prepared for Complex TA/Faculty Dynamics

Addressing issues of diversity successfully often requires efforts that at first glance appear completely uncomfortable or inappropriate to the traditional role of faculty. Because western academic culture still strongly promotes rational/scientific neutrality, the self-reflection required by even well-intentioned faculty members can seem daunting. It is important to acknowledge from the outset that programs focused on teaching, learning, and diversity will most likely differ substantially from disciplinary, content-based presentations. Identifying with their own group memberships, socialization, and prior training, participants will come to these discussions with widely ranging expectations and values. However, careful design and pacing can help the discussions, and even conflicts contribute robustly to the experience rather than compromise it.

The use of team facilitation (i.e., pairs that balance racial representation, sexual orientation, gender, etc.) is an important strategy for diversity training programs. When presenting within departments, it is advisable to copresent with a respected group member in order to respond to discipline-based expectations and provide appropriate examples of useful application. Because of the emotional content of these issues, it also is essential to include opportunity for personal stories and discussion in both homogeneous and heterogeneous groups.

Set Realistic Timelines

A commitment to actively engaging issues of diversity in the classroom is often only a beginning. The multidimensionality of teaching and diversity issues requires the acknowledgment of the whole person. TAs and faculty striving to attend simultaneously to cognitive, affective, and behavioral dimensions of their teaching may need heightened support and a different kind of debriefing. Behaviors that support teaching improvement in general (e.g., observations, coaching, learning new facilitation skills, and gaining feedback from students) take on added meaning when applied to diversity issues. The implementation of change efforts can be fraught with unpredictability, even troublesome encounters. From students, TAs and faculty members can face increased anxiety and resistance to new ideas. Some students also can be slow to welcome changes in teaching methods and intolerant of experimentation. To relieve some of these frustrations, we underscore that most teaching development goals related to diversity are rarely gained immediately and that instructors have their entire teaching careers to make progress. They are allowed, and in fact, encouraged, to go one step at a time toward getting it right.

Finally, when planning diversity initiatives, it is essential to assess each group individually for their unique readiness and then design interventions accordingly. This assessment process is often the most important component of the experience, especially for those TAs who might already feel alienated or left out of the academic mainstream. Participants need time to build trust and have meaningful conversations before pursuing the application of new methods in their courses.

Redefine Success

Incorporating diversity and inclusion issues meaningfully into teaching development programs requires redefining success. We see signs that traditional criteria for success in the academy are giving way to more progressive definitions. For example, the affective component of diversity work has often been perceived as counter to traditional definitions of academic work or the role of faculty. However, the success of innovations addressing the different learning needs of students (e.g., active learning methods, collaborative work groups, and experiential learning activities) clearly demonstrates that a more pedagogically sound learning and teaching environment enhances the quality of the experience for everyone. Acknowledging and responding to diversity in the classroom can enhance the development of self-awareness, critical thinking, dialogue skills, and empathy. As the roles and rewards of TAs and faculty are reconsidered, what we mean by successful teachers, what we mean by student success, and how we evaluate our own efforts, as TA and faculty developers, will change too.

As our values change, so also will our methods. The standard written teaching evaluation handed out at the end of a lecture course still has a place, but it will no longer exist in isolation. We find it enormously helpful to gather feedback regularly, both formally and informally, on the merits of our programming initiatives from TAs, faculty, and students of color across campus. This requires reconsidering our goals, methods, and outreach efforts. For example, we now annually invite a selected faculty member to serve as an associate to the center. The associate is specifically encouraged to engage a network of faculty, TAs, and students from across the campus to review and provide feedback on our diversity and teaching development programs as well as on our print and video resources, workshops, and seminars.

CONCLUSION AND FUTURE CONSIDERATIONS

The challenges to creating TA programs focused on issues of diversity are, at first glance, formidable. Colleges and universities will continue to debate how best to address issues of diversity and multiculturalism in the academy. In the same way, there is no ideal or universal model for responding to social and cultural diversity in the classroom. Although research on best practices is limited (Adams, 1992), there are some promising models for TA development.

This chapter has offered a continuum of types of TA development programs that address teaching and diversity goals. Presented as a continuum, interventions such as the development of instructional resources, workshops, intensive seminars, and individual and departmental consultations offer strategies that focus both on immediate teaching skills and on the development of TAs as future faculty. The challenge will be to extend these models so that faculty development and inclusionary educational practices are explicitly fused in all TA development programming.

There are immediate as well as long-term benefits for individual TAs and institutions in addressing diversity issues and teaching development more synergistically. At a personal level, such programs can help TAs to become more aware of who they teach, how they teach, and how they might teach all students more effectively. At an institutional level, diversity programs can help sharpen the integrity of a campus culture by reminding members of their egalitarian principles, democratic values, and cherished ideals. Improving both the inclusiveness of our own teaching and the valuation of equity in departments, colleges, and the campus is ultimately good for instructors, students, and our institutions.

REFERENCES

Adams, M. (1992). Cultural inclusion in the college classroom. In L. L. B. Border & N. Van Note Chism (Eds.), *Teaching for diversity.* New Directions for Teaching and Learning, No. 49. San Francisco, CA: Jossey-Bass.

Astin, A. (1993). *What matters in college? Four critical years revisited.* San Francisco, CA: Jossey-Bass.

Banks, J. A. (1995). *Multiethnic education: Theory and practice.* Boston, MA: Allyn and Bacon.

Baxter Magolda, M. B. (1992). *Knowing and reasoning in college: Gender-related patterns in students' intellectual development.* San Francisco, CA: Jossey-Bass.

Chesler, M. A. (1993, March). *Intergroup relations: Teaching and training about conflict and multiculturalism.* Preconvention workshop presented at the American College Personnel Association Conference, Kansas City, KS.

Chickering, A. W., & Gamson, Z. F. (1987). Seven principles for good practice in undergraduate education. *The Wingspread Journal, 9* (2), 1-4.

Dovidio, J. F., & Gaertner, S. L. (Eds.). (1986). *Prejudice, discrimination, and racism.* San Diego, CA: Academic Press.

Gaertner, S. L., & Dovidio, J. F. (1981). Racism among the well-intentioned. In E. Clausen & J. Bermingham (Eds.), *Pluralism, racism, and public policy: The search for equality.* Boston, MA: G. K. Hall.

Marchesani, L. S., & Adams, M. (1992). Dynamics of diversity in the teaching-learning process: A faculty development model for analysis and action. In M. Adams (Ed.), *Promoting diversity in the college classroom: Innovative responses for the curriculum, faculty, and institutions.* New Directions for Teaching and Learning, No. 52. San Francisco, CA: Jossey-Bass.

Musil, C. M., Garcia, M., Moses, Y. T., & Smith, D. G. (1995). *Diversity in higher education: A work in progress.* Washington, DC: Association of American Colleges and Universities.

Ouellett, M. L., & Sorcinelli, M. D. (1995). Teaching and learning in the diverse classroom: A faculty and TA partnership program. *To Improve the Academy, 14,* 205-217.

Sax, L. J., Astin, A. W., Arredondo, A., & Korn, W. S. (1996). *The American college teacher.* Los Angeles, CA: Higher Education Research Institute.

Schoem, D., Frankel, L., Zuniga, X., & Lewis, E. A. (1993). *Multicultural teaching in the university.* Westport, CT: Praeger.

Stassen, M. L. A. (1995). White faculty members and racial diversity: A theory and its implications. *The Review of Higher Education, 18* (4), 361-391.

Wlodkowski, R. J., & Ginsberg, M. B. (1995). *Diversity and motivation: Culturally responsive teaching.* San Francisco, CA: Jossey-Bass.

(The videotapes *Teaching in the Diverse Classroom* and *Race in the Classroom* are distributed by Anker Publishing Company, P.O. Box 249, Bolton, MA 01740.)

7

GETTING STARTED WITH TA TRAINING ON YOUR CAMPUS

Frederic Stout

In reviewing the literature on teaching assistant training, one cannot help but be struck by how many of the articles written in the 1980s and before begin with elaborate justifications for the TA training enterprise itself. Increasing student diversity, new information on student learning styles and theories of pedagogy, the challenges of new technologies and shifts in the academic job market, demands by parents and the general public for better educational outcomes—all are cited as reasons why TA training ought to be a high priority for college and university administrators and faculty leaders. Today, many of those arguments seem curiously old-fashioned—indeed, almost quaint in their obviousness—because the widespread success of TA training efforts at colleges and universities nationwide has become a well-established fact and the importance of TA training has become widely accepted. Former Harvard President Derek Bok (1991), the late Ernest Boyer of the Carnegie Foundation (1990), and many others have made the case for the importance of TA training both as a responsibility of the modern university and as an element of modern scholarship. And as Lavon Gappa (1991) has noted, "What is important to the institution, and to higher education as a whole, . . . is that with the training and development of TAs, undergraduate and graduate education are inextricably linked" (p. 84).

Today, then, the issue is not if TA training should be instituted, but how, and the purpose of this chapter is to help those who have been charged with developing a TA training program—or who merely wish to do so—to begin what will almost inevitably become a long-term evolutionary process. You may be a high-level administrator with an institution-wide vision or a faculty member with a departmental perspective, you may be the newly appointed director of a start-up instructional development office or a graduate student looking for ways to improve your own pedagogical skills as well as those of your fellow TAs—whatever your position, you are almost certainly a campus innovator, and the immediate challenges that you face are clear enough. Unless some god-like benefactor has just showered you with a multimillion-dollar grant, your challenge is to initiate a TA training program with limited, often ridiculously limited, initial resources. And one way or another, by hook or by crook, you will need to 1) develop a realistic organizational plan, 2) demonstrate effectiveness quickly, and 3) begin the process of building a constituency base for long-term programmatic growth.

This chapter is not—indeed, it cannot be—a definitive description of what a fully developed TA training program should be or how it should develop. There are many excellent articles and individual program descriptions that can provide useful models for the campus innovator, and in *Preparing Graduate Students to Teach*, Lambert and Tice (1993) describe the TA training programs of some 28 institutions nationwide. But as Wulff, Nyquist, and Abbott (1991) have made clear in "Developing a TA Training Program that Reflects the Culture of the Institution," each TA training program will be unique in that it will be individualized to the needs of the specific campus in question: "TA training that can be grounded in the culture of the institution . . . is safer, more likely to be accepted, and clearly more reassuring for all involved" (p. 121) and "For the individual developing a TA training program in an institution, it is helpful to understand not only the basic assumptions of the institutional culture but also the evolution of those assumptions" (p. 121).

Thus, this chapter cannot offer a universally applicable blueprint. What it does offer is a few guiding principles based on the historical experience of TA training programs nationwide and some commentary on a short list of low-cost, high-impact tools—TA orientations, follow-up programs, methods for building a faculty constituency, and ways of enlisting the TAs themselves—that any new (or nearly new) program can implement fairly easily. Although much of this chapter is based on methods that have proved successful at the Center for Teaching and Learning

(CTL) at Stanford—a research university with its own peculiar institutional culture—the tools and programs discussed have been chosen for their wide applicability and their flexibility. Here, then, are some useful, easy-to-implement tools that may help get your program off the ground. Once airborne, you are on your own!

THE TA ORIENTATION

The campus-wide TA orientation is the easiest, most common, and most obvious feature of most new TA training programs. Usually scheduled for sometime just before the first week of classes in the fall, the TA orientation is an effective way of bringing TAs and faculty members together, of organizing presentations for TAs on information they need to know (important campus policies and resources, guidelines for interactions with students, a TA's essential responsibilities as an officer of the university), and of offering useful workshops that will prepare TAs, especially first-time TAs, for the classroom experience.

The styles and structures of TA orientations vary widely. Some are three-day, four-day, even week-long affairs organized as intensive pedagogy courses with mandatory attendance for all new TAs; others are one-day or even half-day programs where attendance is strictly voluntary, and the goal is merely to concentrate on a few teaching tips and first-day strategies to help TAs negotiate their entrance into the world of teaching.

However one structures the TA orientation, certain key issues are almost certain to arise. For example, how much of the time will be devoted to university policies and TA responsibilities, how much to teaching? For many, the desired focus will be on teaching and teaching only, but in an age when issues of diversity training, disabled access, and gender equity loom large, campus policies and the corporate responsibilities of TAs as employees of the institution will necessarily claim a significant portion of time. Indeed, a graduate dean may take the opportunity afforded by a new TA orientation to load on program elements that might better be dealt within a graduate student handbook or in some other series of informational presentations.

Centralized or Departmental?

Another issue that almost inevitably arises from the TA orientation is how much TA pedagogy can be done centrally—that is, in a single, campus-wide program or by an office that serves the entire school—and how much must be done within the individual departments. In putting together teaching workshops for a campus-wide TA orientation, TA developers inevitably find themselves dealing in pedagogical generalities. Faced with serving a wide constituency—TAs from every department on campus—they can easily develop presentations on very broad topics such as leading discussions, class preparation, and how to deal with common classroom problems. But the more difficult issues—using multiple explanations in science courses, teaching fieldwork research methods in the social sciences, and leading small-group exercises in literature and drama classes—are discipline-specific. They are not just about how to teach, but how to teach physics, or how to teach sociology, or how to teach Shakespeare.

Thus, those organizing a new TA training program will quickly realize that, no matter how well-organized and effective the central TA orientation may be, departmental orientations are a consummation devoutly to be wished for. And, as Christopher Jones (1991) of The Ohio State University has argued, "... both forms of orientation have advantages" (p. 135) and "... these two options, centralized or departmental, are not necessarily incompatible" (p. 136). Thus, if the central program and the departments can work together on developing a process whereby they coordinate their efforts—for example, the central office organizes a morning program and the departments take over in the afternoon—then a "best of both worlds" model for campus-wide cooperation and shared responsibility will emerge and have a very significant impact on the quality of education campus-wide.

The Importance of Ceremony

Finally, a note on the subject of ceremony. All too often, a TA's first teaching experience is nothing more than an assignment, a job. No matter how much preparation a TA receives, he or she—without so much as a hearty handshake—is often merely dispatched to a classroom and expected to assume the responsibility of delivering college-level education to undergraduates. In reality, of course, a TA's first teaching assignment is an extraordinarily important step in his or her professional development. Whether or not the TA goes on to become a faculty member, the actual teaching that the TA does has tremendous value to him or her, to the students in the class, to the department, and to the university. It is most fitting, then, that the TA orientation for first-time TAs should include some sort of ceremony in which the importance of the teaching role is acknowledged and through which the TA is officially welcomed into the community of teaching scholars. This should be a moment of great honor that is treated with due dignity. Ideally, the president, the provost, or some combination of deans and distinguished faculty members should be in attendance and should take the lead in making the official welcome to those who are entering upon the first steps of a critically important and wonderfully rewarding calling. The ritual does not need to be overwhelming—this is not graduation, after all—but a few words, thoughtfully chosen and sincerely offered, can do wonders for a young teacher's morale and sense of self. Why pass up such an opportunity?

BEYOND THE ORIENTATION

The orientation is over. You have read the glowing evaluations and been congratulated by your dean or chair. Now the real work begins.

Building a Comprehensive Program

A whole literature on TA training addresses the issue of "beyond the orientation" and makes the point that orientations are only one part of a fully evolved program and, more importantly, only one part of a developmental process of TA training. Successfully mounting a one-time event is one thing, but developing, nurturing, defending, and maintaining an ongoing process—one that challenges certain elements of the institutional status quo and promises to transform the academy—is quite another.

Sprague and Nyquist (1989) have carefully analyzed the stages of TA development (see Chapter 4) and suggested the ways in which TA pedagogy moves along a developmental continuum from simple skills training to full professionalism as an experienced classroom teacher. The task of the new TA developer is to recognize that continuum and to create a program which responds to and serves the needs of TAs at every stage of their professional development. One approach to TA training that incorporates the broadest possible vision of the professional development continuum is the "preparing the future professoriate" model. This model (see Chapters 15 and 16), pioneered at Syracuse University with support from the Pew Charitable Trusts and the Fund for the Improvement of Postsecondary Education (FIPSE) of the US Department of Education, elaborates the TA training process to include a full range of special programs and initiatives aimed at preparing graduate students to become future faculty members who are competent as researchers, teachers, and institutional leaders (Lambert, 1993; Witherspoon, 1995-96).

Processes and Projects

Choosing how to proceed with TA training on any single campus will entail many difficult, individual choices based on a myriad of variables. Fortunately, there are a number of very useful guides to help make those choices, both as to the general process to follow and the many types of specific programs and projects that might be developed.

At the level of broad program development strategy, both Weimer, Svinicki, and Bauer (1989) and Hiiemae, Lambert, and Hayes (1990) describe clear, workable models for the design and implementation of TA training programs, and Gappa (1991) lays out a detailed, eight-stage TA program design process that is very much worth studying as a step-by-step instruction manual, even if every step may not be necessary or even possible on your campus. Craig and Ostergren (1993) describe the virtues of a voluntary TA training program at the University of Wisconsin-Madison, while Johnson (1995-96) discusses the history of a mandatory program at Texas A & M. And Burkett and Dion (1991) of Washington State University—very much in the spirit of this chapter—explore "shoestring budget" strategies "leading to the establishment of a permanent low-cost TA training program at a medium-sized research institution" (p. 142).

At the level of specific projects that might be pursued, the existing literature is equally rich. Barker (1983) describes the Teaching Fellows Program sponsored by the Instructional Development Program at the University of Rhode Island that brought together both new and seasoned faculty members to provide ". . . a forum for teachers from different disciplines to participate in a common dialogue" (p. 71) and to radically reconceptualize their role in the classroom. Such a faculty program could easily be adapted to include TAs. Gappa (1993) describes the Teaching Associate Program developed by the Program for Instructional Excellence at Florida State University in which experienced TAs are nominated by their departments to serve as mentors, workshop leaders, and institutional change agents. And Wangberg, Nelson, and Dunn (1995) describe the annual three-day teaching colloquium that is the centerpiece of the program of the University of Wyoming's Center for Teaching Excellence. Although the Wyoming program is for faculty, not TAs, the model could easily be expanded to include both faculty and TA participation.

A TA Training Archive

At the stage of deciding what short-term tactics and long-range strategies to pursue, it will often be useful to carry out a general needs assessment based on a survey of programs and resources already existing in the departments. Gappa (1991) describes a "29-item departmental survey" at Florida State University that asked chairpersons the following questions: "What is the number of TAs appointed? What qualifications and experiences were required for the appointment? What were the TAs' assignments and responsibilities? What training was provided by the department? How were the TAs evaluated?" (p. 84).

Clearly, the answers to these questions can be of great help in determining what needs to be done, what priorities to pursue, and so on. At Stanford and elsewhere, such information is updated annually and is stored in a centralized TA training archive which exists both as a storehouse for resources such as departmental pedagogy course syllabi and departmental TA handbooks and as a centralized institutional memory that may sometimes prove invaluable. For example, departmental TA training programs may sometimes rely on the active involvement of a single dedicated faculty member. If he or she should leave the institution, the materials in the TA training archive can help the department chairperson revive a lapsed program by passing archived materials on to new faculty leaders. In addition, members of one department can use the materials from other departments in the TA training archive as models and prototypes for their own efforts.

Big Issues to Grapple with, Pitfalls to Avoid

Building a comprehensive TA training program inevitably raises big questions, and two of those big issues—centralized versus departmental, mandatory versus voluntary—have already been mentioned.

Mandatory programs have the obvious virtue of reaching all the TAs on campus, but the downside is that the TAs may come to regard their training as a duty, perhaps even as a burden. Voluntary programs allow TAs to buy into their training through a process of self-selection, but the suspicion will always remain that many of those who do not come to orientations and workshops are precisely those who need the training most.

As regards centralized versus departmental, the main point has already been made: The two approaches are by no means mutually exclusive. Almost always, the issue will be how to achieve the proper balance between centralized and departmental efforts. At the University of Washington, as Wulff, Nyquist, and Abbott (1991) note, the centralized program offers "no generic or other campus-wide services" and every "interaction . . . is customized for the particular discipline" (p. 116). Other schools use the centralized program to offer broadly applicable workshops and presentations, while assigning more specific training to the departments, which the central program encourages, supports, and sometimes even funds.

Other big questions will emerge as the new program evolves. Should the emphasis be on the improvement of undergraduate education (housing the program in a dean of undergraduate studies office) or on an integrated approach to graduate education (housing the program in the graduate dean's office)? Should the program be narrowly defined as delivering a specific set of pedagogical skills, or should it address the broader issues of the TA's ongoing professional development?

Whatever path the new program follows, experience shows that certain common pitfalls should be avoided at all costs. In order to build broad institutional support, the TA training program should provide the best possible consultation and assessment services to the departments and other clients, but it should avoid becoming—or even being perceived as—the teaching police. The TA developer will of course be regarded as something of a pedagogical expert, but confidence in one's expertise should be tempered by humility and by the insight that there are as many ways to be a good teacher as there are good teachers. When working with any client, whether faculty member or TA, strict confidentiality should be observed. And situations should be avoided where the services of the TA training office are enlisted to intervene in departmental emergencies, especially those of a disciplinary nature.

Another pitfall to be avoided is what might be called the "let George do it" syndrome. Although the central program should strive to be an exemplary and thoroughly professional service organization, those services should never become a substitute for departmental efforts. It almost always happens that some departments will rely much too heavily on the central program and begin to regard TA training as the exclusive responsibility of the university-wide TA developers. In order to achieve and maintain that proper delicate balance between the centralized and departmental approach already mentioned, the new TA training program must always walk the fine line between providing services to the departments and catalyzing change within the departments.

The Business and Politics of TA Training

How, then, does one go about developing a comprehensive TA training program? The initial goals seem clear enough: some modest centralized program doing broadly applicable work while encouraging departments to develop discipline-specific programs . . . and facilitating the process by helping to develop replicable models for orientations, pedagogy courses, handbooks, mentor TA programs, TA awards, resource libraries, portfolio programs, and the like. But to achieve these goals—and to win the confidence of the campus decision-makers—one needs broad institutional support for the work of the TA training program.

In order to create and maintain such support, two development paradigms suggest themselves: 1) the TA developer as an institutional entrepreneur delivering valuable services to a client base, and 2) the TA developer as an academic political organizer militating for structural change within a system requiring reform and renewal. Applying either paradigm—and the truth is, the TA developer will often have to act both entrepreneurially and politically—two constituencies are critical to success: the faculty and the TAs themselves. A part of the TA developer's job, therefore, will be to both serve the needs and speak for the interests of the two key groups in the world of graduate education: the teachers and the teachers-to-be.

BUILDING A FACULTY CONSTITUENCY

One of the key tasks of any TA training program is to nurture a culture of teaching on campus and to promote what Ernest Boyer called "the scholarship of teaching" as an integral element of graduate student education. What better allies to enlist in this cause than the best teachers on campus?

At any institution, there are teaching awards, either school-wide or departmental. In addition, disciplinary professional organizations offer teaching awards, as do student organizations. Thus, a small research effort will reveal a list of names that are worth more than gold to the TA developer: those teachers on campus who have been recognized by the administration, by the students, or by their peers as superior classroom teachers. Some of these will be popular younger teachers who have a special sense of connectedness with the students. Others—the majority, no doubt—will be senior, tenured faculty members who have learned the craft of teaching over years of academic experience and who are influential both as respected researchers and as institutional leaders.

Distinguished Faculty as Natural Allies

One of the mistakes that is sometimes made by TA developers is to fall into the belief that members of the faculty, especially the senior faculty, are the enemy of institutional change on campus, a skeptical, immovably Neanderthal group who are set in their ways and hostile to progressive change. This opinion is never seen in print, of course, but can often be heard murmured by impatient TA training staff members. On a mytho-literary basis, this belief pattern seems to fit some sort of romantic David-and-Goliath conception of the TA developer's institutional political struggle, but it is a very grave misconception and one that will not reward the serious campus innovator seeking support for a start-up program of TA development.

In fact, the faculty—perhaps especially the senior faculty who no longer need to worry about getting tenure or the other professional rewards that come with success in the area of research—can become the TA developer's greatest, most influential allies if only the right approach is followed. Who, after all, knows more about teaching than great teachers? And who will be most gratified by a renewed recognition of great-teacher status coming from a new organization dedicated to improving the quality of teaching campus-wide?

Peter Beidler's *Distinguished Teachers on Effective Teaching* (1986) and John Roth's *Inspiring Teaching: Carnegie Professors of the Year Speak* (1997) are both compendiums of thoughts about teaching compiled from the observations of Beidler, Roth, and their fellow winners of the Carnegie Professor of the Year Award (formerly the Professor of the Year Award of the Council for Advancement and Support of Education). Beidler is also a contributor to Roth's book, authoring a chapter titled "What Makes a Good Teacher?" Both of these excellent sourcebooks provide useful materials that can form the basis of group discussions by

TAs on the purpose and value of their classroom experience. As useful as these books are, an even better compilation, for your purposes, will be the collected thoughts on teaching by the best, most distinguished teachers on your own campus, and this can be compiled, in transcript or videotape form, by sponsoring your own "award-winning teachers" speakers series.

The Award-Winning Teachers Series at Stanford

At Stanford, the Award-Winning Teachers on Teaching speakers series has become an important feature of the centralized TA training program offered by the Center for Teaching and Learning. Approximately three times per quarter, winners of major campus-wide, decanal, or disciplinary teaching awards are invited to speak at informal brown-bag get-togethers, light refreshments provided, with TAs from throughout the university. Although the speakers are free to discuss any topic they wish, CTL suggests that they address some very specific aspect of teaching that will prove immediately useful to their TA audience. The how-to approach is generally the most successful: Titles like "How to Give a Lecture," "Discussion Leading and Small-Group Methods," "Getting Inside Your Students' Heads," and "Teaching Through Problem Solving" have attracted large, eager audiences.

For the past few years, the Award-Winning Teachers on Teaching series has been professionally videotaped—at no cost to CTL—by the campus-based cable television outlet. Similar arrangements, with school or community-based stations, could be pursued at many campuses, and do-it-yourself videotaping is, of course, always an option. CTL keeps a copy of all tapes in the Award-Winning Teachers on Teaching series in a video resource library, and several titles regularly circulate to departments and individual TAs.

In addition, copies are provided to the speaker as soon after the presentation as possible, along with a sincere, detailed letter of appreciation commending the recipient for his or her commitment to the cause of teaching. The point here is not just good manners; it is good politics as well. At Stanford and at other campuses, the speakers series by the award-winning teachers has not just delivered first-rate pedagogy to audiences of TAs; it has also formed the basis of an ongoing alliance between the TA training program and a core group of distinguished and influential faculty members.

ENLISTING THE TAs THEMSELVES

As is often the case, many TA training methods that are low cost are also high impact in terms of effectiveness. Nowhere is this more clear than in the use of TAs themselves in the work of TA training. Politically, the TAs must be the TA developer's number one constituency: Serving their needs is, after all, the name of the game. Still, for many start-up TA training programs, the motto (apologies to John F. Kennedy) should be: Ask not what you can do for the TAs. Ask what the TAs can do for you!

Communicating with TAs via Email

For years, the problem of being able to communicate with every TA on campus has been one of those practical difficulties that has plagued TA developers. Distributing colorful fliers, relying on sometimes sporadic campus mail systems, placing expensive display ads in the campus newspaper—all have been tried as ways of alerting TAs to orientations, workshops, social events, and the like, with varying degrees of success. Today, the miracle of email has largely solved this once vexing problem, and every new TA developer should immediately establish an email "tree" whereby a single message can be sent to a list of TA liaisons (one in each department) who will then send it on to their own lists of departmental TAs. Similar lists should be developed for allied and/or interested faculty members and other campus contacts. A system of TA liaisons is quite simple to create—send a letter to each department chair asking for a nomination—and amazingly effective as an outreach tool for further organizing.

TAs as Program Consultants

One of the clearest ways to enlist TAs in support of TA training programs is to empower them as partners in the training itself. Petrulis, Carroll, and Skow (1993) discuss the advantages and disadvantages of using TAs in TA training programs by reviewing the experience of the University of California, Berkeley, and the University of Washington. Marincovich and Gordon (1991) note that many TA training programs "rely heavily on the contributions of peer consultants" (p. 182)—that is, TAs themselves who have been recruited and trained to carry out many of the essential tasks of centralized programs. Such tasks include giving orientations, establishing mentoring relationships with less experienced TAs, running workshops (either by themselves or with central program staff), and providing classroom consultations and video feedback for TAs who request it. In addition, TAs in some cases have been the prime movers within departments for the development of TA pedagogy courses and have actually recruited faculty members to assist in efforts that have led to the eventual establishment of ongoing, discipline-specific programs.

In analyzing the program of peer training and consultation that has existed at Stanford since 1979, Marincovich and Gordon (1991) discovered that recruiting TAs to participate in the TA training program was beneficial not just for the program itself—providing a valuable boost in the staffing levels available to the centralized program—but to the TAs as well. TA consultants in the Stanford program were found to "perceive their experience as helpful on the job market and helpful in a number of ways in their subsequent careers, whether in or out of academia" (p. 182). They suggest that programs that intend to use TAs as consultants "should make sure that they will have opportunities to enlarge their knowledge of effective teaching and improve their own skills. For recruitment purposes, explicit reference might be made to the professional development benefits that participants can expect" (p. 182).

A TA Survey

One of the most fundamental ways of using TAs in the development of a TA training program is to build your program activities around the expressed needs of the TAs themselves. And the best way to find out what TAs want is simply to ask them. A simple survey of TA opinion, tailored to the specific needs of your institution, can be a means for reaching out to TAs—many of whom may not even know you exist— and for discovering which departments already have the best TA preparation programs, and which the worst. In addition, the very process of formulating questions will help you clarify many issues about your goals as a program, the strategies you want to pursue, your strengths and weaknesses, and so on.

At Stanford, a teaching assistant survey helped the Center for Teaching and Learning update its overall program, both in terms of centralized activities and priorities for departmental outreach. That survey was divided into four parts. The first part ("Who Are You?") asked the TAs to identify themselves by department, gender, degree sought, citizenship, English proficiency, degree of previous teaching experience, and whether or not they intended to pursue academic careers after graduate school.

The second ("Are You Ready to Teach?") asked the TAs to give a self-estimate of their own preparation for teaching and to identify the sources of their preparation. The third ("How Can We Help?") asked the TAs to identify what they felt they needed to know more about and how they wanted to receive that information—handbooks, workshops, pedagogy courses, online services, etc. And a fourth part of the survey ("Your Issues and Concerns") asked the TAs open-ended questions about the demands and rewards of TAing and their general levels of satisfaction.

The results of this survey gave the staff of the Center for Teaching and Learning a clear picture, university-wide and department-by-department, of what was already being done and what still needed to be done in TA training on campus. And just as important, it signaled to the TAs themselves that the CTL staff was not just interested in them and their opinions, but was also prepared to tailor CTL programs to fit TA needs.

The detailed findings of this survey are, of course, campus-specific, but one general finding may have a broader applicability: Stanford TAs reported that they felt confident and well prepared to begin teaching, but almost immediately wanted follow-up support once their teaching duties actually began. Based on these findings, CTL developed its program of follow-up workshops and speakers organized centrally while at the same time working with the departments to create programs that would extend well beyond the orientation. An additional benefit of the TA survey—as well as the other ways TAs were brought into the workings of the TA training process—was that it helped deliver a strong message to the TAs: that the TA training program was not just for them, but by them as well.

Conclusion

The introduction to this chapter ended with the words, "you are on your own," but, of course, nothing could be further from the truth. If this chapter has accomplished anything, it has suggested the vast number of resources and potential allies that anyone just beginning a TA training program can turn to and count on. It has also tried to suggest that TA training is rather like a movement for progressive social change in that it aims to reform the existing state of the academy by improving the quality of teaching and is a common, collective effort being carried out by hundreds of fellow innovators at campuses throughout the United States and beyond.

You Are Not Alone

The resources that follow represent nothing more than a starting point for the successful innovator putting together a campus TA training program for the first time. The real challenge lies with those doing the actual work on the individual campus in question. Each campus program will inevitably find its own way, growing organically over time out of the specific institutional culture, needs, and assets of the individual campus environment. If it should appear, at times, that the process is never-ending, that is probably because it is. We live in what one social commentator has called a "high-flex society," a world in which the prime virtue is the ability to adapt quickly to new circumstances and changing environments. TA training—as much as any other element of today's social environment, probably more than most—will continue as an ongoing process of change and adaptation, growing and evolving along with higher education itself. In setting out on the path of TA training, it is important for the new TA developer to keep this perspective in mind and to remember as well that old saw about mighty oaks and little acorns.

RESOURCES

Organizations

Among the resources available to faculty and administrators just getting started with TA training are professional organizations, their publications, and periodic conferences. Two particularly important groups are:

- Professional and Organizational Development Network in Higher Education (POD), the leading group for faculty and instructional developers. To find out more about POD, contact David Graf at Valdosta State University. His address is Center for the Advancement of Teaching and Learning, Valdosta, GA 31698-0840 or email: dlgraf@valdosta.edu

- National Consortium on the Preparation of Graduate Students as College Teachers, a project of the Pew Charitable Trusts in Philadelphia, PA. For information about current activities of the National Consortium, contact co-coordinators Nancy Chism of The Ohio State University or Marilla Svinicki of the University of Texas at Austin. The addresses are Faculty and TA Development, 20 Lord

Hall, 124 West 17th Avenue, Columbus, OH 43210-5496 (Chism) and Center for Teaching Effectiveness, Main Building 2202, Austin, TX 78712-1111 (Svinicki).

These two groups, in partnership with the American Association for Higher Education (AAHE, One Dupont Circle, Suite 360, Washington, DC 20036-1110), the Council of Graduate Schools (CGS, One Dupont Circle, Suite 430, Washington, DC 20036; (202) 223-3791) and others, have sponsored an ongoing series of National Conferences on the Training and Employment of Graduate Teaching Assistants. Attendance at these conferences will help the new TA developer acquire both a wealth of up-to-date information and a solid network of colleagues at other campuses.

Other important organizations for TA trainers to become familiar with follow:

- American Educational Research Association (AERA, 1230 17th St. NW, Washington, DC 20036-3078)

- Association for the Study of Higher Education (ASHE, Texas A & M University, Department of Educational Administration, College Station, TX 77843-4226)

- International Consortium for Educational Development in Higher Education (ICED, c/o Karron Lewis, Center for Teaching Effectiveness, Main Building 2200, University of Texas at Austin, Austin, TX 78712-1111)

- Society for Teaching and Learning in Higher Education (STLHE, c/o Center for the Support of Teaching, York University, 4700 Keele St., North York, Ontario, M3J 1T3, Canada)

For TA developers working with international graduate students:

- TESOL (Teachers of English for Speakers of Other Languages, 1600 Cameron St., Suite 300, Alexandria, VA 22314)

- NAFSA:AIE (The Association of International Educators, 1875 Connecticut Ave. NW, Suite 1000, Washington, DC 20009-5728)

Journals
Professional journals are other important sources of information for new TA trainers and TA training program developers.

- Members of the AAHE receive the *AAHE Bulletin.*

- Members of TESOL receive *TESOL Matters and Newsletter.*

- Members of POD regularly receive the *POD Network News* and the annual *To Improve the Academy: Resources for Faculty, Instructional, and Organizational Development.*

- The proceedings of the National Conferences on the Training and Employment of Graduate Teaching Assistants include *Institutional Responsibilities and Responses in the Employment and Education of Teaching Assistants* (Chism, Ed., 1987), *Preparing the Professoriate of Tomorrow to Teach* (Nyquist, Abbott, Wulff, & Sprague, Eds., 1991), *The TA Experience: Preparing for Multiple Roles* (Lewis, Ed., 1993), and *Teaching Graduate Students to Teach: Engaging the Disciplines* (Heenan & Jerich, Eds., 1995). A volume from the 1995 conference *The Professional Apprenticeship: TAs in the 21st Century* is forthcoming in 1998. Edited by Laura Border, it will be available from New Forums Press, P.O. Box 876, Stillwater, OK 74076.

- *Journal of Graduate Teaching Assistant Development* is an invaluable resource for the TA developer. Edited by Karron Lewis of the University of Texas at Austin, it is available from New Forums Press.

Other important journals for TA developers include:

- *Journal of Higher Education* (Ohio State University Press, 1070 Carmack Rd., Columbus, OH 43210)

- *Change* (published in association with AAHE)

- *College Teaching* (Heldref Publications, 1319 Eighteenth St. NW, Washington, DC 20036-1802)

- *Journal of College Science Teaching* (1840 Wilson Blvd., Arlington, VA 22201-3000)

- *Innovative Higher Education* (c/o Office of Instructional Development, University of Georgia, Athens, GA 30602)

- *Journal of Staff, Program, and Organization Development* (New Forums Press, P.O. Box 876, Stillwater, OK 74076)

- *The Teaching Professor* (Magna Publications, 2718 Dryden Dr., Madison, WI 53704-3086)

- *National Teaching and Learning Forum* (Oryx, 4041 North Central #700, Phoenix, AZ 85012)

Other Useful Materials

- Wright, D. L. (1989). TA training resources. In J. D. Nyquist, R. D. Abbott, D. H. Wulff (Eds.), *TA training in the 1990s.* New Directions for Teaching and Learning, No. 39. San Francisco, CA: Jossey-Bass. (This is an excellent further source of information about helpful materials for TA developers, including handbooks prepared by major university teaching centers and audiovisual tools.)

- James Rhem has compiled an extremely useful list of discipline-specific pedagogy journals—some eight or nine pages worth—that is available through the *National Teaching and Learning Forum* and online at http://www.ntlf.com (which is an outstanding website for a full range of information on teaching and learning).

- Davis, W. E. (1994, Winter). College teaching periodicals: Resources for the development of graduate student instructors. *Journal of Graduate Teaching Assistant Development, 1,* (3), pp. 127-130. (This offers an informative discussion of how to use discipline-specific pedagogy journals in TA training.)

Books

Finally, a good selection of books on teaching in general and on TA training in particular should form the basis of a TA training resource library. Each person will develop his or her own list of favorites, but two series of titles deserve special mention:

- New Directions for Teaching and Learning. San Francisco, CA: Jossey-Bass (350 Sansome St., San Francisco, CA 94104-1342), under the general editorship of Robert Menges of Northwestern University and Marilla Svinicki of the University of Texas, Austin. Particularly important New Directions titles include:

  Andrews, J. D. W. (Ed.). (1985). *Strengthening the teaching assistant faculty.* New Directions for Teaching and Learning, No. 22.

  Nyquist, J., Abbott, R., & Wulff, D. (Eds.). (1989). *Teaching assistant training in the 1990s.* New Directions for Teaching and Learning, No. 39.

- ASHE-ERIC Higher Education Reports. Washington, DC: The George Washington University, Graduate School of Education and Human Development (One Dupont Circle, Suite 630, Washington, DC 20036-1183), under the series editorship of Jonathan D. Fife. A recent ASHE-ERIC title of interest is:

  Travis, J. E. (1995). *Models for improving college teaching: A faculty resource* .

Other important titles on TA training include:

- Allen, R. R., & Rueter, T. (1990). *Teaching assistant strategies.* Dubuque, IA: Kendall/Hunt.

- Lambert, L., & Tice, S. L. (Eds.). (1993). *Preparing graduate students to teach: A guide to programs that improve undergraduate education and develop tomorrow's faculty.* Washington, DC: AAHE.

- Nyquist, J., & Wulff, D. (1996). *Working effectively with graduate assistants.* Thousand Oaks, CA: Sage.

And on teaching in general, titles that have proven especially useful to TA trainers who wish to counsel young teachers or develop specific workshops are:

- Davidson, C. I., & Ambrose, S. A. (1994). *The new professor's handbook: A guide to teaching and research in engineering and science.* Bolton, MA: Anker.

- Davis, B. G. (1993). *Tools for teaching.* San Francisco, CA: Jossey-Bass.

- Eble, K. E. (1976). *The craft of teaching: A guide to mastering the professor's art.* San Francisco, CA: Jossey-Bass.

- McKeachie, W. J. (1994). *Teaching tips: Strategies, research, and theory for college and university teachers* (9th ed.). Boston, MA: Houghton Mifflin.

- Nilson, L. (1998). *Teaching at its best: A research-based resource for college instructors.* Bolton, MA: Anker.

- Seldin, P., & Associates. (1995). *Improving college teaching.* Bolton, MA: Anker.

- Weimer, M. (1993). *Improving your classroom teaching.* Newbury Park, CA: Sage.

- Wright, W. A., & Associates. (1995). *Teaching improvement practices: Successful strategies for higher education.* Bolton, MA: Anker.

REFERENCES

Abbott, R. D., Wulff, D. H., & Szego, C. K. (1989). Review of research on TA training. In J. D. Nyquist, R. D. Abbott, & D. H. Wulff (Eds.), *Teaching assistant training in the 1990s.* New Directions for Teaching and Learning, No. 39. San Francisco, CA: Jossey-Bass.

Andrews, J. D. W. (Ed.). (1985). *Strengthening the teaching assistant faculty.* New Directions for Teaching and Learning, No. 22. San Francisco, CA: Jossey-Bass.

Barker, W. L. (1983). Ripples on the pond: A teaching fellows program examined. In P. A. Lacey (Ed.), *Revitalizing teaching through faculty development.* New Directions for Teaching and Learning, No. 15. San Francisco, CA: Jossey-Bass.

Beidler, P. G. (Ed.). (1986) *Distinguished teachers on effective teaching.* New Directions for Teaching and Learning, No. 28. San Francisco, CA: Jossey-Bass.

Bok, D. (1991). The improvement of teaching. *Teachers College Record, 93* (2), 236-252.

Boyer, E. L. (1990). *Scholarship reconsidered: Priorities of the professoriate.* Lawrenceville, NJ: Princeton University Press.

Burkett, S. R., & Dion, P. (1991). TA training on a shoestring budget: A cooperative effort by graduate students, faculty, and administrators to achieve a common goal. In J. D. Nyquist, R. D. Abbott, D. H. Wulff, & J. Sprague (Eds.), *Preparing the professoriate of tomorrow to teach: Selected readings in TA training.* Dubuque, IA: Kendall/Hunt.

Craig, J. S., & Ostergren, R. C. (1993). Establishing an effective, voluntary teaching assistant training program in a large, decentralized university setting. *Journal of Graduate Teaching Assistant Development, 1* (2), 75-83.

Davis, W. E. (1994). College teaching periodicals: Resources for the development of graduate student instructors. *Journal of Graduate Teaching Assistant Development, 1* (3), 127-130.

Gappa, L. (1991). A professional teaching assistant program: Custom designing for your institution. *Journal of Staff, Program, & Organization Development, 9* (1), 83-91.

Gappa, L. (1993). The teaching associate program: A collaborative approach. *Journal of Graduate Teaching Assistant Development, 1* (1), 25-32.

Hiiemae, K., Lambert, L., & Hayes, D. (1990). How to establish and run a comprehensive teaching assistant training program. In J. D. Nyquist, R. D. Abbott, D. H. Wulff, & J. Sprague (Eds.), *Preparing the professoriate of tomorrow to teach: Selected readings in TA training.* Dubuque, IA: Kendall/Hunt.

Johnson, G. R. (1995-96). Mandating that new teaching assistants enroll in a college teaching course. *Journal of Graduate Teaching Assistant Development, 3* (2), 77-81.

Jones, C. N. (1991). Campus-wide and departmental orientations: The best of both worlds? In J. D. Nyquist, R. D. Abbott, D. H. Wulff, & J. Sprague (Eds.), *Preparing the professoriate of tomorrow to teach: Selected readings in TA training.* Dubuque, IA: Kendall/Hunt.

Lambert, L. M. (1993). Beyond TA orientations: Reconceptualizing the Ph.D. degree in terms of preparation for teaching. In K. Lewis (Ed.), *The TA experience: Preparing for multiple roles. Selected readings from the 3rd national conference on the training and employment of graduate teaching assistants.* Stillwater, OK: New Forums Press.

Lambert, L. M., & Tice, S. L. (Eds.). (1993). *Preparing graduate students to teach: A guide to programs that improve undergraduate education and develop tomorrow's faculty.* Washington, DC: American Association for Higher Education.

Marincovich, M., & Gordon, H. (1991). A program of peer consultation: The consultants' experience. In J. D. Nyquist, R. D. Abbott, D. H. Wulff, & J. Sprague (Eds.), *Preparing the professoriate of tomorrow to teach: Selected readings in TA training.* Dubuque, IA: Kendall/Hunt.

Nyquist, J. D., & Wulff, D. H. (1996). *Working effectively with graduate assistants.* Thousand Oaks, CA: Sage.

Nyquist, J. D., Abbott, R., & Wulff, R. (Eds.). (1989). *Teaching assistant training in the 1990s.* New Directions for Teaching and Learning, No. 39. San Francisco, CA: Jossey-Bass.

Petrulis, R., Carroll, S., & Skow, L. (1993). Graduate students as instructional consultants: Case studies from two universities. In K. Lewis, (Ed.), *The TA experience: Preparing for multiple roles. Selected readings from the 3rd national conference on the training and employment of graduate teaching assistants.* Stillwater, OK: New Forums Press.

Roth, J. K. (Ed.). (1997). *Inspiring teaching: Carnegie Professors of the Year speak.* Bolton, MA: Anker.

Sprague, J., & Nyquist, J. (1989). TA supervision. In J. D. Nyquist, R. D. Abbott, & D. H. Wulff (Eds.), *Teaching assistant training in the 1990s.* New Directions for Teaching and Learning, No. 39. San Francisco, CA: Jossey-Bass.

Wangberg, J. K., Nelson, J. V., & Dunn, T. G. (1995). A special colloquium on teaching excellence to foster collegiality and enhance teaching at a research university. *To Improve the Academy, 14,* 157-177.

Weimer, M., Svinicki, M., & Bauer, G. (1989). Designing programs to prepare TAs to teach. In J. D. Nyquist, R. D. Abbott, & D. H. Wulff (Eds.), *Teaching assistant training in the 1990s.* New Directions for Teaching and Learning, No. 39. San Francisco, CA: Jossey-Bass.

Witherspoon, P. D. (1995-96). Preparing the university professoriate of tomorrow: An integrated approach to TA education. *Journal of Graduate Teaching Assistant Development, 3* (2), 69-75.

Wright, D. L. (1989). TA training resources. In J. D. Nyquist, R. D. Abbott, & D. H. Wulff (Eds.), *Teaching assistant training in the 1990s.* New Directions for Teaching and Learning, No. 39. San Francisco, CA: Jossey-Bass.

Wulff, D. H., Nyquist, J. D., & Abbott, R. D. (1991). Developing a TA training program that reflects the culture of the institution: TA training at the University of Washington. In J. D. Nyquist, R. D. Abbott, D. H. Wulff, & J. Sprague (Eds.), *Preparing the professoriate of tomorrow to teach: Selected readings in TA training.* Dubuque, IA: Kendall/Hunt.

8

Teaching Teaching: The Importance of Courses on Teaching in TA Training Programs

Michele Marincovich

A s universities' expectations for the teaching quality of both faculty and TAs grow, and as the notion of what constitutes the proper training of TAs develops, universities are moving—or will need to move—from TA orientations and occasional workshops to more substantial modes of teaching preparation for TAs. One of these modes is a one- or two-semester (or longer) course on teaching (also called a pedagogy course). No less an authority than the late Ernest Boyer (1990), formerly president of the Carnegie Foundation for the Advancement of Teaching, argued in his influential *Scholarship Reconsidered* that graduate education should include preparation for teaching and that this should be delivered through for-credit seminars on teaching taught by the regular faculty. Although we will see that courses on teaching can take many forms, be offered by such different university entities as the graduate dean's office or an academic department, and occur at various times in a student's graduate study, their hallmark is a systematic attempt to equip graduate students with both the theoretical and the practical knowledge to be successful university teachers.

In fact, courses on teaching have been around for a long time. Many campuses have offered them since the 1970s and some even before that. Until recently, however, these courses were not generally considered an essential or especially important part of a graduate student's education, and even in the TA training literature they were touched upon rather lightly if at all (Piccinin & Picard, 1994). This chapter focuses on courses designed to teach teaching in an attempt to sharpen our sense of definition, learn from the already considerable history of these courses, and recommend resources and best practices. In this effort, I have drawn on my own experience with the development of departmental pedagogy courses at Stanford, on articles scattered through disciplinary sources as well as in the TA training literature, and on a collection of pedagogy course materials assembled on the World Wide Web in 1995 under the auspices of the Professional and Organizational Development Network in Higher Education (POD) listserv (http://www-ctl.stanford.edu/podmenu.html).

TYPES OF COURSES

Let's look first at what we mean by courses on teaching. The literature suggests that at least four different types of these courses exist on university campuses across the country. There is, first of all, the course on teaching, almost always offered by an academic department, that prepares graduate students to TA or teach a particular course (such as "Introduction to Psychology") or a particular type of course (such as composition). Usually taught by a content specialist—sometimes from the regular faculty, sometimes not—this kind of course tends to focus mainly or completely on a TA's immediate teaching role. Diamond and Wilbur (1990) suggest that the prime purpose of this kind of class is to make sure that TAs teach a particular course "uniformly" (p. 205). For years, foreign language departments and freshmen English programs have offered such courses in recognition of the large degree of responsibility that foreign language and composition TAs have had for the instruction in their sections.

A slightly more generic course on teaching, again usually offered by the department, goes beyond preparing TAs for any one particular course to exposing graduate students to instruction in that discipline. Such courses are usually taught by a content specialist in the department, though again not necessarily regular, tenured faculty, or they can be staffed by a procession of guest speakers coordinated and carefully selected, one hopes, by a course sponsor. These courses can be an ideal venue in which to pursue the scholarship of teaching in that discipline and, indeed, some disciplines have developed an array of resources—

from syllabi collections to publications—to enrich these classes. (The American Sociological Association, for example, has produced several helpful materials for the development of pedagogy courses. Consult its publication web pages [www.asanet.org/pubs/publicat.htm] under "Teaching and Academic Resources," then under "Graduate Education.") Teaching and learning centers can also often provide materials, speakers, and general consultation to the teachers of these classes.

Although many of these courses cover similar issues—student learning, the curriculum of the discipline, and the types of teaching common to the field—there can be significant variations on the theme. Some of these courses, for example, also prepare graduate students for their research and service responsibilities in addition to their instructional responsibilities. A 1993 two-quarter pedagogy course in the religious studies department at Stanford, on the other hand, had a more curricular and course design focus; it featured faculty presenters who brought their course syllabi and discussed with class members both the theoretical and practical issues in the conception and implementation of their regular courses (Gonnerman, 1993). A second offering of the pedagogy course in 1998 will feature not only faculty from Stanford but also religious studies professors from other types of postsecondary institutions discussing the nature of their classes.

Desirable as it may seem for departments to sponsor courses on teaching, some TA trainers make the argument for encouraging TAs to cross departmental boundaries and take courses on teaching that are targeted to disciplinary clusters of the sciences, the social sciences, and the humanities. Through these kinds of groupings, some experts (Nilson, 1993; Schoem, Carlton, Gates, & Black, 1991) have argued that a teaching or TA training center can take responsibility for initiating and standardizing courses on teaching—a commitment that departments may not want or be able to make. In addition, these courses can help TAs to look beyond their specialized area of study and identify themselves less as disciplinary citizens and more as university citizens.

A type of course that intentionally prepares TAs for university citizenship as well as teaching is one that takes higher education as its focus and is usually offered by a school of education, a graduate division, or a teaching and learning center. Piccinin and Picard's (1994) survey of courses on teaching in Canadian universities discovered that this type of course prevailed. Such courses are usually not required but instead are offered on a voluntary basis to that subset of the TA population that intends to pursue a professorial career. The Preparing Future Faculty Programs described in Chapter 16, with their focus on the thorough preparation of graduate students for their future careers as university teachers, have encouraged the growth of these kinds of courses in addition to departmental teaching courses with a disciplinary focus (Gaff & Lambert, 1996).

Finally, I will mention a kind of course, which—while strictly speaking not a pedagogy course—may cover teaching and some aspects of higher education in addition to its concentration on a specific aspect or theme in postsecondary education. One example would be Biological Sciences 325, "Professional Responsibility and Academic Duty" at Stanford, a course taught by the university's president emeritus, Professor Donald Kennedy, that explores ethical dilemmas and possible conflicts of interest for academics. Such courses are not meant to train graduate students for all aspects of their academic careers but can significantly contribute to students' knowledge of important facets of higher education and thus the context in which they may do their teaching.

THE GOALS, OBJECTIVES, AND CONTENT OF PEDAGOGY COURSES

In their review of courses on teaching at Canadian universities, Piccinin and Picard (1994) identified three broad goals for these classes: 1) covering the theory and research on teaching and learning; 2) developing such applied teaching skills as establishing rapport with a class, leading discussions, and building a positive classroom climate; and 3) covering professional, philosophical, and ethical issues in teaching in higher education. As a part of these three objectives, graduate students are also oriented to university policies and resources on teaching and learning, the latter including libraries, teaching centers, and instructional technology.

While most faculty or TAs would probably find little to object to and indeed much to appreciate in this list of goals for pedagogy courses, they might also find these topics to be the bare essentials of how to put this kind of course together. Like any course, pedagogy courses benefit from a clear sense of their specific objectives. In a tremendously helpful collection of materials on pedagogy courses put together by Karron Lewis (1992) of the Center for Teaching Effectiveness at the University of Texas, Austin, Lewis suggests specific objectives appropriate for either a general course on teaching or a course designed to help TAs teach a particular class. I will not list here all of the objectives she outlines, but it might be useful to give their flavor with an example:

> Goal: The students will know how to design a course.
> *Objectives*
>
> - Given a catalog course description, the students will produce, in a paper written outside of class, a set of goals, objectives, and learning activities, and a measure of student achievement.
>
> - The students will be able to write and critique instructional objectives in their own field, both in class discussions and on written exams.
>
> - The students will be able to match learning activities with objectives and suggest appropriate activities when none is given.
>
> - The students will be able to match evaluation methods with objectives and suggest evaluation methods if none is given (p. 9).

The actual topics in a pedagogy course will depend on the instructor's particular goals and specific objectives. However, putting the course topics Lewis suggests together with the topics that appear in the literature (especially Diamond & Wilbur, 1990; Wright, 1987; Vattano & Avens, 1987) and in the syllabi on the POD web-based pedagogy course syllabus site yields the following:

- What is effective teaching?
- The first day of teaching
- Getting to know students, teacher-student relationships, counseling students, student (intellectual) development
- Student learning styles, motivating students, classroom assessment techniques, active learning approaches, helping students improve their ability to learn how to learn
- Developing authority as a teacher, classroom management or dynamics

- Instructional, course, and curriculum design
- Lecturing, giving presentations
- Leading discussions, questions and questioning techniques
- Other teaching situations: laboratories, small group instruction, problem-based learning, review sessions, etc.
- Teaching evaluation and improvement
- Teaching with technology
- Testing and grading
- Diversity issues
- Professional and ethical issues in higher education
- History of the university and/or of university teaching

A first impression of this list is its mix of theoretical and practical topics. Students in most of these kinds of courses are not only exposed to theories of learning but are also expected to be concerned with applying those theories to teaching. This concern for the practical and the applied extends to the activities and assignments of a pedagogy course as well. Much more than other kinds of graduate courses, a pedagogy course expects its students to engage in hands-on, active learning. (Needless to say, pedagogy courses should model what they are teaching about effective instruction—another reason for a large active learning component.) In the same vein, pedagogy courses often work best when the students in it are teaching a course at that same time or are given occasions on which they can practice teach (for example, through microteaching).

Although it is not possible in the space here to suggest active learning strategies for all of the pedagogy course core topics listed above, here are some interesting pedagogy course assignments suggested in the literature or by my own interactions with pedagogy course instructors:

- Developing instructional objectives for a course the TA is teaching or will teach

- Observing one or more classes taught by faculty or TAs who are known for their teaching effectiveness and then interviewing the faculty member or TA

- Reviewing and critiquing videotapes of actual classes

- Analyzing the department's undergraduate curriculum and the place in it of the course a TA is assisting in

- Reviewing and comparing possible textbook selections or other readings

- Designing a particular course and producing a syllabus

- Going over tests, analyzing questions, and developing new exams

- Writing a case study of an actual or significant teaching problem

- Designing course Web pages or another type of instructional media

- Developing a teaching portfolio

The readings for a pedagogy course can vary tremendously, heavily influenced by whether the course has a disciplinary, higher education, or thematic bent. There is also the question, as there is in most courses, of whether or not to have a textbook. Several books appeared more than once in the literature as possible textbooks for these courses. Those most often mentioned include Allen and Rueter (1990), McKeachie (1994), and Neff and Weimer (1990). Since the majority of faculty are still not used to reading in the pedagogical literature, even that related to their own discipline, a teaching and learning center can often be of great assistance in identifying other print (and media) resources. Karron Lewis's (1992) compilation is probably the most extensive resource in this regard. In addition to providing general advice on how to do a departmental pedagogy course, she provides detailed reading lists for both faculty and students on a long list of pedagogy topics. Faculty members charged with developing a pedagogy course on a campus without a teaching and learning center may want to start with the Lewis compilation, one of the possible textbooks just listed, or with the web pages of their professional organization. Those in engineering or science are particularly fortunate since several discipline-specific works have come out in those areas in recent years, including the Committee on Undergraduate Science Education's (1997) *Science Teaching Reconsidered,* Davidson and Ambrose's (1994) *The New Professor's Handbook: A Guide to Teaching and Research in Engineering and Science,* Reis's (1997) *Tomorrow's Professor: Preparing for Academic Careers in Science and Engineering,* and Wankat and Oreovicz's (1993) *Teaching Engineering.*

As important as the topics and activities of pedagogy courses are, a more difficult design question is the intellectual thrust of such courses. While we might want pedagogy courses to be as intellectually challenging and substantial as other courses graduate students are taking, Susan Ambrose (1991)—based on her experiences at Carnegie-Mellon—emphasizes that graduate students respond best when these courses are "technique-driven" (p. 159). At the University of Michigan, the Center for Research in Learning and Teaching staff members who implemented pedagogy courses also reported that it was much easier to involve graduate students in practical questions than in theoretical discussions of teaching and learning (Schoem, Carlton, Gates, & Black, 1991). Although Shirley Ronkowski (1989) of the University of California, Santa Barbara, was not speaking of pedagogy courses, she too found in her research on TA concerns that the majority of both novice and even experienced TAs were much more interested in lower-level, teaching survival issues than in abstract, pedagogical concerns.

Is it possible to make a pedagogy course meaty and intellectually challenging rather than practical and "technique-driven"? Stanford history professor Richard Roberts, who has taught History 305, "Workshop in Teaching History" for four years, has successfully designed his course "around a set of intellectual or organizational themes/problems rather than as a practical guide, although clearly practical aspects of teaching emerge." For him, the secret has been not to "'teach' as much as open students to the PROCESS [his capitalization] of becoming a good teacher" (Roberts, 1997). Working in a research university environment, Roberts also draws parallels in the History 305 syllabus between the research that dominates his graduate students' lives and the teaching the course will focus on:

> Our goals in these workshops on teaching history are to demonstrate that teaching and research actually have much in common, that teaching shares with research similar phases of intellection and delivery, and that research enriches teaching, just as good teaching raises new research questions.

In essence, then, Roberts is exposing his students to the "scholarship of teaching," the phrase and notion first popularized by Boyer (1990). This theme seems a natural and intellectually rich one around which to organize a course on teaching. While it allows the techniques of effective teaching to be addressed, it affords the pedagogy course instructor a much more layered and complex framework to work from.

It can still be a leap of faith, however, for pedagogy course instructors to resist the demands of novice teaching assistants for purely practical courses on teaching. My own sense, however, is that several factors may make it more likely that courses can be other than "technique-driven." Since many of these factors have to do with how such courses are implemented, I turn next to that question.

IMPLEMENTING PEDAGOGY COURSES

Courses on teaching sponsored by entities other than departments and with goals beyond those of preparing TAs to teach a specific course seem a relatively recent phenomenon. Andrews' (1985) influential overview of TA training does not devote any specific attention to them while Parrett's (1987) often-cited ten-year review of TA training programs has only one sentence on them. Although Nyquist, Abbott, and Wulff's (1989) also often-cited volume mentions them, there is no extensive or special treatment of pedagogy courses. Gappa's (1991) more recent article on designing TA programs is silent on them. Thus, the accumulation and sharing of wisdom is relatively recent, and uncertainty continues to surround many aspects of such courses, from who should sponsor them to when they should be given and who should take them. Many of these questions can be decided for any one institution, however, if the development of such courses follows the thoughtful route described by Saroyan and Amundsen (1995) of McGill University. When that university first initiated its general TA training program, those in charge conducted a literature review of the topic, a needs assessment to determine the roles and responsibilities of the TAs and departments involved, careful planning at both the institutional and departmental level, and improvement-oriented evaluation of initial efforts.

Ideally, such courses arise when an institution has made a serious commitment to the thorough preparation of all TAs, not only for their immediate teaching responsibilities but for their future teaching careers. (It can be further argued that even those Ph.D.s who do not continue in academia in some sense "teach" their discipline to others and thus should be as prepared for their teaching role as they are for their research role.) A needs assessment of the TAs and their departments and a review of both the number of TAs involved and the human and financial resources available in various offices should indicate whether such courses should be handled at the departmental level, by a graduate dean's office, by a school of education, or by a teaching and learning center. Arguments have been made for and examples exist of each of these approaches. At the University of California, Berkeley, departments have responsibility for TA (called GSI) training although the GSI Teaching and Resource Center has produced materials (Mintz, 1991) to help departments develop a teaching seminar. The Center for Teaching and Learning at Stanford has followed the same course. It is our conviction that graduate students will respond most favorably when pedagogy courses are housed in the graduate student's own department and have a disciplinary bent.

Opinions also vary on whether such courses should be for or without credit; graded or pass/fail; mandatory or voluntary; prior to, contemporaneous with, or even after an initial TA experience. Since my prejudice is to put these courses on as equal an intellectual and administrative footing as others in a graduate student's schedule, I favor that they carry credit and are graded. The question of whether they should be voluntary or mandatory is more complex. If a course is to expose TAs to the scholarship of teaching in that discipline, then it makes sense that it be required just as research methodology courses are generally required of all graduate students in the department. If, on the other hand, a course is designed to prepare graduate students specifically for an academic career, then it should be voluntary. The course itself will benefit from having only willing participants in it. At one institution, departments tried a variety of incentives to motivate TAs to attend pedagogy seminars, even paying them an honorarium (Dalgaard & Dalgaard, 1977). This seems appropriate only if TAs are required to attend training but are not given any credit for their effort.

The question of the timing of such a course is also complicated. TAs who take a course prior to teaching may be better prepared for their first TA assignment but may also lack enough experience to appreciate some of the issues they are studying. On the other hand, TAs who take a course as they teach may be initially less well prepared to help their students. Dalgaard and Dalgaard (1977) and Humphreys (1987) describe a third approach: Hold some sessions of a pedagogy course just before classes begin so that TAs feel prepared for their initial teaching responsibilities, but schedule most sessions during the semester when TAs are teaching and can immediately apply what they are learning. Nyquist, Abbott, and Wulff (1989) mention another consideration—that seminars on teaching are best taken when TAs have reached the second stage of TA development (colleague-in-training; see Chapter 4 of this volume for a discussion of the stages in TA development) and are past some of their initial preoccupation with survival issues. I would suggest that a course on university teaching is best left until the TA is on the more experienced side but that a course aimed at preparing TAs to teach their discipline can occur successfully prior to their teaching as long as certain practicum elements are built into the course itself.

Regardless of when in a student's curriculum such courses are taken, they should be taught by experienced teachers who can themselves model the theories of effective teaching that the graduate students are learning. When departmentally based, these courses—if their credibility and impact are to be maximized—should be taught by regular faculty, whenever possible, rather than by lecturers or visitors. Although departments may find it hard to find a regular faculty member who initially feels qualified to teach these courses, the faculty member's collaboration with a teaching and learning center can help overcome his or her hesitation. Teaching and learning centers can assist with designing the course, identifying pertinent resources, and supplying presentations on certain general teaching topics. The centers may also either have their own funds or know of funding sources that can help with the time-consuming process of putting the course together initially. This funding can be used to pay an interested graduate student to help locate discipline-specific resources and solve some of the logistical problems of these often more hands-on kinds of courses. The centers can also offer guidance related to early and formative (improvement-oriented) evaluations of these courses.

One problem that we have seen again and again is the disappearance of such courses when the faculty member originally identified with them leaves the university, takes a sabbatical, or changes his or her interests. This is probably inevitable as long as the courses are not firmly rooted in the graduate curriculum of the department and carry no special recognition or reward for those who choose to teach them. If each graduate department has such a course on the books and there are extensive supports available to those who teach these courses, as we see at the University of California, Berkeley (Mintz, 1991), and at the University of Texas, Austin (Lewis, 1992), then presumably the turnover problem diminishes.

EVALUATION OF PEDAGOGY COURSES

The evaluation of courses on teaching, at least as reported in the litera-ture, seems to be through the same end-of-quarter or end-of-semester student rating forms that are used on most other university courses these days. As models of effective approaches to teaching, however, the instruc-tors of these courses should also be careful to use midterm evaluations, classroom assessment techniques, videotaping and consultation, and/or a form of peer evaluation. Peer evaluation approaches pioneered by institu-tions participating in the American Association for Higher Education Peer Review of Teaching Project (Hutchings, 1996a) would seem espe-cially appropriate. For example, instructors of such courses may want to do a course portfolio, tracing the development of the course over time, and ask colleagues to react and comment. Or, if not a full-blown course portfolio, they may want to write at least a "reflective memo" on the ped-agogy course syllabus and ask a peer to interview graduates of the course about issues raised in the memorandum.

Certainly one of the forms of assistance that teaching and learning centers or the graduate dean's office could provide is to bring together the teachers of these courses for focused discussions and mutual exchange. These offices might also want to help instructors or departments compare the student ratings of TAs who have taken the course to the ratings of an otherwise comparable group of TAs who did not take the course. If the TAs who took the course are not receiving higher ratings, then the course may not be achieving one of its major objectives. What would be even more exciting, of course, given that the aim of effective teaching is to pro-duce better student learning, is if TAs taking pedagogy courses are able to induce more student learning. Rickard (1991) reports that University of Alabama undergraduates in psychology sections taught by instructors from a course on teaching performed better on standardized departmental tests than students in sections taught by other teaching staff.

There has not been enough research reported in the literature to make specific suggestions regarding what approaches or content makes a pedagogy course most effective. Although one study (Jerich & Leinicke, 1993) used student ratings to compare the results of different versions of the same pedagogy course, the number of students involved was too small and the details provided too few to determine what made the dif-ference.

Two articles (Schoem, Carlton, Gates, & Black, 1991; Williams, 1991) suggest that the effectiveness of a pedagogy course is enhanced if it includes or is supplemented by classroom observation, consultation, and videotaping. As mentioned earlier, some pedagogy courses include these elements anyway. Although two articles are hardly definitive, it makes sense that a pedagogy course—given its objective to develop both a theoretical and practical grasp of teaching—should include actual teaching practice and skillfully conveyed individualized feedback.

THE BENEFITS OF PEDAGOGY COURSES

In an unpublished manuscript on pedagogy courses at Canadian universities, Piccinin and Farquharson stress several benefits to such classes. They can have a "trickle up" effect on the teaching quality and dedication of faculty and other TAs, they can contribute to the creation of a new generation of scholar/teachers who more equally balance their teaching and research responsibilities, they can produce accomplished TAs who can staff training workshops and orientations for other TAs, and they can be a concrete manifestation of a "culture of teaching." Given the emphasis on teaching ability in today's tight academic job market, it also seems reasonable to suggest that such courses may enhance the job prospects of graduate students who take them. Wagener (1991) mentions something equally significant—that the need to staff such courses and other TA training efforts may create a demand for faculty who can and will teach pedagogical content knowledge. As noted, Rickard (1991) also reported that these courses can mean improved TA teaching and student learning.

At Stanford, we have noticed these benefits but only under certain conditions. Pedagogy courses are influential when regular faculty, and more than one, are importantly involved in the course. If such courses are consigned to TAs or to only one committed faculty member, then they often have little or no "trickle" effect. If the courses are mainly concerned with methodology, carry no or little credit, and are given pass/fail, then they do not make an important statement about the importance of teaching or about the need for future faculty to combine teaching and research responsibilities. And the most obvious impact on graduate students' success on the job market seems to occur when the pedagogy course helps them develop important artifacts of their teaching effectiveness, such as course syllabi or a teaching portfolio.

THE FUTURE OF PEDAGOGY COURSES

Whatever their benefits, pedagogy courses' real value will only manifest itself when they are part of a larger effort to make teaching preparation an integral part of graduate education. When they exist outside of such a movement, whatever good they may do for the departments, faculty, and graduate students involved in them, they are still vulnerable to the changing priorities of individuals or the institution. The pedagogy course movement should benefit enormously, then, from the Preparing Future Faculty Programs, mentioned earlier, and from the spread of the so-called pedagogical colloquium first proposed in 1993 at the AAHE Conference on Faculty Roles and Rewards by Professor Lee Shulman (Hutchings, 1996b), now president of the Carnegie Foundation for the Advancement of Teaching. Shulman conceived of the pedagogical colloquium as the teaching analog of the research presentation expected of candidates for academic jobs. In addition to the academic job talk, candidates should have to do a presentation on a course they have taught, a teaching problem of the field, or some other pedagogical dilemma (Shulman, 1995). Already adopted by some departments and institutions, pedagogical colloquia demand a teaching sophistication that today's graduate education rarely provides. Academic job candidates who realize that they will face such a forum may find themselves eager to take a well-conceived and well-taught course on teaching that is more than "technique-driven."

In Canada, Piccinin and Picard (1994) report that more graduate students are eager to take pedagogy courses than can be accommodated (although it must be noted that at the time they were writing, Canadian pedagogy courses were all centrally sponsored and thus relatively small numbers of graduate students could be admitted). Still, there are signs that in the U.S. as well, it is the graduate students themselves who are recognizing their need for more and better training. The enthusiastic and, in some cases, oversubscribed response of graduate students to the Preparing Future Faculty initiative is a case in point (Gaff & Lambert, 1996). The demand for better preparation for teaching that often accompanies TA unionizing efforts (Leatherman, 1997) is further evidence of growing graduate student interest in their right to teacher training.

In this climate, institutions that do not have pedagogy courses or have not been supportive of them might reconsider how to encourage and support such courses. Even institutions that have courses on teaching may want to explore how to root them more firmly in the values of institutional life and may want to consider how to more fully reward and recognize the faculty who teach them. Courses on teaching may be about to come into their own.

REFERENCES

Allen, R. R., & Rueter, T. (1990). *Teaching assistant strategies: An introduction to college teaching.* Dubuque, IA: Kendall/Hunt.

Ambrose, S. A. (1991). From graduate student to faculty member: Teaching Ph.D. candidates to teach. In J. D. Nyquist, R. D. Abbott, D. H. Wulff, & J. Sprague (Eds.), *Preparing the professoriate of tomorrow to teach: Selected readings in TA training.* Dubuque, IA: Kendall/Hunt.

Andrews, J. D. W. (Ed.). (1985). *Strengthening the teaching assistant faculty.* New Directions for Teaching and Learning, No. 22. San Francisco, CA: Jossey-Bass.

Boyer, E. L. (1990). *Scholarship reconsidered: Priorities of the professoriate.* Princeton, NJ: Carnegie Foundation for the Advancement of Teaching.

Committee on Undergraduate Science Education. (1997). *Science teaching reconsidered: A handbook.* Washington, DC: National Academy Press.

Dalgaard, K. A., & Dalgaard, B. R. (1977, April). *An overview of a teaching assistant training program: Implementation in two settings.* Paper presented at the meeting of the Eastern Economic Association, Hartford, CT.

Davidson, C. I., & Ambrose, S. A. (1994). *The new professor's handbook: A guide to teaching and research in engineering and science.* Bolton, MA: Anker.

Diamond, R. M., & Wilbur, F. P. (1990). Developing teaching skills during graduate education. *To Improve the Academy, 9,* 199-216.

Gaff, J. G., & Lambert, L. M. (1996). Socializing future faculty to the values of undergraduate education. *Change, 28* (4), 38-45.

Gappa, L. (1991). A professional teaching assistant program: Custom designing for your institution. *Journal of Staff, Program, & Organization Development, 9* (2), 83-91.

Gonnerman, M. (1993). Teaching colloquium in religious studies, 1992-93: The setting, a summary and some personal observations. In M. Gonnerman & M. Unno (Eds.), *A guide to teaching in religious studies.* Stanford, CA: Department of Religious Studies, Stanford University.

Humphreys, W. L. (1987). The TA seminar and TA support services at the University of Tennessee, Knoxville. In N. V. N. Chism (Ed.), *Institutional responsibilities and responses in the employment and education of teaching assistants.* Columbus, OH: The Ohio State University.

Hutchings, P. (1996a). *Making teaching community property: A menu for peer collaboration and peer review.* Washington, DC: American Association for Higher Education.

Hutchings, P. (1996b). The pedagogical colloquium: Focusing on teaching in the hiring process. *AAHE Bulletin, 49* (3), 3-4.

Jerich, K. F., & Leinicke, L. M. (1993). A comparative study of the teaching effectiveness for three groups of graduate teaching assistants in accounting. In K. G. Lewis (Ed.), *The TA experience: Preparing for multiple roles.* Stillwater, OK: New Forums Press.

Lambert, L. M., & Tice, S. L. (1993). *Preparing graduate students to teach: A guide to programs that improve undergraduate education and develop tomorrow's faculty.* Washington, DC: American Association for Higher Education.

Leatherman, C. (1997, October 3). As teaching assistants push to unionize, debate grows over what they would gain. *The Chronicle of Higher Education,* A12-A13.

Lewis, K. G. (1992). *Teaching pedagogy to teaching assistants: A handbook for 398T instructors.* Austin, TX: University of Texas, Center for Teaching Effectiveness.

McKeachie, W. J. (1994). *Teaching tips: A guidebook for the beginning college teacher* (9th ed.). Boston, MA: Houghton Mifflin.

Mintz, J. (1991). *Departmental handbook for graduate student instructor training.* Berkeley, CA: University of California at Berkeley, Graduate Division.

Neff, R. A., & Weimer, M. (Eds.). (1990). *Teaching college: Collected readings for the new instructor.* Madison, WI: Magna Publications.

Nilson, L. B. (1993). Training TAs in disciplinary clusters: A cost-effective alternative to departmental programs. In K. G. Lewis (Ed.), *The TA experience: Preparing for multiple roles.* Stillwater, OK: New Forums Press.

Nyquist, J. D., Abbott, R. D., & Wulff, D. H. (Eds.). (1989). *Teaching assistant training in the 1990s.* New Directions for Teaching and Learning, No. 39. San Francisco, CA: Jossey-Bass.

Parrett, J. L. (1987). A ten-year review of TA training programs: Trends, patterns, and common practices. In N. V. N. Chism (Ed.), *Institutional responsibilities and responses in the employment and education of teaching assistants.* Columbus, OH: The Ohio State University.

Piccinin, S., & Farquharson, A. (n.d.). *Preparing graduate students to teach: Credit courses in Canadian universities.* Unpublished manuscript, University of Victoria.

Piccinin, S., & Picard, M. (1994). Credit courses on university teaching for graduate students in Canadian universities. *Canadian Journal of Higher Education, 24* (3), 58-70.

Reis, R. M. (1997). *Tomorrow's professor: Preparing for academic careers in science and engineering.* New York, NY: IEEE Press.

Rickard, H. C., et al. (1991). Teaching of psychology: A required course for all doctoral students. *Teaching of Psychology, 18* (4), 235-237.

Roberts, R. (1997, August 18). Personal communication.

Ronkowski, S. (1989, November). *Changes in teaching assistant concerns over time.* Paper presented at the National Conference on the Training and Employment of Teaching Assistants, Seattle, WA.

Saroyan, A., & Amundsen, C. (1995). The systematic design and implementation of a training program for teaching assistants. *Canadian Journal of Higher Education, 25* (1), 1-18.

Schoem, D., Carlton, S., Gates, B., & Black, B. (1991). Developing and implementing a college-wide TA training program at the University of Michigan. In J. D. Nyquist, R. D. Abbott, D. H. Wulff, & J. Sprague (Eds.), *Preparing the professoriate of tomorrow to teach: Selected readings in TA training.* Dubuque, IA: Kendall/Hunt.

Shulman, L. S. (1995). Faculty hiring: The pedagogical colloquium: Three models. *AAHE Bulletin, 47* (9), 6-9.

Vattano, F. J., & Avens, J. S. (1987). Courses on college teaching. In N. V. N. Chism (Ed.), *Institutional responsibilities and responses in the employment and education of teaching assistants.* Columbus, OH: The Ohio State University.

Wagener, U. E. (1991). Changing the culture of teaching: Mathematics at Indiana, Chicago, and Harvard. *Change, 23* (4), 28-37.

Wankat, P. C., & Oreovicz, F. S. (1993). *Teaching engineering.* New York, NY: McGraw-Hill.

Williams, L. S. (1991). The effects of a comprehensive teaching assistant training program on teaching anxiety and effectiveness. *Research in Higher Education, 32* (5), 585-598.

Wright, D. L. (1987). A seminar on college teaching. In N. V. N. Chism (Ed.), *Institutional responsibilities and responses in the employment and education of teaching assistants.* Columbus, OH: The Ohio State University.

9

International TA Training and Beyond: Out of the Program and Into the Classroom

Ellen Sarkisian and Virginia Maurer

I was really scared to death because, as you know, I am not an English native speaker. The first problem I felt seriously was how to teach native speakers by using a non-native language for me. So I was very scared. But I think I tried very hard to prepare in advance the test of the first teaching. Because first of all language problem [sic], and also there is a cultural barrier too. But because of the language problem, I usually prepare extensively before the section. I usually prepare a lot of handouts. Also I sometimes prepare basic questions I'd like to ask during the section, or what kind of direction I would pursue in the section in written form, so that whenever I feel uneasy speaking English, then I can refer to those written materials.

I think in the United States teaching is a very active interaction between the teacher and the students. Most sections I have taught so far are focused on discussion rather than lecture. It is very different from the kind of teaching I had before I came to the United States. Most of the teaching was largely lectures before I came here. And the sections I have taught here are basically an exchange of ideas between the teacher and the students. This active participation in discussion is very useful in understanding the course materials and the issues at hand, by the teaching assistants and also the students. There's a big difference between teaching in the United States and in most of the other countries.

A Chinese ITA comments about teaching American students[1]

I noticed that he was a foreign TA. I'm sure everybody else in the section did as well. I, and probably a few of my classmates, felt a little bit uneasy about whether we would be able to understand and learn from the section.... I decided to stay because it was evident from the first session that he was very enthusiastic and very interested in making sure that we would keep up with the class work, and understand what was going on. He wanted us to understand. You could tell by the way that he spoke, very slowly, and explained terms very clearly. And was genuinely interested in our learning, and our learning process.... He would ask us each pointed questions and really work a lot on student interaction, getting our feedback from us and listening to our discussions and encouraging them.

I really liked that. You can't ask for much more.... I've had both good and bad foreign TAs. There are problems with their accents, and there are problems with culture, language barriers, and so forth. But I think all of that can be made up for in things like enthusiasm for the subject matter and interest in the students. If you have a TA who really cares about whether the students learn the material or not, who makes himself or herself available for students who are having problems, I think all factors like that can make up for just about anything, any drawback that they might have during section. I think a lot of foreign TAs know that the students are maybe judging them a little bit more critically than, say, American TAs. And they make up for that in having a lot more zeal inside the classroom, really wanting their students to learn.

An American student comments about a Chinese ITA

Fear of the unfamiliar is a powerful force for most people. In many gatherings, people tend to talk to others they already know. Most people, with few exceptions, talk more readily to those who look as if they come from a familiar culture and speak the same language. These tendencies work against foreign graduate students who find themselves teaching in a language that is not their own to a room full of students from a culture that is also not their own. And these tendencies can also work against the students in that classroom. The situation carries a tinge of fear for the teaching assistant, who may have difficulties communicating, and anxiety for the students, who believe they will have difficulty understanding and learning from the teaching assistant.

Easing international teaching assistants (ITAs) into the unfamiliar territory of teaching in English has been the goal of ITA training programs, many of which were established in various American universities in the 1980s, and continues to be the goal for new programs in institutions with an influx of foreign graduate students. Initially responding to student complaints about language, trainers of ITAs rapidly discovered the impossibility of anticipating quick results from a crash course in English as a Second Language (ESL). They further discovered ITAs' great difficulty in expressing themselves appropriately in different contexts (Hoekje & Williams, 1992) and in applying to their teaching the information and skills learned in training programs. Programs have become increasingly sophisticated and practice-oriented in their approach to language, pedagogy, and culture. For those new to this enterprise, as well as experienced practitioners, many books and resources with extensive bibliographies provide comprehensive surveys of the field, current perspectives on ITA language and testing issues, reviews of research, and summaries of issues related to program design, curriculum, and teaching strategies, as well as policy and administration (e.g., Bauer & Tanner, 1994; Briggs et al., 1997; Madden & Myers, 1994; Nelson, 1991; Sarkisian, 1997; Smith et al., 1992). These resources should be consulted for information on several fundamental issues such as the level of English competence expected at different institutions, current methods of screening, and the range of program designs suited to different institutions. In addition, ideas are continually exchanged through national organizations and networks, for example, Teachers of English to Speakers of Other Languages (TESOL) and National Conferences on the Training and Employment of Graduate Teaching Assistants. Many ideas expressed in this chapter come from these conferences and from colleagues at a range of institutions. This chapter will not survey the full range of ITA issues treated in detail elsewhere. Instead it will concentrate on what many experienced practitioners see as the central issue in ITA training—interactive teaching—and will focus on three strategies that effectively translate training into the ITAs' classroom teaching:

- Involving undergraduates in the training process

- Training within academic departments and courses

- Training, feedback, and reflection during the semester

THE IMPORTANCE OF INTERACTIVE TEACHING

Interacting with students through asking questions and giving feedback in problem sessions, labs, or discussion sections is essential to successful teaching (Nelson, 1991; Smith et al., 1992). Beyond short presentations of material, most TAs are expected to facilitate their students' learning by creating a climate conducive to raising questions and exchanging ideas. In a problem session, the TA should coach students, step by step, not simply plug numbers in for them; ask questions; urge students to apply their learning; and invite students to voice their confusion when they are puzzled. In a lab, in addition to giving directions, the TA should move around from station to station asking students what and how they are doing and troubleshooting problems. In discussions, the TA must raise issues, understand and follow up on replies, invite comments, and manage the flow of ideas. American students are educated to express their opinions and to speak up as individuals. They expect the back and forth of an open classroom environment. Professors also increasingly expect interaction in the classroom because they believe that students learn better this way: not simply absorbing texts and lectures, but formulating questions before class, answering questions in class, testing out ideas with others, and applying their learning to new situations. In American classrooms, ITAs encounter activities they may never have imagined: Students are encouraged to talk to each other, to learn from each other, and even eventually to give feedback to the teacher.

A paradox lies at the core of ITA training. Teaching interactively is important for all TAs. Although it can be difficult for any TA, it is especially difficult for ITAs. Yet teaching interactively is probably even more important for them than for their native English-speaking counterparts. Why is it especially hard for ITAs to teach interactively? And why is it so important for them to do so?

Most TAs find it far easier to prepare, practice, and then deliver a talk, unencumbered by interpreting the meaning of a question or thinking on their feet than to follow unanticipated paths in a discussion. This is especially so for ITAs, who typically read and write at a level far beyond their ability to speak or understand the American English spoken by their students. Some exceptional ITAs are very approachable inside and outside the classroom and teach interactively with no guidance. However, other ITAs tend to shy away from initiating contact with individual students and may lapse into teaching by one-way communication rather than teaching interactively. Many ITAs say their greatest problem with teaching interactively is understanding the students' questions. Stories illustrating ITAs avoiding the demands of interactive teaching abound. An Indian ITA, in order to escape from his students before and after math class, simply arrived late and left promptly. A Korean ITA tried asking questions in an economics discussion section, but resorted to lecturing when he found he could not understand students' replies or the questions they asked him.

The most daunting situation of all is an open discussion when ITAs must initiate and sustain conversation. In a large group, with comments and questions crisscrossing the room, following the thread is very hard. Many ITAs hear a student's comment and have no idea how to respond. Others simply cannot listen fast enough to follow the discussion, much less speak quickly enough to manage it.

In addition to the difficulties posed by language, there is typically little in their own educational background to prepare ITAs to teach interactively. The majority have spent years sitting in a classroom with a large number of fellow students listening while the teacher lectures. Their experience typically does not include students asking questions of the teacher (interpreted as a sign of disrespect in some cultures) or students making comments in a discussion (frowned upon in some cultures unless the speakers are absolutely sure of what they are saying). Furthermore, if the formal educational system measures student success only at the end of a very long period of study, keeping up with the work and participating in ongoing discussions are less important than solitary cramming.

Since teaching interactively is so difficult, why is it so important for ITAs? First of all, their students may have trouble understanding them. To find out whether an explanation is clear, they must invite questions and be open to students' interruptions. This will provide an opportunity to clarify a muddled explanation with more examples or express an idea in different words. In addition, by inviting student participation, ITAs will discover how the students understand the material, solve problems, and apply their learning. This is particularly important for ITAs in math and science who are likely to teach over the heads of their students, expecting a higher level of background than the uneven—and often lower—level of most American high school graduates.

Operating in an American environment with expectations that may or may not have been communicated clearly, ITAs may start out with little understanding of their audience—the American students—their educational background in general, their level in a particular discipline, and their expectations of teachers. The challenge for training programs is to give ITAs the skills, along with the underlying rationale and follow-up support, to more effectively teach their students.

INVOLVING UNDERGRADUATES IN TRAINING

Recognizing the difficulty many ITAs have teaching interactively, most ITA training programs incorporate practice teaching into their training. Typically, this practice teaching consists of several microteaching sessions during which ITAs give short, interactive presentations to small groups of fellow ITAs pretending to be students. Yet despite this chance to develop interactive skills, many ITAs still find it difficult to fully appreciate many issues involved in teaching American undergraduates, partly because the classroom behavior of these "students" is artificial.

Interacting with the very audience they will face—undergraduates— is one way to prepare ITAs for the variety of undergraduates' experience and education; the ethnic and racial diversity of American undergraduates; unpredictable student comments and behavior; and unfamiliar situations ITAs will find themselves in. In order to help ITAs recognize the rationale for teaching interactively, and to motivate them to teach this way, many institutions involve American undergraduates as the audience for practice teaching and as participants in formal and informal discussions of teaching and learning.

Students as Audience and Critics

Undergraduates are the most authentic audience for microteaching. At the University of Delaware's ITA training program, undergraduates are instructed to ask and answer questions and to behave as students in class normally do. Following the microteaching, the undergraduates give their reactions. Hearing undergraduates talk in context about what is important to them in the classroom and discussing with them why these things are important gives immediacy to many aspects of cultural norms of the U.S. classroom, especially those which might seem unimportant to an ITA. This direct experience with American undergraduates motivates ITAs to teach in ways well suited to their students.

Even with limited training in giving feedback, undergraduates make comments surprisingly similar to those of teacher trainers, pointing out what ITAs have done well and commenting on one or two essential areas which need improvement. Sincere in their efforts to help ITAs become better teachers, undergraduates focus on what is important when they are in a class trying to learn.

Hearing comments directly from a cross section of the very kinds of people ITAs will teach instead of from a trainer or fellow ITAs is very powerful. Several of the dozen programs that we interviewed for this chapter include undergraduates in their ITA training activities. Program staff reported that undergraduates are both tactful and direct, dealing with subtle aspects of group dynamics and student learning that are reflected in research on ITAs and student learning.

> *When you answered Lydia's question, you looked only at her. You still need to look at all of us. If one person asks a question, you can be sure that there are other people in the class who don't understand either.*[2]

> *That was good the way you tried to find out our thinking process when we got an answer wrong. That gave you the chance to see what our misconceptions were, what the holes in our knowledge were. That helps everybody, not just the person who asked the question.*

> *You showed good wait-time after you asked us questions, which gave us time to think. Keep up the good work!*

Undergraduates also bring specific knowledge of the difficulties in learning a particular subject.

> *The notation you are using is unfamiliar to us. Be sure you know what the conventions are here in the U.S. Otherwise, when we see it, it makes it difficult to relate it to what we already know and are comfortable with.*

> *That was really helpful for me the way you used concrete examples to illustrate Gauss's Law. Abstract formulas are like compressed knowledge and some of us need help to decompress it.*

In addition, students are alert to pedagogical tactics that support clear communication in the classroom.

> *I really appreciated your asking me to rephrase my question when you didn't understand what I was asking. I don't care if you don't understand me, but I do expect you to make sure, with whatever it takes, that you understand. Otherwise, I feel frustrated.*

> *It seemed that when someone asked you a harder question, you spoke more softly and even used less language and just resorted to writing on the board. That makes it more confusing. We still need to hear what you are doing and why, not just to see it.*

> *When Demian answered your question about open sets, you just nodded and pursed your lips and looked unsure. That sent a mixed message and we weren't sure if what he said was right or not. You just went on. That doesn't help.*

Finally, the importance of teaching behavior that might seem insignificant to an ITA takes on deeper importance when undergraduates repeatedly make the point.

> *You used our names, which was great. We want you to learn and use our names, even if it takes you six weeks!*

> *We can't see what you're writing or hear what you're saying when you write facing the board. It makes it hard for us to take notes. Could you try writing standing sideways?*

You looked at us more this time, which was good.

Most undergraduates are not used to listening and speaking to non-native speakers at great length, nor are they accustomed to interpreting the unintended cues or miscues of someone from another culture. ITAs fluent in English still might be misunderstood by students if they act in a way that differs significantly from student expectations (Schneider & Stevens, 1991). ITAs, by practicing teaching skills on the group they will eventually be teaching, can develop styles of interacting with an authentic audience whose reactions reflect the reality of the undergraduate classroom.

After looking over the written undergraduate feedback that he had received after his third session of microteaching, one ITA remarked:

> *What I like best is that the students are really honest in the feedback they give us. They tell us what they like and don't like. Sometimes I feel you [the ITA trainers] say everything in such a positive way that I'm not really sure how I'm doing. You work with foreign students all the time, and you're used to us. It's easy to interact with you. And anyway, it's your job. But before I had the chance to teach something to these American students, I was really afraid of them . . . Would they be able to understand me? Would they like my teaching style? What would I do if I didn't understand them? But now, I see them as real people who want to learn, and I have to do everything I can to help them. Part of that is understanding better how they learn and what they expect.*

Students as Participants in Discussions about Culture

To reduce the social and cultural distance between ITAs and American undergraduates, many institutions have set up ways for ITAs and undergraduates to learn more about cultural differences and how they get expressed in the classroom. These can range from providing conversation partners and having regularly scheduled informal lunch discussions, to holding more focused meetings in which undergraduates and ITAs might role play scenarios involving typical undergraduate-TA interactions (e.g., office hours or handling a complaint about grades).

Michigan State University has established a successful, highly structured ITA-undergraduate Buddy Program. Each semester, ITAs currently teaching are paired with undergraduates whom they meet with weekly during the semester to explore and compare American undergraduate life with student life in the ITAs' home countries. With a guiding structure of assigned weekly activities, the Buddy Program curriculum emphasizes experiential learning. Each pair of buddies engages in a shared process of discovery, learning from each other and observing student life. Afterwards, ITAs say they feel more comfortable and confident relating to their students, and the undergraduates say they themselves benefit from the personal exposure to cultural differences.

Discussions do not have to be structured to be effective. The University of South Florida sets up unstructured discussions among ITAs and undergraduates, making sure that the undergraduates chosen are typical students reflecting a wide range of backgrounds. These discussions provide ITAs with an opportunity to meet people they might not normally meet and allow them to experience the diversity they will be encountering in class. The importance of helping ITAs learn to reach a diverse group of students is underscored by the fact that many of them teach introductory courses in science, where women and minorities are typically most at risk of giving up and changing majors.

Whether the interaction is structured or unstructured, formal or informal, research suggests that involving undergraduates in ITA training can have a positive effect on undergraduate-ITA relations (Plakans, 1997). Furthermore, using undergraduates in a training program has the added benefit of preparing undergraduates for cultural diversity. Many undergraduates who participate view ITAs with new respect and understanding, an attitude that they may pass on to their peers.

TRAINING ITAS WITHIN ACADEMIC DEPARTMENTS AND COURSES

Undergraduates participating in interactive training programs vividly demonstrate to ITAs the need for an appropriate level of teaching and provide clues about the interpersonal side of the classroom. Academic departments offering training provide concrete experience with the specific content and skills ITAs are expected to teach. While some ITA programs offer field-specific training, home departments or disciplines can supplement the general teaching strategies offered in many ITA training programs by focusing on what works well in teaching a particular course (Heenan &

Jerich, 1993). In addition, learning more about teaching with a particular group of colleagues, including faculty members and experienced TAs, reduces the isolation of ITAs and provides a context for support throughout the semester. If the trainers are department faculty and administrators, the ITA can appreciate directly the department's commitment to teaching.

The following two examples of discipline-based TA training come from the chemistry department at the University of Pittsburgh and the mathematics department at Harvard University. While these departments do not view their programs as specifically for ITAs, discipline-based TA training programs are highlighted because they go beyond ITA training programs in familiarizing ITAs with discipline-specific teaching issues and give ITAs the confidence and skills needed to get off to a good start.

Chemistry Department Training Program

The four-day TA training program at the University of Pittsburgh includes developing a philosophy of teaching and dealing with students' problems, along with performing experiments and lab safety. Aspects of the program related to pedagogy begin with general discussions about teaching (on topics such as, "How would you characterize a good teacher?") followed by break-out groups with four or five participants. These small groups are particularly suited to ITAs (about one-fourth of the new TAs in this department), who more readily voice their concerns or fears in this setting. A few days later during microteaching (facilitated by experienced faculty and TAs), the audience includes the now familiar TAs from the small discussion groups.

Several advantages to department-based training are evident in the comments and questions given to ITAs during microteaching. While many comments are not specific to chemistry (e.g., advice to look at the students or to slow down), the audience of TAs who have taught the course before asks the kinds of questions a sophomore with no experience might ask. Furthermore, these TAs and the faculty can assist with very specific course-based tips (e.g., conventions in drawing molecules) and confusion in terminology that a nonspecialist might miss or could not comment on with authority (e.g., avoiding words like "carbocation" because students will not know their meaning).

Hands-on lab training is especially important for ITAs, to familiarize them both with equipment which they may not have had experience with in their own countries and with essential aspects of lab safety which might not be clear with only a cursory introduction. Many ITAs may never have seen, for example, the most up-to-date balance, which they must be comfortable using in teaching. Lab safety takes on added dimensions for ITAs since it ventures into areas of cultural ambiguity. Not only must information be emphatic enough to protect everyone's physical safety, but at the University of Pittsburgh, the program recognizes difficulties foreign graduate students might have with accidents. At their safety seminar, to dramatically emphasize responding to an accident in the lab, a very small Asian female graduate student grabs a very large male student and says forcefully, "You must strip."

Math Teaching Apprenticeship

The teaching apprenticeship in the math department at Harvard University traces its origins to the influx of foreign-trained graduate students in the early 1980s. However, all TAs, irrespective of native language or educational background, participate in the program during the semester before they will begin teaching.

The central feature of the apprenticeship is for the TA to observe and then to teach three complete classes in the middle of the semester in the classroom of an experienced faculty member or successful teaching assistant (called a "coach"). Before they begin teaching, apprentices meet as a group with a faculty member to discuss teaching strategies. Then the apprentice practices the lesson with a few students from the class, observed by the coach. The apprentice later teaches the lesson to the entire class, meeting afterwards with the coach (who observes and gives the apprentice feedback after all three classes). The second class is videotaped and the students fill out a written questionnaire evaluating the class. The apprentice and a viewing partner, selected from a list of department faculty and teaching consultants, review the videotape and the student evaluations together, setting goals for the third class. The goal of the math teaching apprenticeship—to help new TAs gain confidence and develop skills appropriate for teaching lower-level math courses—is particularly appropriate for ITAs, many of whom have no idea what an undergraduate math class in the U.S. is like.

Pairing experienced teachers directly with individual TAs for a series of training or follow-up activities can be complicated to set up and labor-intensive to carry out. However, if staff and resources are available, the benefits of individual attention to ITAs can be enormous.

Both training programs offer follow-up activities for all TAs as they begin teaching on their own. At the University of Pittsburgh, TAs meet regularly with the professor to discuss the course and their teaching; in-class observation and coteaching are available for TAs needing extra help. Additional workshops on general teaching issues, including syllabus development and active learning, are available at the university's teaching center for all TAs. At Harvard, further practice teaching, observing others' classes the first week of term, and review of midcourse feedback are offered in the math department. Close cooperation among the math department, the teaching center staff, and the center's ESL specialist provides a strong and flexible framework to train and support ITAs while they teach.

GUIDANCE, FEEDBACK, AND REFLECTION

Some ITAs move to actual classroom teaching with little difficulty, but many profit from additional follow-up. Their own experience as learners inevitably informs countless decisions ITAs make while teaching. Coming from different teaching and learning environments, ITAs are often unable to decide on the most effective ways to engage undergraduates with the material. Responsibility for a class week after week is a world apart from discussing teaching in the abstract, practicing on others' students, and planning a few classes.

The experience of one Chinese graduate student illustrates some difficulties faced by ITAs in transferring training into a real teaching situation. Li, an ITA in statistics, had taken a presemester, week-long ITA training course. By the end, he was able to conduct a relatively interactive microteaching session, encouraging participation from the group. Four weeks after classes began, the ITA coordinator called Li to suggest having his section observed or videotaped to get feedback on how he was doing. Embarrassed, Li told the coordinator that each week fewer undergraduates had shown up for the section, and only two students were still coming. Demoralized and humiliated, he had no idea what to do. The ITA coordinator asked an experienced ITA from the statistics department to observe Li's section. It was immediately clear that Li had little idea of what to cover in section and was giving the students challenging problems going far beyond the lecture. Li chose material that he believed was essential and not even difficult. The students, needing clarification of the professor's lecture, found the section confusing and irrelevant and stopped coming.

Li's experience illustrates the limitations of training programs without follow-up. Often a gap exists between ITA training and the actual classroom teaching ITAs will be doing. Most ITA training programs can teach the importance of involving students in an interactive class but cannot teach ITAs what should be covered in section, they cannot help ITAs accurately interpret the level of their students' prior knowledge, they cannot help the ITAs grasp the root of undergraduate misconceptions about scientific concepts, and they cannot give explicit suggestions on how to make specific content more accessible to students who are having difficulty.

Many departments and professors assume that once an ITA has taken a training course, the general pedagogy and communication problems will be solved, and the ITA, already knowledgeable in the subject, will be prepared to teach. Even when departments do offer training for all their TAs, this training often does not take into account the special needs of ITAs who, like Li, may hold expectations about course responsibilities and their own teaching that differ from those of their students or course heads. Departments can ensure that ITAs get the support and guidance they need through, for example, weekly TA meetings specifically addressing teaching issues and strategies, midcourse feedback, and class videotaping and consultation.

Weekly TA Meetings

TA meetings are the most obvious vehicle for ongoing training. Although many professors or head TAs meet regularly with TAs, the content of such meetings varies widely from course to course. Some concentrate on administrative issues, while others may involve the ITAs in discussions of the material they should cover. Many TAs comment, however, that TA meetings rarely include discussions about how to teach. Professors may assume that TAs will learn as they themselves did, by trial and error and by modeling their teaching on good teachers they had while undergraduates. This puts ITAs at a disadvantage since the knowledge and experience of how a certain subject is typically taught in the U.S. may not be clear to them. ITAs, in addition, may not understand everything that is said or implied in a TA meeting. Professors can help ITAs come to a deeper understanding of good teaching in their discipline and help prevent a debacle such as Li's by being aware of the assumptions that ITAs bring to teaching (e.g., Li's assumption that the purpose of section was to challenge the students even further); by checking that ITAs have understood everything clearly; by addressing discipline-specific teaching issues in TA meetings; and by discussing effective teaching methods for the particular content of the next class meeting.

Midcourse Feedback

Requiring midcourse feedback from students is an additional way that departments can help ITAs get a clear idea of what is going well and what needs improvement. There are a number of different methods for collecting feedback, but, irrespective of the process, two things are important to consider: First, student feedback can be more effectively interpreted and alternative strategies explored when a teaching consultant goes over the feedback with the ITA and, second, department policies concerning confidentiality must be clear.

ITAs at the University of Missouri must ask their students to fill out feedback forms on the class early in the semester. Completed forms are not seen by the ITA but are sent to the Center for Teaching Excellence where comments are typed and forwarded to an advisor chosen by the ITA, usually a professor or experienced ITA from the same department. The ITAs and their advisors go over the comments together and discuss strategies to respond to the feedback. The ITA is later observed in class or lab by someone from the teaching center, and afterward they discuss the class.

Another way to obtain midcourse feedback is the Small Group Instructional Diagnosis (SGID) used by the Center for Instructional Development and Research at the University of Washington and on many other campuses. A teaching consultant from the center meets with the students in a TA's class and facilitates a discussion about how the class is going. Afterward, the teaching consultant meets with the TA to review the themes that emerged from the discussion. Asking students to articulate in a discussion the strengths and weaknesses of the class has additional benefits since students who have participated in the process seem to develop a better working relationship with their ITAs (Bauer & Tanner, 1993).

Videotaping and Consultation

The opportunity to have a class videotaped and then to view and discuss it with a teaching consultant or an experienced teacher is another effective training tool for ITAs. Typically, before a viewing consultation begins, the ITA talks about how the class went, describing the goals of that particular class and how the class fit into earlier classes. Watching the videotape provides a context for discussing both language and teaching issues particularly relevant for ITAs: Is language used appropriately? Does the ITA accurately interpret the language and behavior of the undergraduates? What is the balance of formality and informality and what does it convey? What does the ITA do after finishing one content segment before moving on to the next? How are main points emphasized, and how are examples used? How is student participation discouraged or encouraged? Viewing their own class can give ITAs a clear sense of the level of student participation in their class and help them build on the interactive teaching strategies they learned in training programs.

CONCLUSION

Interactive teaching is a difficult but essential skill. For many ITAs it goes against the grain of their educational background, but they must learn to appreciate its fundamental importance. There is no single best program for every individual or, for that matter, every institution. But the most effective programs open up channels of communication with students, departments, and colleagues. Since ITAs come from different cultures and are individuals with different strengths and weaknesses in the classroom, a variety of training activities and flexible follow-up will increase their confidence and provide skills and background to help most adjust to this new and unfamiliar classroom environment.

ENDNOTES

[1] These quotations were taken from the transcript of the videotape, *Teaching in America,* produced by the Derek Bok Center for Teaching and Learning, Harvard University, and available from Anker Publishing, P.O. Box 249, Bolton, MA 01740-0249.

2 These and other quotations, unless otherwise indicated, were drawn from feedback forms filled in by Harvard undergraduates participating as practice students in the Spring 1997 Teaching in English program.

REFERENCES

Bauer, G., & Tanner, M. (Eds.). (1994). *Current approaches to international TA preparation in higher education: A collection of program descriptions.* Seattle, WA: University of Washington, Center for Instructional Development and Research.

Bauer, G., & Tanner, M. (1993). Insights into ITA instruction in problem solving courses through student perceptions at midterm. In K. G. Lewis (Ed.), *The TA experience: Preparing for multiple roles.* Stillwater, OK: New Forums Press.

Briggs, S., Clark, V., Madden, C., Beal, R., Hyon, S., Aldridge, P., & Swales, J. (1997). *The international teaching assistant: An annotated critical bibliography* (2nd ed.). Ann Arbor, MI: University of Michigan, English Language Institute.

Heenan, T., & Jerich, K. (1993). *Teaching graduate students to teach: Engaging the disciplines.* Urbana-Champaign, IL: University of Illinois, Office of Conferences and Institutes.

Hoekje, B., & Williams, J. (1992). Communicative competence and the dilemma of international teaching assistant education. *TESOL Quarterly, 26* (2), 243-269.

Madden, C., & Myers, C. (Eds.). (1994). *Discourse and performance of international teaching assistants.* Alexandria, VA: Teachers of English to Speakers of Other Languages (TESOL).

Nelson, G. L. (1991). Effective teaching behavior for international teaching assistants. In J. D. Nyquist, R. D. Abbott, D. H. Wulff, & J. Sprague (Eds.), *Preparing the professoriate of tomorrow to teach: Selected readings in TA training.* Dubuque, IA: Kendall/Hunt.

Plakans, B. (1997). Undergraduates' experiences with and attitudes towards international teaching assistants. *TESOL Quarterly, 31* (1), 95-119.

Sarkisian, E. (1997). *Teaching American students: A guide for international faculty and teaching assistants in U.S. colleges and universities* (Rev. Ed.). Cambridge, MA: Harvard University, Derek Bok Center for Teaching and Learning.

Schneider, K., & Stevens, S. (1991). American undergraduate students as trainers in an international teaching assistant training program. In J. D. Nyquist, R. D. Abbott, D. H. Wulff, & J. Sprague (Eds.), *Preparing the professoriate of tomorrow to teach: Selected readings in TA training.* Dubuque, IA: Kendall/Hunt.

Smith, R. M., Byrd, P., Nelson, G. L., Barrett, R. P., & Constantinides, J. C. (1992). *Crossing pedagogical oceans: International teaching assistants in U.S. undergraduate education.* (ASHE-ERIC Higher Education Report No. 8). Washington, DC: The George Washington University, School of Education and Human Development.

10

HELPING TAS
IMPROVE UNDERGRADUATE WRITING

Jack Prostko

In the last four decades, we have witnessed the creation of diverse and far-reaching programs designed to improve the writing skills of undergraduates. During this period, writing centers, laboratories, peer tutorial programs, online writing labs, and writing-across-the-curriculum (WAC) programs have appeared, supplementing standard undergraduate offerings in composition and rhetoric. Much has been written on these programs, focusing on changes brought about by student-centered teaching methods and the skills needed for faculty to adopt new classroom strategies, in addition to suggestions for program administrators delivering faculty training in these strategies.

At the same time, faculty and TA development programs have also blossomed and become part of the academic institutional structure. As this volume illustrates, much has been written about the pedagogy of university-level teacher training, exploring its theoretical assumptions and providing specific suggestions for training, support, and evaluation.

Given these nearly simultaneous developments, one wonders what connections between these initiatives have been pursued to provide graduate TAs with systematic support in fulfilling one of the more common aspects of their teaching role: responding to and evaluating undergraduate writing. If we think of writing as only pertaining to composition courses, then the answer is simple, since for years TAs have received extensive training in how to organize and teach writing classes. Indeed, the term

"TA" seems a misnomer when referring to these graduate students, who more properly should be called "instructors," because they are often fully responsible for their own classes. Composition instruction, like language instruction, has a rich pedagogical history—with journals and organizations focusing solely on the best methods of improving students' writing. Graduate students teaching in composition programs are, as a matter of course, introduced to this field of study. (For examples of graduate training programs in composition, see Lambert & Tice, 1993.)

But the majority of TAs teaching in disciplines that require students to write receive almost no formal preparation outside of occasional workshops. If TAs are being introduced to the subject of evaluating writing, the connections that ought to exist between writing center administrators and TA trainers seem to be haphazard and remain largely unexamined in the literature of TA training. There is little to indicate that TAs across the board are receiving substantial training in the evaluation of writing, and little to suggest that writing programs are systematically preparing TAs to respond to students' written work even in writing-across-the-curriculum programs.

Given this situation, it seems appropriate to suggest some goals and strategies for teaching assistant training efforts. After reviewing basic issues in graduate education and the teaching of writing, I will suggest methods for improving training either at the departmental or university-wide level.

GRADUATE STUDENTS AS WRITERS

Most graduate students have had some assistance improving their writing during their undergraduate years. Yet it is clear that many graduate students, entering into a new professional stage of their education, are uneasy about their own writing skills. In the National Study of Teaching Assistants conducted by Syracuse University in 1987, 54% of TAs responding said they wanted more preparation in developing their own writing skills (Diamond & Gray, 1987). Moving from being a competent undergraduate writer to a professional writer within a discipline (with a distinct culture and set of expectations) is difficult for most graduate students. Ph.D. candidates are well aware that a dissertation waits at the end of their classwork and apprenticeship, and that writing for publication is essential for professional success. Yet few schools or departments provide specific advanced training in writing at this stage of a student's career. It is assumed that the graduate faculty will individually attend to graduate students' writing concerns and mentor them through this phase of their professional development—or that without such attention graduate students will learn to adapt to professional standards by whatever means possible. As those in writing centers working with graduate students in the midst of dissertations know, this isn't the most pragmatic or far-sighted approach to helping graduate students with their writing.

Since most graduate students feel some discomfort with their own writing, any attempt to provide TAs with skills to improve undergraduate writing should acknowledge this fact. Training must address graduate students as writers and recognize their needs, which will at the same time provide an understanding of the basic issues confronting undergraduate writers. It is not difficult to instruct graduate student teachers in writing at the same time they are being given the theoretical and practical background to meet the needs of their students, for writers at all levels of sophistication confront many of the same issues. Indeed, having instructors look at how the refinement of writing skills circles back repeatedly to certain fundamental issues allows them to assist students at many levels, and lets them see how their own writing concerns are mirrored in the written work they evaluate. Feedback from faculty workshops designed to help faculty teach WAC courses, for example, indicates that workshop faculty participants themselves "gain confidence in their writing which extends to their professional work," an "unexpected benefit" which would indeed be a welcome outcome for many TAs (Young & Fulwiler, 1986, p. 244).

THE FOCUS OF WRITING INSTRUCTION

While research in the pedagogy of writing instruction over the last several decades is complex and far from producing universal assent on basic principles, two generally accepted notions provide sufficient basis for organizing assistance to both undergraduate and graduate writers—and for providing TAs with a focus for their own work with undergraduate writing. Writers can improve if 1) writing is considered a process of learning, not a mechanical skill; and 2) major problem areas (e.g., invention, organization, style, clarity) receive attention rather than basic issues of "correctness."

Undoubtedly, the greatest shift to take place over the last few decades in the general approach to teaching composition is the focus on writing as a process rather than simply on the product of composition—that is, that "rhetoric is being reconceptualized as an activity" (Young, 1987, p. 1). Within an academic culture increasingly emphasizing student learning as the measure of good teaching, researchers in composition have argued that writing is not the final presentation of information learned, but an essential part of the learning process itself. Janet Emig's influential 1977 essay, *Writing as a Mode of Learning,* focused attention on how "writing uniquely corresponds to certain powerful learning strategies" (p. 69), and highlighted a sea change in composition studies. (For an early brief summary of this development, see Fulwiler, 1982.) This now dominant paradigm laid the groundwork for the Writing-Across-the-Curriculum movement and is increasingly the focus of disciplinary studies in writing instruction (Connolly & Vilardi, 1989; Sorcinelli & Elbow, 1997). Graduate students, having had undergraduate instruction based on this paradigm, may yet need to have the pedagogical assumptions supporting the "writing to learn" approach made explicit, as well as be reminded of the principles of student-centered approaches to education. Indeed, it would serve faculty and administrators well to regard such matters as eminently applicable to graduate education, as Haworth and Conrad (1996) have recently done in a discussion of assessing graduate program quality on the basis of student learning.

Working under the assumption that writing exercises are an integral part of the learning process itself, instructors have redesigned writing courses in several respects. Instead of focusing on one or two major papers during a course, writing takes a greater role in the weekly course structure, so that the kinds of writing required of students include "workaday" or informal writing, free writing, and journals (Tchudi, 1986, p. 18). In short, assignments are designed to offer students a chance to think through ideas. More informal assignments also encourage an exchange of ideas, so that more constant and wide-ranging feedback for the writer is emphasized, including peer response and self-reflection on the process of organizing and composing essays.

Outside of composition classes themselves, this holistic and developmental approach to writing has been most fully realized in writing-intensive courses generally gathered under the rubric of Writing Across the

Curriculum. From the outset of the WAC movement, training has been offered to instructors whose primary task had been disciplinary teaching, not the teaching of writing. Aspects of the training process for these instructors offer some help in developing a training model for graduate TAs, but are not entirely satisfactory in addressing the specific needs of instructors who are neither designing courses nor deciding how writing will be integrated into general course goals. Some work resulting directly from the WAC endeavor, however, focuses less on university-wide organizing structures for WAC programs and more on "what individual instructors do with writing in their own classes," (Tchudi, 1986, p. 7) and is therefore quite helpful.

Besides focusing on writing as a process, instruction in writing needs to concentrate on holistic issues of organization and style, rather than on "correctness." A common complaint among TAs asked to grade student writing is that they are not experts in grammar, and therefore have nothing to say about the writing itself, as if content is somehow divorced from its presentation in language. But new TAs are also generally relieved to hear that evaluating writing is not synonymous with correcting grammar and that the merely technical issues of grammar or spelling are a relatively minor concern in helping students improve their writing. It does not take an expert in grammar to understand when an essay is incoherent, illogical, or incomplete; and it requires little time to notice systematic technical errors and point students toward necessary resources for improvement. For most university students, difficulties in writing primarily center on the generation of compelling ideas, the organization of these ideas, the selection and use of sufficient evidence to justify arguments, the understanding of audience and use of an appropriate tone, and the use of vivid and clear language. Even discipline-specific forms of presentation, while they play a role in writing for graduate students and for the students they teach, are of secondary importance in the final production of readable writing. Graduate students will be aware of either basic or disciplinary aspects of writing, both for their own careers and in the classes they teach, but asking TAs to attend principally to them can result in what has been called "grammar across the curriculum" or "packaging information across the curriculum" rather than a genuine attention to the process of producing effective writing (Rideout, 1983, pp. 31-32).

Training Issues for TAs

In working with novice instructors, trainers are inevitably caught between handing out much sought teaching tips and explaining pedagogical theory which produces sound teaching. Negotiating these waters often means satisfying neither the audience longing for immediately applicable survival instructions nor the instructor focused on principles of effective practice. Survival tips, of course, only have lasting value within a framework of pedagogical goals. In working with student writing, TAs require an approach which concentrates on general principles applicable to aiding students to improve their performance of specific writing tasks, not simply a method of marking stacks of essays.

And like most of the training for new instructors, help in working with student writing should be delivered over time, as instructors prepare for and actually engage in working with students. This is the kind of ideal preparation offered by a mentored relationship, in which an experienced teacher monitors and guides novices through some of the basics and helps them put into practice strategies only first understood in the abstract. While unfortunately few TAs receive this kind of attention when it comes to the basics of teaching, it is fundamental to their training when working with student writing, where assignments, feedback, and evaluation happen over time as a complex series of steps.

Without a mentored practicum, there are still ways of adequately preparing graduate students to work with undergraduate writing, through intensive day-long workshops or, more fruitfully, through an integrated series of workshops over the course of a semester. Attempting to offer assistance in the evaluation of writing in one brief introductory workshop at best simply raises complex issues and provides simplistic tips to get TAs started. With the assistance of WAC or writing center instructors, if they are available, and existing WAC models for training, experienced TAs can be trained as workshop leaders and mentors, to provide the discipline-specific or course-specific context for general writing principles (Graham, 1984).

Because the individual's writing process is such a personal, unexamined, and shifting collection of practices and beliefs, the assumptions underlying the possibilities of improving writing require explanation and exemplification through attending to our own practice first. One approach often used in WAC training workshops is to start by examining participants' own writing attempts and difficulties; beginning this way has the advantage of uncovering assumptions that must be explicit from the outset if training is to be beneficial.

Either through a general discussion of graduate student writing or a brief writing and feedback session, instructors should discuss the following kinds of issues:

- How do we define "good" writing within our disciplines, and how have we come to this conclusion? TAs can look at their own writing processes and the training they have had as writers to consider what has helped them improve their writing.

- Though TAs are most frequently seeing only the final product of a student's writing process, they must be reminded that such writing is part of an undergraduate's academic career and therefore part of a skills and disciplinary learning process. In this way, diagnostic considerations should not be ignored, and students must be encouraged to improve through specific, thoughtful commentary.

- For writers to improve, clear explanations of the tasks assigned are necessary, and precise and guided feedback is essential.

- If it is the TAs' responsibility to evaluate student papers, the goal of improving students' writing skills must be integrated with the other essential pedagogical goals of the course and made explicit.

- Since evaluating writing takes place within a departmental and course context, specific standards must be discussed among instructors and TAs.

- There is a significant difference between helping students improve their writing and simply copyediting their papers. Helping TAs learn to teach writing skills and help undergraduates improve these skills requires a balancing act that TAs need to be conscious of: Not everything they might say about an essay is serving the student's needs, and laboring over the correction of papers may little serve the interests of the TA.

WORKSHOPS TO PREPARE TAS TO TEACH WRITING

After a discussion of assumptions about writing and the instructor's role in the teaching of writing, TAs can then turn to the practical tasks that confront them in their teaching. Any training program ought to include, at a minimum, a sequence of at least five discussions focusing on the following:

1) Explaining the role of writing in the context of learning specific course material

2) Making assignments and offering guidelines

3) Reading and marking assignments

4) Composing written feedback and assigning grades

5) Handling problem papers, including plagiarism

1) Explaining the Role of Writing in the Context of Learning Specific Course Material

Even though TAs have little say in the design of the courses in which they teach, they should examine the rationale for including writing in these courses and discuss ways writing can effectively promote learning in their field. While the larger philosophical issues involved here may be left until later in a TA's career, most instructors will benefit from examining courses in their disciplines which integrate content goals with writing goals, and also from understanding how writing promotes discipline-specific learning. Research on the context-specific aspect of writing improvement has grown enormously in recent years, and a discussion of the problems of introducing students to disciplinary practices should not be oversimplified, since TAs will benefit from this discussion both as graduate students engaged in writing and as instructors. As Anson (1988) points out, "If the situation were simply a matter of matching each discipline with a clear set of conventions and processes for writing, students would have far less difficulty growing as writers than they do now" (p. 22).

To make this larger philosophical discussion relevant to the teaching task at hand, the workshop should use course syllabi and actual writing assignments to examine the rationale for certain kinds of writing tasks—that is, how they promote the kind of learning sought in the course. Bloom's taxonomy, or other measures of pedagogical intent, help TAs understand how different assignments can achieve different learning goals, and examples like those suggested by Farris (1987) are extremely useful.

2) Making Assignments and Offering Guidelines

While TAs do not commonly have sole responsibility for creating assignments and determining how students properly fulfill them, they often have input in these areas and should confront the fact that poor assignments rarely generate excellent writing. Examples of good and poor assignments can be analyzed to distinguish effectively presented tasks from those that are confusing or invite misinterpretation.

A discussion of assignments should also cover how to properly explain the writing task to students. Workshop facilitators can cover how to give students guidance in approaching assignments and how to model phases (outlines and drafts) or aspects (thesis statements, argumentative structure, and evidence) of the process. Discussion should also cover areas such as: ways of explaining the discipline-specific demands of structure, tone, and citation; how to construct handouts for assignments that fully explain the requirements and goals; how to provide models that students can read to understand the conventions of the assignment; where to find resources students can turn to for information on good writing in general and within the discipline; how to explain the drafting process, and whether students can receive feedback on an initial draft from the TA; and whether peer review will be part of the assignment, or whether peer tutoring assistance is available (and allowed). And while TAs know that preparing students properly for writing assignments should include communicating grading criteria, a full discussion of grading issues is best reserved for a workshop discussion of its own.

3) Reading and Marking Assignments

Pencil in hand, inexperienced TAs faced with the task of grading exams or essays appreciate information about methods for making sense of these intimidating piles of paper. Sharing the working methods of experienced graders helps TAs get a sense of the advantages of various systematic approaches. How should goals for the assignment be identified and kept in mind? Should there be any marking on a first reading? Can a first reading give a general sense of the breakdown of grades which can then be checked by a second, more careful reading? Should marking and grading be blind? If several TAs are sharing grading responsibilities for a course, can there be a system to cross-check grading standards? Will effort primarily go into marginal comments, a summary of critical points at the end, or some reasonable combination of the two? How can comments be worded to encourage further reflection pointing toward revision, rather than to praise or criticize? Can a predetermined marking checklist be designed to assist the reader in easily explaining problems to the writer (and simplifying the marking of essays)? Davis (1993) summarizes two checklists which can provide a starting point for developing criteria for specific course assignments (pp. 223-224).

After covering these broad issues, TAs should be given the opportunity to mark actual essays from courses similar to those they will teach, in order to begin the discussion of how much marking is sufficient—and how much marking is too much. Writing instructors are aware that the overmarking of papers does not lead to better essays, and that "many teachers tax themselves unnecessarily with copious written commentary" (MacAllister, 1982, p. 61). Emphasizing holistic criteria that cover argument and organization, TAs can learn to suppress the urge to correct each minor mistake and instead determine how best to produce limited comments which help writers improve their writing. At this point too, TAs can get a better sense of how much time marking assignments should take and can discuss methods for evaluating legitimate course demands and identifying unrealistic expectations.

4) Composing Written Feedback and Assigning Grades

Written comments in the margins, and especially global end comments, most fully identify for the writer success in—and problems with—communicating ideas. Since, as Hodges (1997) has shown, "written feedback fails more often than not, largely for reasons that are avoidable" (p. 78), TAs need practice in relating marginal corrections to final summary statements, and isolating in hierarchical fashion the most crucial feedback. Issues that can be discussed include offering positive as well as corrective feedback, using descriptive rather than prescriptive comments, offering specific examples to illustrate general writing or course principles, framing questions that stimulate thinking, and suggesting methods of and resources for improving. TAs can also discuss the advantages of holding individual writing conferences to provide feedback and elicit immediate responses from students.

Since the corollary to marking essays is assigning a grade, students as well as TAs usually are concerned about criteria, fairness, and consistency in grading. Undergraduates often assume that writing can only be evaluated subjectively, and therefore explain their own success or failure on papers as due less to their writing skill than to the grader's eccentricities. Writing then becomes less a process of communicating ideas than simply an attempt to figure out how to please the teacher. Such guesswork, and the kind of writing it produces, can be minimized by clear assignments which include the criteria by which writing will be judged. Either generic holistic scales or assignment-specific descriptions can provide students with a clear sense of characteristics distinguishing high quality work from merely acceptable and unacceptable writing. If research is required, if citations must be included, if two or more texts or experiments must be compared, students can know in advance how such requirements affect the final paper grade. The significance of the thesis, the quality of support for an argument, and the applicability of examples can all be discussed in ways that reduce the notion that successfully meeting the criteria is a hit-or-miss proposition.

5) Handling Problem Papers, Including Plagiarism

Finally, the kinds of problems which may not be addressed fully in other sessions must be reviewed or discussed in a general workshop on problems to anticipate with written assignments. Some of the issues most frequently encountered by writing instructors include confronting papers with such fundamental writing problems that content cannot be addressed, and basic skills need to be taught; handling the essays of writers for whom English is a second language; grading essays which miss the mark in some essential way, by either being off the topic or not following the details of the assignment; setting policy about accepting, penalizing, or refusing late assignments; working with students with writer's block; recognizing or responding to plagiarism; and handling grade disputes.

PROVIDING RESOURCES

Helping TAs across disciplines work with student writing requires specific examples and help from their own fields. General texts on teaching composition will only occasionally provide examples of assignments and essays that are useful in training TAs. As a result of WAC programs and research, various fields are offering more materials for improving instruction in writing. Trainers can consult disciplinary associations to discover materials directly aimed at helping graduate students develop skill in teaching writing. In addition, Davis (1993) provides a brief bibliography of discipline-specific guides (pp. 208-209), which can be supplemented in the sciences by Bowen and Schneller (1991), McMillan (1988), and Pechenik (1993).

Many of the essays gathered in collections generated by the WAC program offer specific kinds of advice for making assignments and evaluating essays, though the focus on informal writing as an aspect of class design makes them less immediately useful to TAs. Essays in Griffin (1982), Sorcinelli and Elbow (1997), and Connolly and Vilardi (1989) are particularly helpful.

For a starting place for general information on basic aspects of writing, see the 12 bibliographic essays in Tate (1987). For information about writing programs, see Connolly and Vilardi (1986). And for a comprehensive bibliography on WAC programs, see Anson, Schweibert, and Williamson (1993).

REFERENCES

Anson, C. M. (1988). Toward a multidimensional model of writing in the academic disciplines. In D. A. Jolliffe (Ed.), *Advances in writing research, Vol. 2: Writing in academic disciplines.* Norwood, NJ: Ablex.

Anson, C. M., Schwiebert, J. E., & Williamson, M. M. (Eds.). (1993). *Writing across the curriculum: An annotated bibliography.* Westport, CT: Greenwood.

Bowen, E. C., & Schneller, B. E. (Eds.). (1991). *Writing about science* (2nd ed.). New York, NY: Oxford University Press.

Connolly, P., & Vilardi, T. (Eds.). (1986). *New methods in college writing programs: Theories in practice.* New York, NY: Modern Language Association.

Connolly, P., & Vilardi, T. (Eds.). (1989). *Writing to learn mathematics and science.* New York, NY: Teachers College Press.

Davis, B. G. (1993). *Tools for teaching.* San Francisco, CA: Jossey-Bass.

Diamond, R., & Gray, P. (1987). *National study of teaching assistants.* Syracuse, NY: Syracuse University, The Center for Instructional Development.

Emig, J. (1977). Writing as a mode of learning. *College Composition and Communications, 28,* 122-28.

Farris, C. (1987). Helping TAs respond to student writing. In N. V. N. Chism (Ed.), *Institutional responses and responsibilities in the employment and education of teaching assistants.* Columbus, OH: The Ohio State University, Center for Teaching Excellence.

Fulwiler, T. (1982). Writing: An act of cognition. In C. W. Griffin (Ed.), *Teaching writing in all disciplines.* New Directions for Teaching and Learning, No. 12. San Francisco, CA: Jossey-Bass.

Fulwiler, T. (1986). Reflections: How well does writing across the curriculum work? In A. Young & T. Fulwiler (Eds.), *Writing across the disciplines: Research into practice.* Upper Montclair, NJ: Boynton/ Cook.

Graham, J. (1984). What works: The problems and rewards of cross-curriculum writing programs. In B. L. Smith (Ed.), *Writing across the curriculum.* Current Issues in Higher Education, No. 3. Washington, DC: American Association for Higher Education.

Griffin, C. W. (1982). *Teaching writing in all disciplines.* New Directions for Teaching and Learning, No. 69. San Francisco, CA: Jossey-Bass.

Haworth, J. G., & Conrad, C. F. (1996). Refocusing quality assessment on student learning. In J. G. Haworth (Ed.), *Assessing graduate and professional education: Current realities, future prospects.* New Directions for Institutional Research, No. 92. San Francisco, CA: Jossey-Bass.

Hodges, E. (1997). Negotiating the margins: Some principles for responding to our students' writing, some strategies for helping students read our comments. In M. D. Sorcinelli & P. Elbow (Eds.), *Writing to learn: Strategies for assigning and responding to writing across the disciplines.* New Directions for Teaching and Learning, No. 69. San Francisco, CA: Jossey-Bass.

Lambert, L. M., & Tice, S. L. (1993). *Preparing graduate students to teach: A guide to programs that improve undergraduate education and develop tomorrow's faculty.* Washington, DC: American Association for Higher Education.

MacAllister, J. (1982). Responding to student writing. In C. W. Griffin (Ed.), *Teaching writing in all disciplines.* New Directions for Teaching and Learning, No. 12. San Francisco, CA: Jossey-Bass.

McMillan, V. E. (1988). *Writing papers in the biological sciences.* New York, NY: Bedford/St. Martin's.

Pechenik, J. A. (1993). *A short guide to writing about biology* (2nd ed.). New York, NY: HarperCollins.

Rideout, C. (1983). Applying the writing-across-the-curriculum model to professional writing. In B. L. Smith (Ed.), *Writing across the curriculum.* Current Issues in Higher Education, No. 3. Washington, DC: American Association for Higher Education.

Russell, D. R. (1991). *Writing in the academic disciplines, 1870-1990.* Carbondale, IL: Southern Illinois University Press.

Sorcinelli, M. D., & Elbow, P. (1997). *Writing to learn: Strategies for assigning and responding to writing across the curriculum.* New Directions for Teaching and Learning, No. 69. San Francisco, CA: Jossey-Bass.

Tate, G. (Ed.). (1987). *Teaching composition: 12 bibliographic essays.* Fort Worth, TX: Texas Christian University Press.

Tchudi, S. N. (1986). *Teaching writing in the content areas: College level.* Washington, DC: National Education Association.

Young, A., & Fulwiler, T. (1986). *Writing across the disciplines: Research into practice.* Upper Montclair, NJ: Boynton/Cook.

Young, R. (1987). Recent developments in rhetorical invention. In G. Tate (Ed.), *Teaching composition: 12 bibliographical essays.* Fort Worth, TX: Texas Christian University Press.

11

TECHNOLOGY AND TA TRAINING

Michael J. Albright

Instructional technology has had a presence in academe since faculty first used films and lantern slides nearly a hundred years ago. For most of this era, the story of audiovisual and media technologies has largely been one of unmet or unrealistic expectations, underfunding, rejection, and bitterness. The Carnegie Commission on Higher Education (1972) found faculty resistance second only to the lack of funding as the most severe obstacle to the adoption of new technologies. In his highly influential text on faculty development, Gaff (1975) described the "knee-jerk reaction of many faculty members who dismiss any idea that emanates from media centers" and observed that "disdain for technological 'aids' runs deep in faculty culture" (p. 73). Even as late as 1988, McNeil lamented that the vast majority of faculty members were either apathetic about or openly resistant to the use of computers and videotapes as instructional tools.

That picture is slowly changing. According to a 1995 national survey by the Corporation for Public Broadcasting, 43% of faculty at doctoral universities and 56% at comprehensive institutions used videotapes at least once an academic term, and 11% and 14%, respectively, used multimedia in the classroom (CPB, 1995). Sixty-six percent of all students and 75% of all faculty now have Internet access, and 25% of all college classes had electronic mail components in 1996 (Green, 1996). Green also found that nearly 30% of faculty now use presentation software to create handouts, transparencies, or computer-generated graphics. During the 1990s, numerous universities have reorganized their instructional support services to place stronger emphasis on newer technologies and have established senior positions to provide instructional technology leadership.

Many faculty now see technology as a means of solving instructional problems and providing learning opportunities for students that were inconceivable just a few years ago. For example:

- An English professor has converted her technical writing course to a web-based format with no face-to-face meetings. The course web site is designed as a floor plan, with a "library" for reading assignments, a "help room" for tutorial assistance, a "lounge" for online discussions, a "bulletin board" for course announcements, a "post office" for submission of assignments, and other features. Course evaluations have revealed high levels of student achievement and enthusiasm for the course offered in this format.

- A biology department digitized over 5,500 images from existing photographs, slides, and videotapes, supplemented them with additional graphics and animations, and mounted the collection on a department server. Faculty now create customized files for each class period, access them directly from the server during lectures, and download the files after class to a different server accessible to students for further study.

- A professor of hotel, restaurant, and institution management saw that many of the international (mostly Asian) students in her quantity food preparation class had trouble understanding Western food concepts. She developed a CD-ROM illustrating over 200 different foods and food preparation processes, including photographs and descriptions, phonetic pronunciations, short video clips, and cross-referenced recipes. Students view the CD-ROM in a learning lab prior to class.

- An agricultural economics professor accumulated a large collection of unpublished, copyright-cleared documents illustrating the development of agribusiness in countries adapting to market-driven economies. He created a web site containing digitized versions of these papers, maps of the target nations, digitized video clips, case studies, files providing background information, and links to the World Bank and other resources. The site is used by students for analysis, in-class and online discussions, and resource materials for class projects.

These are not isolated examples of cutting-edge technology use by innovators and early adopters. They are typical of the practical applications of technology that may be found on almost every university campus today. This is the environment that our new teaching assistants are entering, although "low tech" certainly is still in widespread use and can be powerful as well. An effective training program at the beginning of their careers will help TAs use technology in their teaching and recognize its potential for solving the instructional challenges they will face.

TECHNOLOGY'S FOUNDATIONS IN GOOD TEACHING

Resistance to change has been so prominent over the years that a body of literature has evolved describing "barriers" to technology use. Common barriers include lack of funding for technology and uneven access from one department or college to another, lack of time available to faculty to learn about technology and develop materials, inadequate campus support services, the rapid pace of technological change, and outright technophobia (Lewis & Wall, 1988). Perhaps even more important are institutional issues such as conservative structures that inhibit change, faculty commitment to traditional teaching methods, reward systems that discourage faculty from spending time on instructional improvement (McNeil, 1988), and the lack of recognition by administrators and faculty of the value of technology as an integral part of the curriculum and undergraduate experience (Green, 1991). As these examples suggest, some of these barriers are eroding, but at academe's typically glacial pace.

If teaching assistants (TAs) are to use today's teaching tools effectively in the classroom, some commitment to technology must be evident both in their departments and in the individual professors for whom they work. However, many faculty themselves still need to be convinced that technology is a sufficient improvement over current teaching methods to be worth their time and effort. If students are indeed mastering course material to a satisfactory degree and are able to generalize and apply this material to real-life situations, then nothing needs to be changed. However, if students are not learning to the maximum extent possible—probably the case with most college courses—then present teaching methods may need to be reviewed. Any decisions regarding technology should be made within the context of teaching strategies for the entire course, or at least the course segment being reconsidered. The key question is, "How can we help students learn this material to the degree we feel they should know it?" Technology may be part of the answer, and it may not.

Knapper (1982) emphasized that "no technical innovation, no matter how sophisticated, will succeed educationally if it is based upon faulty, or nonexistent, pedagogical foundations" (p. 82). Effective use of technology begins with a well-conceived, well-designed course. Teaching is the process of leading students through a sequence of learning experiences that enables them to reach course goals and objectives. Traditionally, these learning experiences have included listening and note-taking during lectures, textbook reading, term paper writing, large and small group discussions, and homework assignments. Collaborative learning activities have become popular in recent years, as have other methods such as case studies. Learning experiences could also include interaction with course content and other students via some form of instructional technology. It is no coincidence that these technologies are referred to as "media," because their purpose is to serve as the medium by which students experience and interact with the substance of a course.

That point cannot be overemphasized. Instructional technologies represent resources or teaching methods that facilitate learning within the broader context of a carefully structured educational environment (Albright & Graf, 1992). For example, if the faculty member or teaching assistant feels that discussion of course content outside of class would help further understanding, the group could meet together additional hours, but technology might provide a better alternative in an asynchronous setting such as a class Internet mailing list. Students studying oratory could read the text of Dr. Martin Luther King's "I Have a Dream" speech, but watching the film of the actual event and sensing the emotion with which it was delivered might be a much more effective learning experience. Business faculty or TAs could acquire and photocopy (if the department budget permits) a corporate annual report for students to study and discuss, or students could access the report directly on the company's web site and not only print it themselves but also learn more about the company and be able to put the report into context by studying other information on the site. In each of these examples, technology enhances the learning experience to a degree that might be difficult or impossible without technology.

CONVENTIONAL CLASSROOM TECHNOLOGIES

How does a TA determine when it is appropriate to use some form of technology? Instructional technology should be selected to perform specific functions within the context of a well-planned lesson. Conventional classroom technologies such as videotape, slides, and overhead transparencies have for the most part been incorporated into lectures and used on a large group basis with students to provide a common learning experience for all. Even when students view these media in libraries and learning labs, the functions are essentially the same. The following list certainly is not all-inclusive.

- Provide an organizational structure and facilitate notetaking. Overhead transparencies have long served to help students put lecture notes into an organizational framework and identify key lecture points.

- Provide visualization of course material. This is probably the most common of all functions of media technologies. If first-hand observation is not possible or practical, media can provide visual representation, demonstrate processes and procedures, and illustrate concepts far more effectively than a lecture, textbook readings, and chalkboard sketches by themselves. Numerous studies have shown that visualization of course content facilitates learning.

- Take students where they otherwise could not go. From documentaries and simulated field trips to live video showing microscopic images on the large screen, videotapes and other media can provide learning experiences that are impractical or impossible for students to have in person.

- Provide historical documentation. Media technologies can provide a record of events and resources that may not otherwise be available to future classes.

- Provide stimulus for class activities. Videotapes and other media can serve as the stimulus for class discussions, practice activities, and test items.

Until the lecture becomes obsolete, these functions will remain quite valid, and conventional classroom technologies will continue to play an essential role in university teaching. Realistically speaking, the lecture will not disappear from academic culture anytime soon.

Emerging Technologies

With new media, however, have come exciting new opportunities for providing learning experiences to students. Emerging technologies, such as multimedia and the Internet, allow faculty and TAs to involve students intellectually with course material in more personal and productive ways. These technologies can be used in the face-to-face classroom in various forms but are more likely to be found in independent learning and small group settings.

Their appearance has coincided with and greatly facilitated the transition from a teacher-centered instructional paradigm to a learner-centered paradigm. Oblinger (1994) sees the following transformations taking place:

- From lecturing to coaching
- From taking attendance to logging on
- From distribution requirements to connected learning
- From credit hours to performance standards
- From competing to collaborating
- From multiple choice to portfolio assessment
- From library collections to network connections
- From passive learning to active learning
- From textbooks to customized materials

Barr and Tagg (1995) drew similar conclusions. As Table 11.1 indicates, the focus in the learning paradigm shifts from the delivery of instruction and courses, passive learning, and competition to the creation of learning environments, active learning, and cooperation. Learning comes under the control of the student, the time at which learning takes place becomes variable, and a "live" teacher may no longer be required. The newer, more individualized, interactive technologies seem particularly well suited for use in a learner-centered instructional paradigm and permit faculty to make more substantive changes in the structure of a course (Gilbert, 1994).

Table 11.1
Comparing Educational Paradigms

INSTRUCTION PARADIGM	LEARNING PARADIGM
Mission and Purposes	
Provide/deliver instruction	Produce learning
Transfer knowledge from faculty to students	Elicit student discovery and construction of knowledge
Offer courses and programs	Create powerful learning environments
Improve the quality of instruction	Improve the quality of learning
Criteria for Success	
Curriculum development, expansion	Learning technologies development, expansion
Quantity and quality of resources	Quantity and quality of outcomes
Teaching/Learning Structures	
Time held constant, learning varies	Learning held constant, time varies
50-minute lecture, three-unit course	Learning environments
One teacher, one classroom	Whatever learning experience works
Covering material	Specified learning results
Degree equals accumulated credit hours	Degree equals demonstrated knowledge and skills
Learning Theory	
Learning is teacher-centered and controlled	Learning is student-centered and controlled
"Live" teacher, "live" students required	"Active" learner required, but not "live" teacher
Classroom and learning are competitive and individualistic	Learning environments are cooperative, collaborative, and supportive
Nature of Roles	
Faculty are primarily lecturers	Faculty are primarily designers of learning methods and environments
Faculty and students act independently and in isolation	Faculty and students work in teams with each other and other staff

Adapted from Barr & Tagg, 1995.

The Internet

Electronic mail allows students to discuss assignments or course material outside of class. For example, a professor at a midwestern university maintains an Internet mailing list for his meteorology course. Recently, a student posted a question to the list that the professor could not answer, so he forwarded the message to a colleague at another university. Within six hours after the student posted the query, she had a response sent to the entire class by the world's leading authority on that particular topic. This is a powerful use of a relatively simple technology, widely available on most campuses.

The online newsletter, *Internet Index,* calculated in 1995 that if growth rates at the time were continued, everyone on earth would have access to the Internet by the year 2004 (Treese, 1995). The prediction was tongue-in-cheek because obviously 1995 growth rates could not be sustained, but the Internet is rapidly becoming ubiquitous in academic, business, and governmental settings all over the planet. The "net" allows a class to expand its discussions to virtually unlimited dimensions, with participants involving leading experts in the field joining in from anywhere in the world. Electronic mail and groupware, mailing lists, and newsgroups can easily be set up to provide threaded discussions among class members as a whole or within smaller groups working on collaborative projects, promoting further intellectual involvement with the course material.

With more than two million servers and over 100 million pages of information, the WWW has opened a whole new dimension of learning opportunities. Without question, the web presents filtering and critical thinking challenges to students, but quality sites out there in virtually every subject area, coupled with the extraordinary opportunities the web provides for student interaction with course content and each other, offer serious implications for curricular content and the basic structure of course activities. By 1996, about 9% of all college classes were using some form of web-based resources to support instruction (Green, 1996), and that figure is growing rapidly.

At least a dozen different organizations now market web-course software packages that provide course development, content presentation (including web access), individual and group communication, testing and assignment submission, and course management tools, all with convenient user interfaces (Albright, 1997). These systems can be used both for virtual courses as well as supplements to conventional face-to-face courses.

How can faculty members, TAs, and students conveniently obtain current information related to the subject matter of a course or discipline? The answer is "push" technology. Web users must seek out information, employing search tools that often turn up more chaff than wheat. With push technology software such as *PointCast*, service providers do the searching. They scan numerous news (e.g., *New York Times*, *Reuters*) and industry sources and "push" relevant information to the user's client software via the Internet. Users specify the industries and content areas to be scanned and determine the download times. Both the client software and the services are free, paid for by advertisers. Class discussions and student projects can focus on industry trends and significant current events, and can be based on the very latest information available, literally up-to-the-minute.

Multimedia

Multimedia products such as CD-ROMs provide interactive learning opportunities that can be customized to a student's unique learning needs. Kozma and Johnston (1991) examined over 700 multimedia software packages submitted to the EDUCOM/NCRIPTAL Higher Education Software Awards competition and identified seven different ways in which multimedia technologies are changing the ways in which students learn:

- From reception to engagement. Students are moving from being passive receptors of information to active participants in the construction of knowledge.

- From the classroom to the real world. Kozma and Johnston cited a videodisk simulation in which law students learn how to manage a case, from client interviews to courtroom defense.

- From text to multiple representation. Through technology, students are learning to express, understand, and use ideas in a variety of symbol systems.

- From coverage to mastery. This trend builds upon one of the historic functions of technology by providing drill and practice activities.

- From isolation to interconnection. According to Kozma and Johnston, technology allows us to shift our perception of learning as an individual act done in isolation toward learning as a collaborative activity.

- From products to processes. Technology provides students with new insights into the processes that create knowledge because they are able to use the same tools as scholars, and in the same ways.

- From mechanics to understanding in the laboratory. Kozma and Johnston point out that the scientific lab is one of the most expensive instructional areas of the university. New technologies provide highly effective simulations of lab experiments at a greatly reduced cost.

Distance Education

Technology has enabled universities to reach out to new student populations, extending the campus to worldwide dimensions. Distance education is now the fastest growing component of academe, and many TAs are now assigned to assist with the development and delivery of such courses. By the 1996–97 academic year, more than half of all four-year institutions in the United States provided off-campus courses to over a million students, and explosive enrollment increases were anticipated (Gubernick & Ebeling, 1997). Today's interactive video and Internet-based delivery systems have vastly improved instructional capabilities over the educational television systems of past years. An added benefit is that the same technologies that deliver courses to remote students can also be used to bring a wealth of off-campus resources to students in our conventional classes.

Other Applications

Even something as mundane as word processing lets faculty and TAs rethink the ways in which they use student written assignments as learning tools. Ehrmann (1995) described how word processing permits the assignment of projects developed in stages, with multiple drafts at each stage. Such an activity was unthinkable when student papers had to be typed. Assignments like these promote active learning through complex projects, rethinking of assumptions and positions, and collaboration with other students in the development of a finished product (Ehrmann, 1995).

FAMILIARIZING TAS WITH CAMPUS TECHNOLOGY RESOURCES

With all these options available to teaching assistants, how can faculty help their TAs use technology effectively in their teaching? TA training workshops should include an orientation to campus technology resources, as well as a general overview of the roles technology can play in the context of university teaching. Experienced instructional technologists should be available from the faculty development center or other campus units to serve as session facilitators.

The resources available will vary greatly both from one campus to another and within the institution from one college or department to another, and can only be addressed in general terms here. A comprehensive guide describing facilities, resource personnel, processes, and policies can be quite helpful to TAs. A template can be prepared listing campus-wide resources, for sharing by all departments that employ teaching assistants. Individual campus units can then customize the guide to include resources of particular interest or available only to their own TAs.

What information should be included in a TA training session or resource handbook? The following list provides some ideas but certainly is not all-inclusive. Some of these suggestions may not be applicable or desired. Technology training should follow workshop sessions on general teaching methods, so that participating TAs will better understand the context for technology use.

Departmental Teaching Support

- Teaching methods and technology applications found to be successful in the department

- Suggestions for successful applications of technology in the department's curriculum

- Useful media resources and other forms of instructional technology existing in the department, for example, transparency-making and classroom media equipment

- Access to computers, software, and upgrades within the department

- Identity of department computer and/or telecommunications coordinator(s) and other sources of information and assistance

Classrooms and Labs

- Identification of classrooms typically used by the department for its teaching and permanently installed technology maintained in these rooms

- Sources of technology needed but not maintained in the classrooms

- Sources of assistance in learning to use that equipment

- Availability of live connections to the campus network and Internet, information on how access to an active data jack can be obtained if needed

- Identification of persons to contact about classroom environmental problems that have a detrimental effect on learning

Computing Resources

- Availability of computer and/or learning lab facilities for TA and student use

- Information about general campus computing services available to faculty, TAs, and students

- Information about obtaining an ID and account to use the campus network and Internet

- Procedures for accessing the Internet via the campus network

- Availability of software to enable TAs and students to access the Internet from off-campus locations

- Availability of software that is site-licensed for your campus

- Availability of online statistics packages used by the department

- Procedures for setting up a course Internet mailing list or newsgroup

- Procedures for setting up a course web page, and availability of support services

Library Resources

- Availability of library resources, both online and within the library itself

- Availability of assistance in using library resources effectively, both for TAs and their students

- Information about library policies and procedures for electronic reserves

Media/Audiovisual Services

- Identification of campus units providing centralized media services or audiovisual support

- Availability of consultation services to help TAs use technology effectively in their teaching

- Location of centralized collection of videotapes and other media resources

- Location of centralized collection of media equipment available for TA and/or student use

- Availability of production services to help TAs create learning materials

- Identification of office to contact if classroom media equipment is faulty

Miscellaneous Technology-Related Topics

- Availability of technology-related services from other campus offices

- Availability of training programs offered on a campus-wide basis that help TAs use technology effectively in their teaching

- Information about campus copyright policies and identification of source of authoritative advice regarding copyright

Using Technology in Training

The same technologies employed in the education of undergraduates can also be used in TA training. Video is perhaps the most common tool. Many excellent tapes have been produced that provide both orientation—particularly for international TAs (ITAs)—and examples of effective teaching. The videotaping of microteaching sessions for evaluation purposes is another common training technique. Campus networks and the Internet have also become widespread TA training tools, as illustrated by the following examples:

- The University of Wisconsin-Madison maintains mailing lists for communication, coordination, and training of TAs serving two introductory courses in communicative arts.

- The University of Georgia has created a web site to supplement a face-to-face training program for TAs, including study materials, case studies, and links to other web sites relevant to course topics.

- The University of Texas at Austin produced a videotape explaining an assessment test required of all international teaching assistants, then digitized the tape and placed it on the web for viewing by ITAs before they leave their home countries.

- The University of South Florida has a unique activity in which ITAs and undergraduate student consultants engage in an anonymous, live chat session using Daedalus software in a single computer lab. The participants discuss the ideal academic relationship between students and instructor while online, then move to a large conference table in the center of the room to talk about the chat experience in a face-to-face setting.

SUMMARY AND CONCLUSIONS

As teaching assistants develop their courses, many for the first time, they need to think through the learning tasks conceived for their students and consider carefully the match between these tasks and the teaching strategies available. It is difficult to suggest the formulation of course goals and learning objectives because these are unpopular notions in many corners, but having the target student behaviors clearly identified can be a tremendous help to TAs in planning the learning experiences designed to get students there.

If those lesson plans include some form of technology, TAs should recognize that on most campuses an infrastructure is in place to support them, from faculty/instructional development units to academic computing, media centers, and the campus library. Professionals should be in place to provide both pedagogical and technical assistance. TAs should not hesitate to ask for help.

This chapter would be remiss without some mention of the rapid pace of technological change, since it was identified as a barrier. For some faculty, the evolution of technology serves as a deterrent. To be sure, each new equipment item, software application, and version presents its own unique challenges. For the most part, though, one technology evolves from another. Learning one tool provides the foundation for learning the next. Faculty and TAs should not be intimidated. Perhaps the most difficult step is the first.

INTERNET RESOURCES ABOUT TEACHING WITH TECHNOLOGY

Many excellent resources are available on the Internet to help teaching assistants learn more about teaching effectively with technology. The following are suggested starting points, according to a TA's personal needs.

World Wide Web Sites

- Institute for Academic Technology
  http://www.iat.unc.edu
  Facilitates widespread use of technology in higher eduction. Site contains numerous academic and technical papers, newsletters, online forums, and other resources to help faculty use technology effectively in their teaching.

- SyllabusWeb
  http://www.syllabus.com/
  Maintained by the publishers of *Syllabus* magazine. Contains articles, case studies, news, and resources related to technologies used to enhance education. Aimed at faculty and administrators.

- The Faculty Connection
  http://faculty.creativeanalytics.org
  Articles and links maintained by Creative Analytics, Inc., an Indiana company specializing in helping faculty and other clients learn about and use technology. Has novice, intermediate, and expert tracks.

- Computers in Teaching and Learning
  http://www.staffs.ac.uk/cital/welcomenf.html
  Links maintained at Staffordshire University covering a wide range of topics related to computers and learning.

- Teaching with Electronic Technology
  http://www.wam.umd.edu/~mlhall/teaching.html
  Maintained by Michael Hall at the University of Maryland. Provides extensive list of links to web-based courses, papers, resources, and projects related to teaching with technology.

- ERIC Clearinghouse on Information and Technology
    http://ericir.syr.edu/ithome/
  Provides searchable index of over 850,000 documents and journal articles published since 1966 and related to instructional technology. Includes full text of monographs and digests, archives of instructional technology-related mailing lists, and other resources.

- Technology Tools for Today's Campuses
    http://horizon.unc.edu/projects/monograph/CD
  Collection of 72 case studies describing innovative faculty projects using technology in teaching, grouped in seven different categories by discipline and technology type.

Internet Mailing Lists

- AAHESGIT (listproc@list.cren.net)
  Sponsored by the American Association for Higher Education (AAHE), discusses various roles played by technology in facilitating educational change. Closely tied to the AAHE Teaching, Learning, & Technology (TLT) Group.

- INFOBITS (listserv@unc.edu)
  Monthly newsletter for the Institute for Academic Technology describing sources of information about teaching with technology.

REFERENCES

Albright, M. J. (1997). Web course authoring and management systems. *MC Journal: Journal of Academic Media Librarianship* [online], *5* (1), 14-23. Available: http://wings.buffalo.edu/publications/mcjrnl/v5n1/inter.html [1997, July 24].

Albright, M. J., & Graf, D. L. (1992). Instructional technology and the faculty member. In M. J. Albright & D. L. Graf (Eds.), *Teaching in the information age: The role of educational technology.* New Directions for Teaching and Learning, No. 51. San Francisco, CA: Jossey-Bass.

Barr, R. B., & Tagg, J. (1995). From teaching to learning: A new paradigm for undergraduate education. *Change, 27* (6), 13-25.

Carnegie Commission on Higher Education. (1972). *The fourth revolution: Instructional technology in higher education.* New York, NY: McGraw-Hill.

Corporation for Public Broadcasting. (1995). *Study of communications technology in higher education.* Washington, DC: Corporation for Public Broadcasting.

Ehrmann, S. G. (1995). Asking the right question: What does research tell us about technology and higher learning? [online] *Change, 27* (2), 20-27. Available: http://www.aahe.org/technology/TLTR-ch.2.htm [1997, January 14].

Gaff, J. G. (1975). *Toward faculty renewal: Advances in faculty, instructional, and organizational development.* San Francisco, CA: Jossey-Bass.

Gilbert, S. W. (1994). If it takes 40 or 50 years, can we still call it a revolution? *Educational Record, 75* (3), 19-28.

Green, K. C. (1991). A technology agenda for the 1990s. *Change, 23* (1), 6-7.

Green, K. C. (1996). *The national survey of information technology in higher education* [online]. Available: http://ericir.syr.edu/Projects/Campus_computing/1996/index.html [1997, July 25].

Gubernick, L., & Ebeling, A. (1997, June). I got my degree through e-mail [online]. *Forbes.* Available: http://www.forbes.com/forbes/97/0616/5912084a.htm [1997, July 13].

Knapper, C. K. (1982). Technology and teaching: Future prospects. In C. K. Knapper (Ed.), *Expanding learning through new communications technologies.* New Directions for Teaching and Learning, No. 9. San Francisco, CA: Jossey-Bass.

Kozma, R. B., & Johnston, J. (1991). The technological revolution comes to the classroom. *Change, 23* (1), 10-23.

Lewis, R. J., & Wall, M. (1988). *Exploring obstacles to uses of technology in higher education.* Washington, DC: The Academy for Educational Development, Inc. (ERIC Document Reproduction Service ED 304 073).

McNeil, D. R. (1988, September). *Status of technology in higher education: A reassessment.* Paper presented at the Second Annual Conference on Interactive Technology and Telecommunications, Augusta, ME. (ERIC Document Reproduction Service ED 307 860).

Oblinger, D. G. (1994). *Transforming the academy to improve delivery of services: Redesign for reallocation* [online]. Available: http://www.hied.ibm.com/news/whitep/technote/hied/oblinger.txt [1997, January 15].

Treese, W. (1995). *Internet Index,* No. 9 [online]. Available: http://www.openmarket.com/intindex/95-09.htm [1997, July 28].

12

Evaluating TAs' Teaching

Beverly Black and Matt Kaplan

The purpose of evaluating a TA's teaching is twofold: 1) to provide information that can be used for improvement and development purposes (generally called formative evaluation); and 2) to make personnel decisions (called summative evaluation). To convey our notion of the nature of formative evaluation, we would like to borrow a description from Braskamp and Ory's (1994) definition of assessment, based on its Latin root *assidere*, "to sit beside." When we use the term *formative evaluation* in this chapter, we intend it as a process of sitting together.

> "To sit beside" brings to mind such verbs as to engage, to involve, to interact, to share, to trust. It conjures up team learning, working together, discussing, reflecting, helping, building, collaborating. It makes one think of cooperative learning, community, communication, coaching, caring, and consultation . . . "Sitting beside" implies dialogue and discourse, with one person trying to understand the other's perspective before giving value judgments (p. 13).

In this chapter, we use this definition of formative evaluation to refer to the process used to help TAs develop their skills and understanding of teaching and learning. *Summative evaluation* refers to the process of making a value judgment for administrative purposes. In practice, the two are rarely clearly separate activities. However, only by understanding the differences can we make them work together to ensure that TAs receive the feedback and assistance they need and that departments are confident of the quality of teaching done by TAs.

EVALUATION FOR IMPROVEMENT PURPOSES

Departments can help TAs become effective teachers by fostering a collaborative, trusting atmosphere in which colleagues "sit beside" new TAs as they take their first steps in learning to teach. This process includes helping TAs determine whether their teaching is effective for the students in their class and providing a variety of resources to help TAs develop the skills they need.

In this section we look at the kind of information that informs a TA's efforts to improve teaching. In obtaining this information, it is essential that TAs work with a consultant, at least in the early stages of their development. McKeachie (1987) has identified three advantages that a consultant can provide to an instructor:

> First, he or she can help identify particularly important information provided in the data, separating critical information from superficial information. Second, the consultant can provide hope and encouragement. All too often feedback fails because it discourages the individual and increases his or her sense of anxiety and hopelessness. And, third, a consultant can provide suggestions about what to do about the data, for example, suggestions about alternative methods of teaching that may be more productive than those used in the past (McKeachie, 1987).

The consultant can be a faculty member, an experienced upper-level graduate student, a peer, or a teaching center staff member. Each of these individuals brings a different emphasis to the feedback process. When departmental faculty and colleagues act as consultants, there is evidence that some give a narrow view of what improvement is needed, based on their own approach (Stodolsky, 1990; Weimer, Kerns, & Parrett, 1988; Millis, 1992) and that feedback is less likely to be effective if there is a power differential between the recipient and the departmental observer (Brinko, 1993). In contrast, teaching center specialists are more likely to have extensive knowledge and experience in a wide range of teaching strategies and more likely to be trained in observation techniques (Millis,

1992). However, faculty and TAs in the department bring a knowledge of the discipline and can give feedback on ways to effectively teach a particular concept, giving suggestions on activities or methods that have worked for them. They can be even more effective if they have been trained in giving nondirective, supportive feedback and have experience in using a variety of teaching methods in their own classrooms.

Regardless of who plays the role of the consultant, the process for evaluating a TA's teaching should include a planning meeting with the TA, the gathering of data or information, an analysis of the data by the consultant, and another meeting with the TA to discuss the data and any changes that should be made in response to the feedback. Each of these steps will be discussed next.

Planning Meeting

The consultant meets with the TA prior to the feedback process to discuss the process and gain a knowledge of the class. A planning meeting will give the TA a measure of control and a feeling of collaboration while helping her or him to become reflective about and aware of important elements of good teaching. The consultant will also benefit from such a meeting. She will be more aware of the TA's needs if she has a context within which to view the class or analyze the data presented by the students. In this meeting, the consultant and the TA set the ground rules for the goals of the feedback process and for the means being used to gather data. In a planning meeting the consultant can:

- Establish a relationship of trust and credibility.

- Have the TA talk about the class. What are the goals for the class? Who are the students? If it is a discussion or lab section, how does it relate to other parts of the course?

- Get the instructor thinking and talking about his or her teaching. What are the TA's perceived strengths? Perceived weaknesses? Is there something in particular the TA would like feedback on? What kind of feedback would he or she like?

- If it hasn't been decided before, mutually agree on the method or methods that will be used to gather information.

- Have the TA discuss the class session that will be observed (if observation is to be part of the process). What will be taught? What are the goals for the class? What are the students expected to learn in the class? (Sometimes TAs may not have thought about having goals for a particular class nor thought of what they want students to learn. This is a good opportunity to help them think along these lines.)

• Set a time and place for the collection of information.

Gathering Data or Information

In order to make decisions about their teaching, TAs need accurate information about what is going on in their classes. Their own impressions are, of course, one source of valuable data; however, it is difficult for instructors to be objective and systematic about a class while they are immersed in the process of teaching, especially when they are first learning to teach. In this section, we briefly describe methods for collecting meaningful data to help TAs think systematically about their teaching and student learning.

Observation. To make a classroom visit useful for the TA, it is important to record objective information that is descriptive rather than evaluative, specific rather than general, and focused on behavior rather than the person. To follow are a few methods that a consultant might use (individually or in combination) to collect objective data.

• Keep a written record. Get to the class early and take notes on the environment, interactions, and reactions: how the students come into the room, how they interact with each other and the instructor, how the instructor starts the class, the types of questions he or she asks, etc. Pay close attention to the students, and record their behavior throughout the class. Try to keep opinions out of the recorded data and be as specific as possible.

• Draw a map of the room and the students and record interactions. Drawing a map that gives a visual image of classroom dynamics is fairly easy and can provide a wealth of information. Since instructors are often preoccupied with the details of teaching, they might not notice patterns in how they interact with students. For example, a TA may pay more attention to one side of the room or call on a larger proportion of men than women. TAs tend to be quite enthusiastic about seeing a diagram of their classroom, and they will often discuss at length a map and the individual students represented there. Figure 12.1 has an actual classroom diagram that was used to give feedback to the instructor. You might use it as a guide in developing your own

FIGURE 12.1
Sample Class Map, Discussion Section

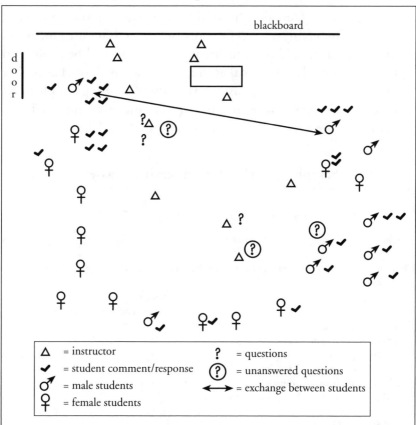

△	= instructor	?	= questions
✔	= student comment/response	⑦	= unanswered questions
♂	= male students	⟷	= exchange between students
♀	= female students		

This map shows about 35 minutes of an anthropology discussion section, excluding a small group activity. The TA focused first on the three unanswered questions, indicating that she had felt uncomfortable when no one responded and had rephrased the questions immediately. She was adamant about not answering the questions herself, and we discussed waiting periods and levels of questioning. She discovered from the map that students separated themselves by gender, and initiated discussion of how she might structure the small groups differently in future classes to avoid this. She was also concerned that most of the answers came from one side of the room (with the exception of two talkative students), and we discussed eye contact, use of classroom space, and strategies for getting quieter students to participate and more vocal ones to listen.

From *Handbook on Departmental GSI Development,* Center for Research on Learning and Teaching, University of Michigan, 1997.

symbols and information that will be meaningful to the TAs you work with.

- Use a checklist. Develop a list of behaviors that one would expect to see when observing an excellent instructor, and use it to focus the observation. In addition, make note of exceptional behavior and concrete examples of areas that might be examined for change. If a checklist is to be used, go over it with the TA during the planning meeting and make sure that his or her concerns and needs are addressed. See Figure 12.2 for an example of a checklist.

FIGURE 12.2
Sample Checklist for Observing Classes

Instructor _____ Course_____ Section_____

Observer_____ Date of Visit_____ Class Size_____

Characterize the TA's performance on each of the following items using the three-point scale provided.

	Needs Improvement	*Satisfactory*	*Well Done*
I Lesson Planning			
1. Evidence of lesson plans	1	2	3
2. Warm-up used	1	2	3
3. Overview given to each activity	1	2	3
4. Transitions between activities	1	2	3
5. Mixture of new and familiar material	1	2	3
II Techniques Used			
6. Amount of teacher talk to student talk	1	2	3
7. Small group activities included	1	2	3
8. Uses target language throughout period	1	2	3
9. Personalizes the material	1	2	3
10. Correcting: cues for student self-correction	1	2	3
III Classroom Climate			
11. Established a warm, supportive atmosphere	1	2	3
12. Sensitive to the needs of individual students	1	2	3
13. Students prepared for class	1	2	3
14. All students active during the class period	1	2	3
15. Set limits in a non-threatening, non-rejecting way	1	2	3

Adapted from the University of Michigan Department of Romance Languages TA development materials. Used with permission.

Videotapes for data collection. TAs who watch a videotape of their classes gain a fresh perspective on how they come across to their students and how students respond to their instruction. In the process of examining what worked and what did not, TAs can recognize their strengths as teachers and begin to identify areas in which they could be more effective.

To make the tape as useful as possible for feedback, both the camera person and the instructor need guidelines about the process. General guidelines for videotaping a class might include the following:

- Have the TA tell the students ahead of time that the class will be videotaped so that the TA can get feedback on his or her teaching.

- Have the camera person arrive early in order to videotape students as they come into the room. Watching how students interact with each other and the instructor before class begins can provide insights into the atmosphere of the class and the instructor's relationship to the students. This also helps the students get used to the camera.

- Be sure that the camera person focuses on both the students and the TA during the class. A TA can learn a lot about her or his teaching by watching the students. For example, in a discussion section, a shot of students looking involved and alert during a discussion or, conversely, two or three students falling asleep, will provide a good basis for reflecting on the strategies used in the class.

A videotape made for formative evaluation purposes should never be used for summative evaluation unless the TA authorizes that use.

Peer observation. In this process, TAs exchange classroom visits and then meet to share observations, give feedback, and discuss teaching and learning issues of mutual interest and/or concern. In addition to providing early feedback for each of the TAs, this process exposes TAs to alternative teaching styles, gives TAs an opportunity to observe students and their reactions to different methods of teaching, and encourages them to exchange ideas about teaching with their peers.

Some departments have the TAs focus their observations on the students. The anxiety of a peer critique tends to decrease when both parties discuss the specifics of student responses and activities. The process focuses attention on the learning that is taking place (rather than the teaching), which, after all, is the primary goal of our classroom activities.

To ensure success of the peer observations, TAs need background preparation, including:

- An explicit statement of the goals of peer observation.

- Guidelines for observation and feedback: what to discuss with the peer partner before visiting the classroom, how to observe someone teaching (including the usefulness of a classroom map), and how to structure a feedback session.

- An idea of timing: Mutual observations should be scheduled close together and discussed as soon after the observations as possible.

Immediately following the peer observations, some faculty members facilitate a discussion with the TAs so that they learn from each other's experiences. This type of discussion can be less threatening if faculty have the TAs focus on their observations of students or on the strategies and methods they found particularly successful.

Early feedback from students. Collecting student feedback has benefits for both the students and the TAs who teach them. If student input comes early enough in the semester, a TA can respond to suggestions and consider changes that would benefit the students who participated in the evaluation. Moreover, asking students to think about what might help them learn more effectively has the potential to make them more reflective about how they learn. TAs will get the most out of student feedback if they do the following:

- Let students know in advance why, when, and how feedback will be collected and emphasize that student responses will not affect grades.

- Collect student feedback early enough in the semester so that changes are still possible but late enough for students to have a clear sense of how things are going.

- Leave the room while students complete the feedback activity.

- Discuss the feedback with an experienced TA, a supervisor, or a consultant from the teaching center.

Collecting student feedback. Three methods of collecting student feedback are the small group method, written feedback, and ratings forms.

1) *Small group method.* This method of gathering student feedback is patterned after a process called the "small group instructional diagnosis" or SGID (Redmond & Clark, 1982). Following a planning meeting with the TA, a consultant arrives a few minutes before the class period begins and observes (taking objective data) until there are approximately 20 minutes left. At that time the instructor turns the class over to the consultant and leaves the room. The consultant explains the procedure and its purpose and then divides the class into groups of four or five students. Each group receives a sheet with the following questions:

- List the major strengths in this course. (What is helping you learn in the course?) Please explain briefly or give an example for each strength.

- List changes that could be made in the course to assist you in learning. Please explain how suggested changes could be made.

Students are then asked to come to a group consensus on responses to each of these questions; a recorder, chosen by each group, writes down the responses. After five to eight minutes, the groups take turns sharing their responses about the strengths of the course while the consultant posts them on the chalkboard or an overhead transparency. Other students are encouraged to comment if they disagree with a particular response; the consultant might also ask for clarification or more specific information. When the groups have volunteered as many strengths as they choose to, the process is repeated for the suggested changes. The consultant and the TA meet one or two days later to discuss the feedback.

Small-group feedback has at least three advantages: 1) The questions are open-ended so that the instructor finds out which issues students think are most important; 2) because the process involves consensus building, it eliminates the isolated and often harsh comments that can be very distracting for instructors who collect written feedback from each student; and 3) consultation is built into the small-group feedback process.

2) *Written student feedback.* TAs can ask students for written feedback by posing questions on specific aspects of a course or by simply asking students to respond to: What is going well, or what is helping you

learn? What suggestions do you have for improving the course? (Some instructors at the University of Michigan have used this method successfully at the end of each week.)

Written feedback can offer TAs insights into their students' perceptions of the course (or section) that may have otherwise gone unspoken. If the form is completely open-ended, then the students will be listing their major concerns. If the form asks about specific items, students can offer suggestions that might prove quite useful for making changes or improvements in the way the course is taught.

The disadvantage of written feedback is the time it takes to compile and interpret the responses. Student comments for each question need to be organized into major categories in order for the TA to discern patterns of responses rather than focusing on individual comments. TAs may also have to reconcile seemingly contradictory student reactions to the same aspect of the course.

3) *Ratings forms.* TAs can use midsemester forms similar to the end-of-the-semester student ratings forms. Questions can focus on any aspect of the course about which a TA would like student feedback. An early feedback rating form might also include a space for written feedback to some general questions. See Figure 12.3 for an example of an early feedback form.

Rating forms are relatively easy to fill out and to compile. As a result, they will be particularly useful for TAs who have limited time or have a large number of students. There are two drawbacks to using rating scales alone: While low scores can point out areas that need improvement, they do not offer any advice about how to make changes; and if TAs use closed-ended questions exclusively, they will not find out if students have concerns other than the ones they were asked about.

End-of-semester student ratings. End-of-semester ratings forms generally consist of some combination of items that ask students to rate instructors on a numerical scale and to respond to open-ended questions. Much of what we said earlier about collecting early feedback can also apply to end-of-semester ratings, if they are to be used solely for improvement purposes. In order to make the information as useful as possible, TAs should choose questions that provide feedback on the various components of good

FIGURE 12.3
Early-Semester Student Rating Form

Course _____ _____ Section_____ TA's Name _____
      (department)   *(number)*   *(number)*

EARLY FEEDBACK FORM

Dear Student: Thank you for taking the time to fill out this confidential questionnaire thoughtfully. The information will be used solely by your TA to assess student satisfaction while the course is still underway.

Please rate the following on a scale of five (strongly agree) to one (strongly disagree). NA= Not applicable.

	strongly agree	agree	neutral	disagree	strongly disagree	
This teaching assistant:						
1. is well prepared for class/lab.	5	4	3	2	1	NA
2. communicates the subject matter clearly.	5	4	3	2	1	NA
3. provides helpful comments on exams, assignments, etc.	5	4	3	2	1	NA
4. encourages class discussion.	5	4	3	2	1	NA
5. is responsive to students' questions.	5	4	3	2	1	NA
6. uses effective examples to illustrate points.	5	4	3	2	1	NA
7. is enthusiastic.	5	4	3	2	1	NA
8. is friendly and approachable.	5	4	3	2	1	NA
9. is helpful during office hours.	5	4	3	2	1	NA
10. overall, is an excellent teacher.	5	4	3	2	1	NA

Please complete the following:

11. My attendance at this section has been approximately _____ %.

12. I have visited this TA during office hours _____ times.

13. What have been the best aspects of this course/lab?

14. What aspects need improvement? Any suggestions?

15. Additional comments for the TA

Adapted from *A Guidebook for University of Michigan Graduate Student Instructors,* 6th ed., Beverly Black and Matthew Kaplan, Eds., Center for Research on Learning and Teaching, 1997, p. 104.

teaching (such as organization, grading, workload, rapport, and enthusiasm). Questions that ask about concrete and changeable behaviors should also be included. For example, the section on organization in the University of Michigan rating system includes "The instructor had everything going according to schedule" and "The instructor followed an outline closely."

Unfortunately, many TAs see student ratings as a source of anxiety rather than as a diagnostic tool that can help them with their teaching. TAs may experience this reaction because they look at their ratings alone, without any type of consultation. They find it difficult to make sense of the numbers and the possibly conflicting comments. Other TAs focus solely on one or two negative responses and become discouraged about their teaching. As with other forms of feedback, student ratings will be more likely to lead to improvement when they are combined with consultation (Cohen, 1980).

Materials and grading. TAs should get feedback on the materials they develop for their course: first-day handouts, written assignments, quizzes, etc. In addition, early feedback on how TAs grade students' work can head off a number of problems. TAs should hand in student work that they have graded and should receive feedback on both the positive aspects of their grading and on changes that could increase effectiveness.

Portfolios. (See Chapter 13.)

Analyze the Data in Preparation for Giving Feedback

Before meeting with the TA, a consultant should review and analyze the information gathered and think about how it can be organized. To make the feedback useful rather than overwhelming, the consultant can find two or three aspects of the TA's teaching that seem to be successful and two or three aspects that do not seem to be consistent with the TA's goals. Next, the consultant can prepare suggestions for how the TA could further exploit his or her strengths and reconcile discrepancies between stated goals and actual teaching practices.

After the consultant has analyzed the data, she should organize and type feedback from students along with key observations to give to the TA as a record. TAs will get the most from written comments if they are organized so that they reveal trends rather than idiosyncratic responses. A fairly simple method of organization is to divide positive comments from suggestions and then, within these broad categories, group together specific comments that relate to the same topic or aspect of teaching (such as organization, testing, or group work).

Meet with TA to Give Feedback and Exchange Ideas on Teaching

An essential part of the feedback process is the meeting between the TA and the consultant after the data are collected. The goals for this session are to:

- Help the TA develop or maintain a positive sense of what he or she is already accomplishing.

- Collaborate on analyzing the data in order to get a clear picture of what is happening in the class.

- Assist the TA in becoming reflective about teaching and the students' learning.

- Expand the TA's view of what is possible in the classroom.

- Help the TA identify two or three areas that he or she can work on to become a more effective teacher.

- Assist the TA in identifying resources and next steps to facilitate improvement.

The consultant and TA should meet to discuss the feedback one day (or no more than two days) after the data were collected, while the details of the class are still fresh for both. The TA may be nervous, so it is important to put him or her at ease. The consultant might begin by thanking the TA for the opportunity to observe the class and possibly talking about an aspect of the class that seemed especially interesting.

Much of the literature stresses that feedback is most useful when the consultant uses a nondirective approach and helps the TA draw on his or her experiences to discover changes that could be made in light of the information gathered. In this way, the consultant shows respect for the instructor's knowledge about teaching and learning and trusts that the instructor has a repertoire of experiences to draw on (Carrol & Goldberg, 1989; Brinko, 1993). In practice, the consultant may find that more direction is needed. This is especially true with new instructors who may have a single mental image of what teaching is and may be so invested in conforming to that image they may not be able to see when something is not working. In this case, TAs may have a limited repertoire of experiences to draw upon, and the consultant may need to make explicit suggestions for development (Brinko, 1993; Fowler, 1996).

Following is an outline that might be used to plan the meeting. (In practice, if the consultant really listens to the TA and respects his or her needs, the meeting may go much differently than planned. It is, however, essential to have a plan.)

- Have the instructor talk about the goals for the class session observed. (This may have been done in the preobservation meeting, but it is good to reiterate it here.)

- Ask for the instructor's perceptions of the class (how the session went for him/her, was it typical, etc.) and share recorded information that reinforces the TA's view.

- Share other information gathered. Discussing a map of the classroom might be a good place to start.

- If there is a videotape to view, set it up with the control between the consultant and the TA to allow either one to stop the tape and discuss different aspects of the classroom as they arise.

- Have the instructor discuss the information collected in light of his or her goals. What was successful? What might be changed to more fully reach the goals?

- Encourage the instructor to reflect on why things might be happening the way they are. Why were some parts of the class successful? How would she or he change a particular activity, situation, etc., to make it better?

- Encourage the instructor to reflect on what is happening in the classroom from the students' point of view.

- Reinforce insights by citing evidence or specific examples from the different sources of data.

- Ask the instructor which two or three areas of feedback are most interesting or cause the most concern.

- Assist the TA in developing a plan of action.

- Summarize what has been discussed.

If the feedback came from students through the small group method, have the TA set aside class time—as soon after the feedback session as possible—to discuss the results with them. This discussion should include a summary of both positive comments and suggested changes, a plan for how the TA will make certain changes, and an explanation for why particular suggestions cannot be adopted.

It is important that TAs go away from a session with, at most, two or three ideas that they can take action on to improve their teaching. With a long list of changes, TAs may feel overwhelmed and may not know where to begin. They should also have a list of resources and places they can go for help.

Videofeedback. A feedback session using a videotape as the source of information can be similar to the procedures just outlined. The difference is that videotape provides more direct and more copious information (both verbal and nonverbal) than data collected in other ways. With a vibrant picture in front of them, TAs can easily ignore their strengths and focus instead on everything they perceive as wrong, including their appearance. This can be devastating for TAs who are still developing confidence in themselves as teachers. Thus, it is essential for them to view the tape with someone who has had instruction in the feedback process (Taylor-Way, 1988). When the viewing is completed, the videotape should be given to the graduate student or erased. The TA should have control over whether or not the tape will be shown to other people.

If TAs are to view their tape by themselves for some reason, provide them with a video self-analysis form that contains some combination of open-ended questions and checklists. Such forms help TAs concentrate on teaching goals and behaviors related to those goals, rather than on obsessing about appearance or idiosyncratic speech (see Figure 12.4 for an example).

SUMMATIVE EVALUATION OF TAS' TEACHING

We turn now to the other purpose of evaluation: judging TAs for administrative purposes, such as reappointment and selection for teaching awards. Summative evaluation is a difficult subject. Often the faculty member in charge of TA development will work with TAs as they gain the skills and knowledge necessary to be effective teachers.

FIGURE 12.4

Getting the Most from Your Videotape

Characterize your performance on each of the following items
using the three-point scale provided.

	Needs Improvement	Satisfactory	Well Done

A. Class Structure. The structure and organization of your class should be clearly evident on the videotape. If they are not evident, your students probably missed them as well.

1. Clearly states the objectives of the class (what the students will gain from the class today).	1	2	3
2. Relates the day's materials to content from previous classes and the underlying themes of the course.	1	2	3
3. Checks frequently with students to ascertain if they are following the logic of the lecture, discussion, or learning activity.	1	2	3
4. Summarizes the major points of the class.	1	2	3

B. Exciting Student Interest. At minimum, students should be alert and paying attention throughout the class, but you should always strive for a higher level of involvement.

5. Addresses students by name.	1	2	3
6. Uses techniques that require students to do something in class.	1	2	3
7. Class activities are challenging, forcing students to reach above their previous level of understanding.	1	2	3
8. Class activities center on the important questions and issues in the field, and not just factual content.	1	2	3

C. Questioning Techniques. Questioning enhances student learning in powerful ways. Questions in class challenge students to analyze and synthesize information and to exercise informed judgment.

9. Asks factual questions to determine student preparation.	1	2	3
10. Asks questions that require students to apply information or principles from the course.	1	2	3
11. Asks questions that require students to exercise analysis or judgment.	1	2	3
12. Asks follow-up questions (to clarify and interpret the concepts under consideration).	1	2	3
13. Waits at least 10 seconds for a student to formulate an answer.	1	2	3
14. Responds to confusing (or wrong) answers honestly, but without insulting the students who offered them.	1	2	3
15. Redirects some student questions to other members of the class.	1	2	3

Adapted with permission from *TAs and Professors as a Teaching Team: A Faculty Guide to TA Training and Supervision,* Center for Teaching and Learning, University of North Carolina at Chapel Hill, 1992.

The collegial relationship that results from this type of mentoring can seem at odds with the task of making a value judgment about a TA's competence as a teacher. However, such decisions are necessary for several reasons: to help departments ensure the quality of courses taught by TAs, to decide which TAs to assign to which courses, to identify TAs for departmental and university teaching awards, to provide information for letters of recommendation for academic jobs, and to identify experienced TAs who can help out with departmental training of new graduate students.

To be effective, summative evaluation needs to be systematic and fair. Systematic means that the department has developed and shared with TAs a clear set of procedures for how and when evaluation of a TA's teaching will take place, how the information will be used, criteria for reappointment, etc. Fairness relates both to the overall system (how clear criteria for evaluation are, how consistently they are followed, whether the information gathered gives an accurate picture of TA teaching, etc.) and to the actual components of the system (use of student ratings, observations, portfolios, etc.). A detailed set of guidelines for evaluation and decision-making can help maintain the quality of undergraduate teaching while avoiding misunderstandings or haphazard decisions.

Early in their work as instructors, TAs need to receive a clearly stated policy on evaluation. The following questions should guide the development of such a policy:

- What are the TAs' responsibilities, and what are the basic standards for meeting these responsibilities? The more specific a department is in describing what is expected from TAs, the easier it will be to judge whether they are fulfilling their duties.

- How should a department get this information? Multiple sources of data should be used to provide a full picture of a TA's teaching performance.

- How will TAs be kept informed about their standing? It is unfair to wait until the end of the semester to give a TA feedback that his or her teaching is unacceptable. TAs need frequent feedback before they are evaluated, clear indications of what needs improvement, and suggestions for how to make changes.

- What resources will TAs have to help them improve? It will be easier for TAs to respond to feedback if they are given a number of options for help. Possibilities include: departmental meetings/course meetings, observing others teaching the same course, early feedback from students coupled with consultation, working with graduate student mentors, attending instructional workshops, and readings on teaching.

- How will decisions be made about whether or not to reappoint TAs? What constitutes unacceptable performance (i.e., what combination of negative evaluations and inability to improve despite feedback)? Who will make this decision: the faculty member in charge of TA development, the course supervisor, or the department chair? When will decisions be reached? A TA who is not reappointed will need time to look for other means of support. It would be helpful for the department to advise graduate students who are not reappointed on where they might turn for other funding.

- Under what circumstances will a TA be able to apply to be reappointed?

The following sections provide suggestions for using various sources of data as part of the decision-making process: student ratings, observations by supervisor, examination of materials, and information from course supervisors.

Using Student Ratings for Decision-Making

When student ratings are used to make administrative decisions, a TA supervisor will need to follow formal procedures to ensure fairness and accuracy. Results of considerable research indicate that, when used correctly, student ratings provide one accurate measure of an instructor's performance. There is also a broad consensus (Cashin, 1995; Braskamp and Ory, 1994; Marsh, 1984) that they should never be the only source of data used in personnel decisions.

Selecting questions. A few simple principles should guide the selection of questions for student rating forms:

- Be sure that all questions actually apply to the type of teaching done by TAs in the unit.

- When possible, give TAs some say in which questions are included.

- Students are not in a position to make judgments about a TA's knowledge of the subject (Theall & Franklin, 1991).

Administering student ratings. The department should develop standard procedures for handing out, explaining, and collecting student ratings.

- Since ratings should be anonymous, the TA should leave the room while students fill out the forms.

- Make clear to students that the TA will not see the ratings until after grades have been posted.

- Rating forms should be administered during the last week or two of classes, although preferably not on the last day.

- Students should fill out the forms at the beginning of the class period and should have sufficient time to complete the form.

Interpreting results. The following guidelines should assist in interpreting fairly the results of student ratings:

- For decision-making purposes, it is best to look at global items (e.g., "Overall this is an excellent course," "Overall this is an excellent instructor").

- Decisions should be based on data collected over time rather than on the results from only one course.

- In general, any item rated by ten students or fewer should be viewed with caution (Cashin, 1995). Similarly, data should not be used for decision-making unless most of the students in a class have completed the survey: 80% for small classes with five to 20 students; 75% for classes of 20-30; 66% for classes of 30-50; and 50% for classes larger than 50 (Theall & Franklin, 1991).

- Comparative data can establish a useful context for interpreting ratings results; however, such data must be used carefully. It is best to 1) compare TAs teaching in the same course over time, 2) compare TAs' scores to similar courses in the same department, and 3) compare TAs' scores to courses in related disciplines.

- When using comparative data, small differences in ratings results should not be overstated.

Observations for Decision-Making Purposes

Observation of a TA's class is one of the essential elements in an evaluation process. A consultant can follow the same procedures as those outlined immediately above, with the following additions:

- TAs should know well in advance that the results will be put in their file and used as part of their evaluation.

- Observations for evaluation should be done toward the end of the semester by a faculty member.

- Graduate students should not be put in the position of evaluating their peers.

- Observations from more than one semester should be used to make summative evaluations.

- To ensure consistency, a checklist or a standard method for collecting data should be used and shared in advance with TAs.

- The TA should know when the observation will take place.

In all cases, TAs should receive early feedback to help them develop their skills before they are summatively evaluated.

Other Sources of Information

Materials that TAs have developed (syllabi, assignments, activities, quizzes) and teaching portfolios are good sources of information for evaluation purposes. TAs should have feedback on early versions of any material that will be part of an evaluation. In addition, departments should develop clear criteria for the evaluation and share them with TAs. (For more information, see Chapter 13.)

SUMMARY

The combination of formative and summative evaluation is essential in helping TAs develop the skills they need to become effective college teachers and to ensure a high quality learning experience for the undergraduates in their classes. By "sitting beside" TAs as they learn about teaching and students' learning, TA supervisors and consultants will assist them in building their confidence as teachers. The process will also help create a community of faculty and graduate students who collaborate and engage in conversations about teaching as well as research.

When TAs receive respect, collaboration, coaching, and dialogue on their teaching, they can become reflective teachers and view evaluation not as a burden or surprise, but as part of the ongoing process of improvement that will continue throughout their careers in the academy.

REFERENCES

Braskamp, L. A., & Ory, J. C. (1994). *Assessing faculty work.* San Francisco, CA: Jossey-Bass.

Brinko, K. T. (1993). The practice of giving feedback to improve teaching: What is effective? *Journal of Higher Education, 64* (5), 574-593.

Carrol, J. G., & Goldberg, S. R. (1989). Teaching consultants: A collegial approach to better teaching. *College Teaching, 37* (4), 143-46.

Cashin, W. E. (1995). *Student ratings of teaching: The research revisited.* Manhattan, KS: Center for Faculty Evaluation and Development, Kansas State University.

Cohen, P. A. (1980). Effectiveness of student-rating feedback for improving college instruction: A meta-analysis of findings. *Research in Higher Education, 13* (4), 321-341.

Fowler, B. (1996). Increasing the teaching skills of teaching assistants through feedback from observation of classroom performance. *The Journal of Graduate Teaching Assistant Development, 3* (3), 95-103.

Marsh, H. W. (1984). Students' evaluation of university teaching: Dimensionality, reliability, validity, potential biases, and utility. *Journal of Educational Psychology, 76* (5), 707-754.

McKeachie, W. J. (1987). Can evaluating instruction improve teaching? In L. M. Aleamoni (Ed.), *Techniques for evaluating and improving instruction.* New Directions for Teaching and Learning, No. 31. San Francisco, CA: Jossey-Bass.

Millis, B. J. (1992). Conducting effective peer classroom observations. *To Improve the Academy, 11,* 189-206.

Nyquist, J. D., & Wulff, D. H. (1996). *Working effectively with graduate assistants.* Thousand Oaks, CA: Sage.

Redmond, M. V., & Clark, D. J. (1982). A practical approach to improving teaching. *AAHE Bulletin, 34* (6), 8-10.

Stodolsky, S. S. (1990). Classroom observation. In J. Millman & L. Darling-Hammond (Eds.), *The new handbook of teacher evaluation.* Newbury Park, CA: Corwin Press.

Taylor-Way, D. (1988). Consultation with video: Memory management through stimulated recall. In K. G. Lewis (Ed.), *Face to face: A sourcebook of individual consultation techniques for faculty/instructional developers.* Stillwater, OK: New Forums Press.

Theall, M., & Franklin, J. (1991). Using student ratings for teaching improvement. In M. Theall & J. Franklin (Eds.), *Effective practices for improving teaching.* New Directions for Teaching and Learning, No. 48. San Francisco, CA: Jossey-Bass.

Weimer, M. G., Kerns, M., & Parrett, J. L. (1988). Instructional observations: Caveats, concerns, and ways to compensate. *Studies in Higher Education, 13* (3), 285-293.

13

Teaching Portfolios as a Tool for TA Development

Pat Hutchings

Teaching portfolios have become a prominent feature on the higher education landscape. Their use by faculty is on the rise (Seldin, Annis, & Zubizarreta, 1995), and, as evidenced by the inclusion of this chapter in this volume, they have benefits to offer TAs as well, in two ways. First, a properly constructed portfolio can assist TAs to reflect upon and therefore improve their practice as teachers—both in the short run and through the inculcation of lifelong habits of reflective practice and improvement. Second, as a vehicle for documenting teaching, portfolios can help bring greater recognition and reward to teaching as a form of scholarly, professional work. My purpose in what follows is to lay the groundwork for achieving these two potential benefits.

A Short History of the Teaching Portfolio

Portfolios are not new. Professionals in fields such as architecture and photography have used them for years to document and display their best work. But since the late 1980s, portfolios have also begun to catch on among teachers looking for better, more "full-bodied" ways of representing their pedagogical work.

Pioneering work on teaching portfolios has come from a number of quarters. During the mid-1980s, Lee Shulman and his Stanford University colleagues developed prototypes of portfolios that are now used to assess K-12 teachers who come before the National Board for Professional Teaching Standards. Shulman's vision of the portfolio as shaped by key intellectual tasks that effective teachers need to be able to perform— for instance, planning a course or evaluating student work—has since been advocated for higher education as well, in a 1991 monograph (Edgerton et al.) from the American Association for Higher Education, *The Teaching Portfolio: Capturing the Scholarship in Teaching.* The important work of Peter Seldin also deserves mention in this regard—*The Teaching Portfolio* (1991), *Successful Use of Teaching Portfolios* (1993), and *The Teaching Portfolio,* 2nd ed. (1997).

In addition, pioneering work has been done on campuses. The Evergreen State College, for instance, has used portfolios for several decades, and a number of Canadian campuses have similar, long-time experience. Indeed, "The origins of the construct, as well as the use of the specific term, ... can be traced back to an initiative of the Canadian Association of University Teachers (CAUT) in the early 1970s" (Knapper, 1995, p. 45). Reacting to the exclusive use of student ratings as a means of evaluating teaching, a CAUT committee recommended alternatives that put the faculty member more directly in charge of documenting his or her work, which led eventually to the CAUT publication, *A Guide to the Teaching Dossier: Its Preparation and Use* (Shore, et al., 1980), a valuable document even today, much cited in subsequent publications.

Since then, portfolio use has grown and taken various directions. In some settings, portfolios are required for promotion and tenure decisions; in others, they are a grassroots initiative of faculty looking for ways to reflect upon and improve their teaching. On many campuses, teaching portfolios have also become an important part of the preparation of graduate students.

TEACHING PORTFOLIOS FOR TEACHING ASSISTANTS

It is hard to know just how extensive the use of portfolios is among graduate teaching assistants, but certainly it is increasing. The variety of uses, as well as cross-cutting themes, are suggested by a sampling of current and emerging practice.

Syracuse University
Portfolios are increasingly in use among faculty at Syracuse University, but in many departments it was graduate teaching assistants who pioneered

the idea. As part of "The Future Professoriate Project," funded by the Pew Charitable Trusts and the Fund for the Improvement of Postsecondary Education, the university invited departments to devise strategies to prepare graduate students for the full range of faculty responsibilities that they would one day face. These strategies vary considerably from department to department, but prominent in the mix is the teaching portfolio, which is seen both as a tool for self-reflection and as a way of documenting experience and effectiveness for future employers.

Having been at this work for some time, the Syracuse campus has learned a number of lessons about TA portfolios: 1) the need to employ different formats for different purposes and audiences; 2) the power of the portfolio's reflective components; 3) the critical nature of personal interactions between graduate students constructing portfolios and their faculty mentors; 4) strategic use of the portfolio in the academic job hunt, where it can be helpful but can also backfire; and 5) the importance of collecting artifacts from day one—a habit, by the way, that most current faculty did not develop in their graduate training, though it is taken for granted that they keep careful records of their scholarly work in other areas (Anderson, 1993).

University of Wyoming

At the University of Wyoming, graduate students pursuing an academic career are invited to apply for The Program in College Teaching, a five-part sequence of requirements, jointly sponsored by the graduate school and the Center for Teaching Excellence, which includes the development of a portfolio. Its design is determined by the TA in consultation with appropriate faculty mentors, but one general (and distinctive) feature of Wyoming portfolios is that TAs are asked to document not only their actual teaching experiences but other work done as part of The Program in College Teaching—for instance, research on an important pedagogical issue in the field or work with a faculty mentor on the development of course software. (One participant's special project in the program was to develop a web site on teaching portfolios, accessible at [http://grad.uwyo.edu/pict/portfoli.htm].)

Completed portfolios are assessed as part of a credentialing process. (Syracuse employs a similar strategy.) Students who successfully demonstrate achievement of all five components receive a certificate recognizing their work.

Northern Arizona University

TA portfolios are particularly prevalent in composition programs, no doubt because they are familiar teaching and assessment tools in that culture and are often required of undergraduate students. The Northern Arizona University composition program is a case in point.

Under the leadership of director Geoffrey Chase, portfolios are part of a set of activities and requirements devised to enact the program's motto: "Teaching is a public act." All TAs in the program prepare teaching portfolios, which are shared with others at the end of their first semester of teaching; in subsequent semesters, the portfolios are updated and refined.

Throughout the portfolio-development process, the purpose is growth and development, Chase (1996) notes: "We do not use them for evaluation [but] as a means of raising questions about how [TAs] can develop more fully the vital interplay between teaching and scholarship" (pp. 87-88).

Once a graduate student leaves the NAU program, this development portfolio takes on a more evaluative function since it is used as part of the job search process.

Stanford University History Department

Teaching is central to the experience of graduate students in the Stanford history department, and portfolios play a role. Following a series of preparatory experiences, TAs develop items agreed upon by the department as essential portfolio components: a one- to two-page statement about their teaching goals; a self-criticism of a course they have taught, focusing on what did and did not work and what they will do to improve in the future; and feedback from their students, which is provided through the services of Stanford's Center for Teaching and Learning.

An important contextual note here is that in 1995 the department instituted a pedagogical colloquium (which it describes as "an informal discussion of teaching and curriculum") in which candidates for faculty positions in the department are asked to discuss their approach to the teaching of history. Graduate students attending these events quickly see that the portfolio (and other preparation provided by the department) will serve them well in their own future job search experiences (Roberts, 1996).

University of Wisconsin-Madison, College of Engineering

Like many programs, the College of Engineering at the University of Wisconsin-Madison sees considerable turnover among TAs, making it difficult for the program to learn from and build on teaching practice from semester to semester. To address this problem, a group of TAs recently proposed and pioneered the use of course portfolios.

The contents of these portfolios are familiar: an account of course goals, learning activities, assessments, and examples of student work. What makes them different is that they belong not to the individual TA but to the program, becoming part of a public resource for subsequent TAs in the program.

Benefits of the course portfolios are currently under study, but early experience suggests that the process of their development helps TAs reflect on their teaching and their students' learning. Additionally, portfolios are expected to be useful in accreditation.

For a look at the program's handbook for creating course portfolios, see [http://www/cae.wisc.edu/~tafellow]. (You will need Acrobat Reader software to read the handbook.)

THE BENEFITS OF TEACHING PORTFOLIOS FOR TEACHING ASSISTANTS

As evidenced in several of the previous section's examples, one benefit of portfolios comes when TAs enter the faculty job market. Having teaching-related credentials and materials to show to campuses that place high value on good teaching is almost bound to be a boon. Moreover, the thinking that goes into the portfolio's development (quite apart from the tangible final product) makes it easier for TAs to talk intelligently about their teaching in pedagogical colloquia and other occasions that campuses are increasingly using to assess teaching in the hiring process.

Second, portfolios help graduate students develop a conception of teaching as scholarly, intellectual work. Teaching is often conceived of and treated as a set of techniques, and technique is indeed important. But teaching is also a scholarly activity, an intimate reflection of how one thinks about one's field, and what it means to know it deeply. The portfolio, by inviting intellectually coherent, reflective documentation of one's teaching, reconnects scholarly substance to teaching technique, and treats teaching as engaging intellectual work, worthy of the scholar's time and attention and, like other scholarly work, appropriate for collegial exchange—important lessons early in a teaching career.

Third, portfolios foster habits of reflection and ongoing improvement. We all know the phrase "teaching load," and we know that teaching is often thought of as a sort of spin-off task, dependent only on knowing the field well. Portfolios embody a different ethic (for that is what it is)—that teaching is an activity in which one is a lifelong learner, welcoming and seeking out self-assessment, examination, and improvement. William Massy (1995) of Stanford talks about faculty's habit of "satisficing" around teaching—doing it just well enough to get by—while seeking excellence in research. Portfolios promote a parallel ethic of excellence in teaching.

Fourth, portfolios encourage an attitude of professional responsibility for quality control. As things now stand in many settings, the evaluation and improvement of teaching appear to be "somebody else's" job: Faculty are the objects of evaluation, not its agents. In contrast, the portfolio is a way of saying that teachers can and should be responsible for documenting, assessing, and improving their own practice—an attitude that could usefully be part of the professional socialization of graduate students, who will otherwise, as faculty, face increasingly bureaucratic forms of accountability imposed from outside of academe.

Fifth, portfolios point the way to richer, more authentic, situated portrayals of what teachers know and can do, a significant advance on prevailing practice, which depends almost exclusively on student ratings. Kieg and Waggoner (1994) argue: "... when faculty and administrators allow student ratings to be the only real source of information about teaching, they unwittingly contribute to a system in which too much emphasis is placed on evaluating superficial teaching skills and not enough is placed on more substantive matters" (p. 1).

The aim of portfolios is not, it should be said, to replace student voices, but rather to supplement, complement, and round out the picture. Indeed, this more situated, fuller picture may be especially important to apprentice teachers who are sorting out the vicissitudes of the classroom for the first time.

PORTFOLIO DESIGN

Whether the above five benefits are realized through the use of teaching portfolios depends on institutional context, culture, leadership, resources—that is, on a number of factors. But it also depends on how, exactly, the portfolio is conceived and designed. A rose may be a rose, but not all portfolios are equally useful in achieving the promise they hold.

Often the issue of design begins with the question, "What should I put in my portfolio?" At one level, the answer to this question depends on purpose and audience: One might put things in a portfolio intended for trusted friends and colleagues that one might not put in a portfolio aimed at future employers. But certain categories of evidence, and certain principles of design, are crucial regardless of purpose.

Categories of Evidence

Artifacts of teaching. These are materials and products generated in the process of teaching and learning which reveal the TA's approach to the teaching of his or her field. Among these are syllabi (though in some fields, and in some contexts involving TAs, the syllabus may not be designed by the individual instructor), assignments, examinations, student papers and projects, video- or audiotapes of class discussions or presentations, lecture notes and/or overheads, software developed for the class, hard copy of electronic exchanges with and among students, etc. Materials will vary by field and by type of course, but essential among them are items that sample not only what the TA does as teacher but what the students accomplish as learners.

Reflection. Many "portfolio-ers" have found that a longer reflective essay on course design or philosophy is a particularly valuable document, both for the teacher/writer and the reader. But also useful are shorter, reflective annotations attached to particular artifacts and materials. In general, the purpose of reflective components is to uncover the TA's "pedagogical thinking" and to answer questions about why various items are included and what they tell about his or her teaching. As John Murray (1995) notes, "much of the portfolio should be devoted to reflection on how behaviors are congruent with beliefs" (p. iv).

Self-assessment. This may overlap with reflective components. That is, the portfolio should not only explain and document but also evaluate; it is an opportunity for the TA to take stock of what is working, how he or she can improve, and what steps he or she might take toward possible improvement. This is an important element in portfolios at all career stages but a particularly pertinent one for TAs and others newly entering the field.

Items intended as reader aids. These include a table of contents, a description of the contexts of teaching dealt with in the portfolio (which courses, with how many students, required or elective, etc.), and perhaps an executive summary and statement of the portfolio's purpose. Additionally, some portfolios are color coded, with different categories of evidence in different colors to help orient the reader.

A final point is relevant to all four of the above categories: Less is more. The power of the portfolio comes in large part from the process of selective sampling rather than from amassing every possible scrap of evidence. And in order to select and sample wisely, one needs an organizing principle.

Finding an Organizing Principle

One of the possible pitfalls of portfolios is that laundry lists sometimes overwhelm larger purposes. "Too often . . . supporting documents dominate portfolio creation," Millis (1995) observes. Faculty focus on "a shopping list of possible portfolio items and determine which ones are most accessible. An emphasis on the 'what' rather than the 'why' may result in a superficial compilation of unrelated documents" (p. 68). The antidote to this problem is a controlling idea, an organizing principle, around which the right materials can be selected, organized, and reflected upon.

Key tasks of teaching the field. This is the model proposed in an AAHE monograph on the teaching portfolio which suggests four fairly generic tasks: course planning and preparation; actual teaching (classroom practice); evaluating student learning and providing feedback; and keeping up with the professional field in areas related to teaching performance (Edgerton, Hutchings, & Quinlan, 1991). But tasks may vary with the field. For instance, TAs in chemistry might want to include the teaching of laboratory skills. TAs in programs that entail team teaching might want to include tasks of collaboration with other teachers. There is no right list of tasks; the idea here is that an appropriate set of tasks, whatever it might include, is one way to give needed structure and coherence to the portfolio.

Teaching goals (or goals for student learning). If the central goal of a teacher of literature and writing is to develop students' ability to analyze a text critically, this goal might also be a sort of thesis for the portfolio; one might select artifacts that speak directly to this goal and reflect upon them in ways that illuminate the TA's thinking about its achievement.

Analogy with a scholarly project. This is a model embraced by the course portfolio working group of an AAHE project on the peer review of teaching. As suggested by the name, a course portfolio focuses not on a full teaching career but on the teaching and learning in a particular, selected course. Since many TAs teach only one course, this model may be a natural—even a necessity. Its defining feature is, however, not simply one of scope but of conception.

Following from the argument of Ernest Boyer's 1990 report, *Scholarship Reconsidered,* that teaching is a form of scholarly work, members of the AAHE working group have developed portfolios that entail, like a scholarly project, three basic components:

- Goals and intentions

- Implementation or enactment

- Results

A more extended discussion of course portfolios is included in Chapter 5 of *Making Teaching Community Property* (Hutchings, 1996).

A SPECIAL NOTE ABOUT TECHNOLOGY AND TEACHING PORTFOLIOS

As technology makes its way into classrooms and other instructional settings, it is also beginning to affect the development and use of teaching portfolios.

To begin with, technology makes the processes of teaching and learning public in a way they have not traditionally been (Bass & Batson, 1996). Departmental home pages often include syllabi and materials from courses offered by program faculty; many faculty are developing courses that are at least partly web-based; exchanges between students and faculty, or among students, that were once private are now out there on course listservs and in chatrooms. Thus, many of the components of portfolios are now widely accessible, thanks to technology.

Moreover, one can now find complete teaching and course portfolios on the web. A national project directed by American studies faculty member Randy Bass at Georgetown University entails the electronic development and posting of course portfolios, case studies, and curricula [www.georgetown.edu/crossroads/conversations/html]. Some members of the AAHE working group are similarly turning to the web to share their products: Steven Dunbar, a faculty member in mathematics at the University of Nebraska-Lincoln, is developing an online portfolio for his calculus course, at [http://www.math.unl.edu/CalcHTML/106f97.html].

A number of scholarly societies now sponsor electronic listservs and interactive web sites that include portfolio-like materials, as well. (See Chapter 9 in AAHE's *Making Teaching Community Property* [Hutchings, 1996] for addresses and further information.)

While not all of the above precisely fit the image of the teaching portfolio mentioned earlier, these materials are nevertheless "in the spirit" of portfolios and are useful resources for TAs and others looking to learn from the experience (and materials) of others.

SOME SUGGESTIONS FOR EFFECTIVE USE OF PORTFOLIOS AS TOOLS FOR TA DEVELOPMENT

A good bit of "how-to" literature now exists for faculty who wish to develop teaching portfolios. But what suggestions might aid TAs? The six that follow seem especially worth noting.

Balance Noble Ambitions against Realities of Time and Circumstance

Portfolios may be appealing in theory, but for most graduate students (and, for that matter, faculty) an immediate roadblock is time. As graduate programs attempt to prepare students for a fuller range of faculty tasks, the demands on time multiply, and TAs may reasonably ask: "Where will I find the time not only to teach but to document my teaching?"

There is no easy answer to this question, but it may be useful to say that even a modest step is better than none. One step in the right direction (as noted in lessons from the Syracuse experience above) is simply to begin collecting and saving the artifacts of one's teaching: a handout prepared here, a set of overheads there. Note, too, that the task of portfolio development may not be as daunting as it sounds; one faculty member in the AAHE group recorded the time devoted to his course portfolio at 15 hours, averaging about one a week.

Finally, it should be said that the issue of time is an issue of values, and ultimately one must balance benefits against costs. Great quantities of time are dedicated to research with no questions asked; an increment of attention to teaching might just be worth the expense in terms of practical benefits and personal satisfaction.

Adapt the Idea to Fit Local Circumstances
Portfolios may seem a natural and useful activity for graduate students who have the opportunity to teach their own course, but what of those who do not—those for whom instructional opportunities may be restricted to grading exams or monitoring a laboratory section? Clearly, the latter circumstances would require that portfolios be adapted and more narrowly focused. Indeed, the portfolio will be a mismatch in some situations, in which case TAs might usefully be introduced to the idea but with no expectation of immediate implementation.

Do No Harm
Graduate education is a time for learning the norms and conventions of the field, but in the case of portfolios there are few widely held agreements about good practice. What should a teaching portfolio in chemistry look like? What are the appropriate standards for judging a portfolio in anthropology? These are unresolved questions, and it is important that TAs developing portfolios recognize this reality. One danger, for instance, is putting forward a portfolio which is somehow ahead of the curve in terms of the field's thinking about pedagogy. Another lies in making public aspects of teaching that have (rightly or wrongly) been private and sacrosanct. It is crucial, therefore, that those working with TAs be candid about potential risks and explicit about the need to clarify (for oneself and with others) the portfolio's purposes, how the information will be used, who owns it, and what is at stake.

Use the Portfolio to Help Foster Colleagueship
It is possible to imagine a TA working in her office, behind a closed door, producing a fine portfolio. But she would miss much of the potential benefit which comes from working with others, be they peers, more advanced graduate students, or faculty mentors. Jim Wilkinson (1993), director of the Derek Bok Center for Teaching and Learning at Harvard University, notes:

We have begun to assemble portfolios for and with some graduate students about to enter the job market. Here we have found, as Peter Seldin and others predicted, that *the consultations that go into selecting materials for the portfolio are perhaps the most valuable part of the process* (p. 45).

Those promoting and directing portfolio use by TAs need to build into the process deliberate occasions for this kind of exchange and mentoring.

Connect Portfolios to Other Program Elements

It goes without saying that portfolios will be less powerful if they are trains on their own track, pursued in isolation from other aspects of the graduate education experience. It is important, then, to look for ways to embed the use of portfolios in program activities and requirements. This might mean making portfolio development an aspect of departmental course work, or it might mean that mentors (peer or faculty or both) assigned to assist TAs with teaching would also consult about portfolio development. No doubt there are numerous possible arrangements. The bottom line is that the more integral the portfolio is to the other scholarly work of graduate preparation, the more powerful it will be.

Think of Portfolios as the Beginning of Lifelong Habits and Practices

It is easy to get focused on the portfolio-as-product but what is equally important is the reflection, self-assessment, documentation, and planning that are embodied in the process of portfolio development—habits and practices that TAs will be well served by, both in the short run and throughout their careers. In this spirit, it may be useful for campuses and departments to develop case studies of the experience of TAs who develop portfolios, which can then point the way for the subsequent efforts of others.

A LEVER FOR LARGER CHANGE

Perhaps it goes without saying—but it needs saying and bears repeating—that portfolios are no silver bullet. Their use will not magically turn TAs into master teachers, and they will not ensure employment where there simply are no jobs to be had. As part of a larger, longer-term program of attention to teaching, however, they can be powerful tools not only for individual development but for fostering a culture of teaching and learning by encouraging more scholarly, public exchange about teaching. Indeed, if change in the character of graduate education itself is an aim (as it will be for many of the readers of this volume), the culture- and community-building potential of portfolios is one of the strongest arguments for their use.

REFERENCES

Anderson, E. (1993). *Campus use of the teaching portfolio: Twenty-five profiles.* Washington, DC: American Association for Higher Education.

Bass, R., & Batson, T. (1996). Teaching and learning in the computer age: Primacy of process. *Change, 28* (2), 42-47.

Boyer, E. (1990). *Scholarship reconsidered: Priorities of the professoriate.* Princeton, NJ: Carnegie Foundation for the Advancement of Teaching.

Chase, G. (1996). A professional development program for graduate students: Fostering collaboration in the writing program at Northern Arizona University. In P. Hutchings (Ed.), *Making teaching community property: A menu for peer collaboration and peer review.* Washington, DC: American Association for Higher Education.

Edgerton, R., Hutchings, P., & Quinlan, K. (1991). *The teaching portfolio: Capturing the scholarship in teaching.* Washington, DC: American Association for Higher Education.

Hutchings, P. (1996). *Making teaching community property: A menu for peer collaboration and peer review.* Washington, DC: American Association for Higher Education.

Keig, L., & Waggoner, M. (1994). *Collaborative peer review: The role of faculty in improving college teaching.* ASHE-ERIC Higher Education Report No. 2. Washington, DC: The George Washington University, School of Education and Human Development.

Knapper, C. (1995). The origins of teaching portfolios. *Journal on Excellence in College Teaching, 6* (1), 45-56.

Massy, W., & Wilger, A. (1995). Improving productivity: What faculty think about it—and its effect on quality. *Change, 27* (4), 10-21.

Millis, B. (1995). Shaping the reflective portfolio: A philosophical look at the mentoring role. *Journal on Excellence in College Teaching, 6* (1), 65-73.

Murray, J. (1995). *Successful faculty development and evaluation: The complete teaching portfolio.* ASHE-ERIC Higher Education Report No. 8. Washington, DC: The George Washington University, School of Education and Human Development.

Roberts, R. (1996). The pedagogical colloquium: Focusing on teaching in the hiring process in the Stanford University history department. In P. Hutchings (Ed.), *Making teaching community property: A menu for peer collaboration and peer review.* Washington, DC: American Association for Higher Education.

Seldin, P. (1991). *The teaching portfolio.* Bolton, MA: Anker.

Seldin, P. (1997). *The teaching portfolio* (2nd ed.). Bolton, MA: Anker.

Seldin, P., & Associates. (1993). *Successful use of teaching portfolios.* Bolton, MA: Anker.

Seldin, P., Annis, L., & Zubizarreta, J. (1995). Answers to common questions about the teacher portfolio. *Journal on Excellence in College Teaching, 6* (1), 57-64.

Shore, B., et al. (1980). *The teaching dossier: A guide to its preparation and use.* Montreal, Quebec: Canadian Association of University Teachers.

Wilkinson, J. (1993). Harvard University. In P. Seldin & Associates, *Successful use of teaching portfolios.* Bolton: MA: Anker.

14

EVALUATING TA PROGRAMS

Nancy Van Note Chism

Both those who staff teaching assistant (TA) development programs and those who fund or use them quite legitimately want to know how these programs are faring: Are they effective? efficient? credible? These questions can be asked with different purposes in mind, described traditionally by program evaluators as formative and summative evaluation (Scriven, 1973). Those focusing on the formative purpose seek evaluative information during the enactment of the program for the purpose of making improvements while those focusing on the summative purpose are concerned with decisions that must be made at given intervals, such as continuation of the program, funding increases, and the like. This chapter will look at both kinds of program evaluation in TA development programs, describing documentation of such evaluation in the literature, issues involved in evaluating TA programs, and practical approaches that can be used for conducting evaluations.

FINDINGS FROM THE LITERATURE

The literature on TA development, or on the larger domain of faculty development generally, provides some information on the incidence of program evaluation activity, the types of evaluations that have been conducted, and what these evaluations have revealed.

Types of Program Evaluation Activity
An initial and sometimes ongoing TA program evaluation activity is

needs analysis, which seeks to identify the kinds of initiatives that should be undertaken in a given context. Usually these are performed as a program is instituted, but elements of a needs analysis are often incorporated into ongoing evaluation through such questions as "What topics would you like to see in this series in the future?" Examples of needs analyses conducted before the initiation of a program that are reported in the literature are Ford (1993) and Piccinin and Fairweather (1996-97).

With respect to ongoing program evaluation, Chism and Lumpkins (1995) suggested several kinds of questions that could be asked in evaluating TA development programs:

- What is the extent of program usage?

- What is the satisfaction level of the TAs themselves?

- What effects does the program have on the teaching of the TAs?

- What effects does the program have on the learning of the TAs' students?

These same four questions were used to frame the Chism and Szabó study (1996) that explored the extent to which faculty and TA development programs evaluate their effectiveness. The survey found that most programs collect data on users, can report percentages of use and, to some extent, can provide a descriptive portrait of their users. Programs also reported high levels of evaluation activity dealing with user satisfaction. Open- and closed-ended survey instruments were found to be used most frequently in determining satisfaction. This finding is consistent with several studies from Centra (1976) to Rubino (1994) that find high use of survey instruments and user satisfaction as the measure of success in evaluations of faculty and TA development programs.

Chism and Szabó (1996) found much less reported evaluation activity on the final two questions, dealing with effects of services on teaching and on the learners of the teachers who used the services. When effects on teaching were explored, they were most often assessed by survey or interview of the user but sometimes by follow-up observation, results of student evaluation, or other measures. Program evaluation activity that focused on ascertaining effects of the program on student learning was found to be almost nonexistent.

Incidence of Program Evaluation Activity

Descriptions of how routinely TA development programs are evaluated are not available as such in the literature, but several studies (Boice, 1989; Centra, 1976; Chism & Szabó, 1996; Gaff, 1975; McMillan, 1975; Rubino, 1994; Weimer, 1990) describe the extent to which faculty/instructional development programs evaluate their services. Since these services are similar and, in many cases, the faculty and TA development programs are combined, this literature is informative. The studies vary in their assessments of the amount of evaluation activity, with two studies (Boice, 1989; Centra, 1976) reporting that only 14% of programs engage in program evaluation to several studies that report higher incidence (Gaff arrives at a 56% figure; McMillan's is 45%). Rubino (1994), who conducted a more recent and more directly related study, comes up with higher percentages, although these are not reported in a way that is comparable with the other studies. Rather than asking his respondents about overall evaluation activity, he asked them how they evaluate their programs, finding that 34% relied on participant satisfaction measures, about 12% on more direct measures of impact, and 54% on combined methods. Since overlaps and unique choices were not reported, an overall activity figure is not available, although it is safe to say that it is 54% or higher, which corresponds with Gaff and McMillan. Chism and Szabó (1996) found much higher percentages when they specified type of service evaluated, reporting that 88% of the programs in their sample of both faculty/instructional and TA programs evaluated mentoring programs routinely or occasionally; 86% evaluated events such as workshops routinely or occasionally; 77% evaluated consultations routinely or occasionally; and 47% evaluated publications they distributed routinely or occasionally. When only the "routinely" designation is reported, the percentages are 50% for mentoring, 49% for events, 25% for consultations, and 17% for publications. When TAs-only programs were isolated for this study, there were too few to provide sound conclusions, but they showed patterns consistent with the overall figures.

Several factors make it difficult to estimate overall TA program evaluation activity: the blending of TA and faculty/instructional development programs and types of institutional settings in the samples; the different ways in which studies ask about and report on levels of activity; and the ways in which practices and programs continue to change in the years between studies. However, the studies show that a moderate amount of activity is in place. The Chism and Szabó (1996) study further found that, although this level of evaluation activity is reportedly taking place, very few programs publish the results of these efforts, so evaluation activity is not readily apparent, leaving programs open to charges of not engaging in evaluation.

Results of Studies

Chism and Szabó (1996) found that their respondents were able to document positive program effects. In terms of user satisfaction, ratings were uniformly high, and when effects on teaching were studied, high or moderate impacts were associated with most services. Respondents could not generally report effects on learning.

A body of reports on the effects of specific TA training interventions (as opposed to overall program evaluation) exists in the research literature. Carroll (1980) conducted an early review of such studies, concluding that small positive gains were associated with TA development interventions. However, he found fault with most of the studies, arguing that they had not been conducted scientifically.

Gardener (1985) also reviewed TA training effects studies, finding that studies of training in specific areas (such as asking questions) generally reported improvement and that such improvements positively impacted student evaluations of teaching. She found that studies of general training concluded that such training produced mixed results on whether training interventions influenced TAs' attitudes, such as enjoyment of teaching.

The review by Abbott, Wulff, and Szago (1989) added further support for positive findings associated with components of TA development programs but echoed past recommendations that research be conducted more systematically.

Lewis's 1997 review of research on TA development documented consistent changes in teaching performance associated with development efforts, but no significant difference in the one study she cited that dealt with the effects of training on student learning.

Other major reviews of general faculty development interventions (Levinson-Rose & Menges, 1981; Weimer & Lenze, 1991) support findings in the TA development program evaluation literature in concluding that although studies more frequently rely on measures of user satisfaction than formal experimental design focused on outcomes, they generally find positive effects associated with interventions to improve teaching.

WHAT ARE THE ISSUES?

Several issues arise in discussing the evaluation of TA development programs. Among these are 1) What are appropriate questions for the evaluation to address? 2) Practically speaking, what resources are available to conduct evaluations? 3) With whom should results be shared? and 4) What methodological approaches are feasible and appropriate in conducting program evaluations?

Appropriate Questions

At a minimum, program evaluations are descriptive. They document the main goals of the program, its activities, and how the activities were implemented. Included in this evaluation would be an overview of the resources used by the program and the number and kind of clients served. It would appear, if results of the Chism and Szabó study (1996) are descriptive of TA programs in general, that such overviews are undertaken by most programs for annual reports or other institutional purposes and that most can answer the basic questions about goals and activities.

In addition to descriptive information, questions concerning user satisfaction and the effects of the program on the teaching of the users seem quite appropriate. As indicated above, there is good evidence throughout all the reviews that user satisfaction is routinely assessed and found to be positive overall. Since effects on teaching are more difficult to explore, there is less activity in this area, but programs are in agreement that this is an important question to deal with and is not impossible to do.

More problematic is a question often asked of development programs: Did your program improve student learning? As several commentators agree, this question, while compelling and seemingly relevant, implies that second-order effects of often very limited interventions can be traced in very complex environments. Chism and Szabó's (1996) respondents also found fault with this question. One said, "It is estimated that the teacher makes about 25% of the impact on learning. If this is true and we estimate that faculty developers may have a similar percentage of impact on teaching, it makes it a small connection to identify in an objective way (about 6% at best)." Another replied, "You are asking whether student learning is improved because faculty used our services. A long, long reach. I can't imagine a program that could answer this question with full confidence."

One solution, articulated by Weimer and Lenze (1991), is that formal research on learner effects be conducted by educational researchers who have the necessary resources and can employ the controls needed to do these studies. The results can then be extrapolated to program settings, rather than initiated or replicated by development practitioners.

Resources Available for Program Evaluation

Chism and Szabó (1996) found that the most common limitation on program evaluation activity related to the resources necessary to conduct such studies. Their respondents' list of insufficient resources included time; staff with necessary methodological expertise; and funding for studies that involve transcription, postage, consumables, or other research resources in addition to time. Most TA development programs operate on tight funding and are likely to fit the profile reported in the study. Institutional research offices or other staff are seldom available to units who wish to evaluate.

Again, the Weimer and Lenze (1991) proposal, arguing that the most ambitious studies be done by professional researchers, and the more immediate, limited explorations be done at the program level, offers a practical solution to this issue.

Methodological Considerations

The distinction between basic research studies and program evaluation enters the picture yet again when research methods are considered. While past reviews of the effects of TA development interventions call for more systematic research, usually using controlled experimental design as the criteria for a good study, these reviews are focusing on results of specific interventions, rather than on program evaluation. Their intention is to generalize across settings rather than to assess a specific setting. In assessing TA development programs, methods that can be used in a natural setting, that are accessible to those without intensive background preparation in research, and that can generate patterns readily are most appropriate, at least for formative evaluation. It is no accident that TA programs have traditionally built their evaluation plan on the use of survey forms that can be collected following an activity and quickly tabulated to find mean ratings, or on responses to open-ended questions that can be summarized with minimal effort. These are approaches that work within the setting. Other approaches, such as telephone interviews, observations of teaching performance following a consultation, and analysis of subsequent student evaluations of teaching, are similarly more feasible in a program evaluation setting and for the purposes of program evaluation. They also reflect a shift in the educational research community over the past 20 years that has increasingly recognized the usefulness of naturalistic methods and action research in practice settings (Bogdan & Biklen, 1998).

DEVELOPING A PLAN FOR FORMATIVE EVALUATION

Since the overwhelming driving force for most faculty and TA program evaluation is the desire on the part of those involved to improve the program (Chism & Szabó, 1996), a primary consideration in developing an evaluation plan is the identification of strategies that will provide a continuous flow of information on how the program is performing relative to its goals. The information, when compared with goals, can help to assess progress, alert staff to unintended positive or negative effects, and promote reexamination of goals. Basic information systems on usage rates, the flow of resources, and user satisfaction are all important, as is pilot testing of new interventions.

To monitor usage rates, many programs have developed systems to track the number of TAs who use program services and some basic information on the TAs, such as their department or gender. Staff who work with the TAs can keep such records and submit them monthly, participants at workshops or seminars can sign in on an attendance sheet, and records of responses to publication requests and the like can be kept by staff. At given intervals, these data can be typed into a computer with the use of a simple database package that provides a template for entering the participant information and type of service. These records can be aggregated and sorted to generate monthly, quarterly, or yearly reports, which can easily be compared to previous periods to note changes. Such comparisons generate discussions about the nature of the services offered and the responses to them.

Similarly, ongoing fiscal controls, such as assigning an activity code to expenditures, can enable the program to track the resources that are being devoted to an activity. While this is cumbersome to apply to personnel, which is the main category of expense for most programs, it can be used quite easily with supplies and services categories, which are also the more flexible categories. Finding, for example, that the honorarium and travel expenses of an outside speaker at an event attended by 50 TAs resulted in a cost of $30 per participant and that a four-session seminar series on portfolios for 20 participants that involved $40 in copying and $80 for refreshments cost $6 per participant can help staff to discuss the benefits of each relative to their costs. Such ongoing discussions are crucial for continuous planning efforts.

Immediate user satisfaction is another kind of data that can inform ongoing efforts. While short, scaled, or open-ended item questionnaires administered at the time of service are most frequently employed to provide quick feedback on program effectiveness, other methods are available as well. Some programs use call-back systems following an event, assigning a student clerical assistant or other staff member to call participants a few days after an event or service to ask for their immediate feedback on the quality, usefulness, and other aspects of the service. Electronic mail can be used similarly. Some programs employ a variation of the popular Small Group Instructional Diagnosis (Clark & Bekey, 1979) at an event, assigning a TA or faculty member to hold a short oral feedback session at the end of the event, during which participants itemize what they found most and least effective and what suggestions they have for future changes.

Pilot testing of new interventions is also important as a formative evaluation approach. If seminars are to be offered repeatedly or a new publication is drafted, it makes sense to view the first offering or draft as tentative and to seek as much feedback from users so that the model or text can be revised in accordance with the perceptions and responses of the TAs. A simple feedback form attached to a publication draft or a short discussion held at the end of a pilot seminar can be useful vehicles for suggesting improvement.

Staff can discuss results of all of these continuous data collection strategies at periodic meetings and retreats for the purpose of making modifications or undertaking new directions.

DEVELOPING A PLAN FOR SUMMATIVE EVALUATION

At periodic intervals, decisions need to be made about the future direction of a program, its funding, its organizational position, or the like.

Often outside decision-makers, such as administrators or funding agencies, will be seeking information to make these decisions. This information will come from summative evaluation activities. Even though most of the information sought for formative evaluation is for a different purpose, when it is aggregated in the form of annual reports or trend data, it can be a source for summative evaluation as well. Developing a summative evaluation plan, therefore, entails finding ways of building on past data collection activities as well as conducting some new activities.

Generally, while formative evaluation activities usually are conducted by staff of the TA program, summative activities ideally rely on outside evaluators, such as consultants or appointed review committee members. Such activities usually begin with a self-study prepared by the program being evaluated. A clear statement of mission and goals is needed to frame the study. Performance information is also required. Again, data from ongoing usage, expenditure, and satisfaction documentation can form the basis of this report. Outside evaluators will also want to supplement these data with information collected specifically for their study. Frequently, outside evaluators rely on information gathered either from focus groups of faculty, TAs, administrators, or students or by interviews with stakeholders. They might also survey these constituencies or examine records kept by the program.

When sufficient information has been collected, the next task involves comparing the results with the goals of the program, expectations of administrators, and the performance of comparable programs within the institution or nationally and issuing a report or oral analysis that can be used to make decisions about the program's future. Svinicki, Kristensen, and Menges (1995) describe how such evaluations can be done by visiting teams.

Instances of such systematic summative evaluation reported by participants in Chism and Szabó's (1996) study were rare. A main reason given for the absence of formal summative evaluation was that funding is not generally available to pay consultants to do such evaluations. In light of this, one alternative is to convene a committee to perform an evaluation; another is to arrange for a reciprocal audit by a colleague in the field, exchanging self-studies and providing evaluative responses for each other. A graduate research assistant who is somewhat removed from the program's services can also be asked to collect data for summative purposes. Even when it is impossible to secure an outside evaluator, it is important to summarize ongoing patterns and ask broader questions periodically. These may sometimes be appended to climate surveys, institutional needs analysis instruments, or other information-gathering devices used by another office at the institution.

RECOMMENDATIONS

Many programs have already recognized the benefits of formative evaluation. It remains for them to continue to find ways to routinize ongoing data collection, devise practical ways of collecting additional information, and pursue occasions to reflect on these data in ways that will lead to program improvement.

As Chism and Szabó (1996) document, summative evaluation, entailing the expense of a more formal study, is performed systematically by fewer TA programs. In addition to expense, many programs assert that there are no institutional requirements for such evaluation, so they are under no pressure to arrange for summative evaluation. Even so, it is important to stress the benefits that periodic outside perspectives can bring to the work of TA development in a given setting. Advocacy as well as program enhancement can result, and while there may be no current pressures on the program to demonstrate its value, such evidence is often demanded on short notice. Having recent summative evaluation information is indeed an asset for any program.

In thinking about both formative and summative evaluation, it is important to review the literature for discussions of conceptual issues and for models. There are several discussions of design considerations in program evaluation in faculty and TA development settings that can stimulate thinking. These include Chism and Lumpkins (1995), Davey and Marion (1987), Ferren and Mussell (1987), Menges and Svinicki (1989), and Smith and Beno (1995).

It is more difficult to find models of program evaluation, since results of such evaluations are usually applicable only to the institution. (Smock is an example of one program description that does treat evaluation in some detail.) However, there are studies of specific program components that may be informative in program evaluation design. Proceedings from each of the national TA conferences (Chism, 1987; Heenan & Jerich, 1995; Lewis, 1993; Nyquist, Abbott, Wulff, & Sprague, 1991) are sources for such studies. For example, Duba-Beiderman (1991) studied effects of consultations that employed midterm analysis of teaching; Lenze (1993) studied effects of instructional preparation seminars; Jerich (1993) studied the effects of consultation using a clinical supervision model; and Jerich, Leinicke, and Pitstick (1995) studied the relative effects of a general course on teaching and a discipline-specific workshop. Some doctoral dissertations have also been done in this area, such as Oppenheim (1996), who studied the effects of an orientation for international teaching assistants. Other examples can be found throughout issues of *The Journal of Graduate Teaching Assistant Development.*

A final recommendation concerns resources. While it will always be important to find efficient and economic ways of conducting program evaluation, it is important to recognize in budgeting programs that some amount of funding has to be designated for this purpose. A rule of thumb with funded projects is 5% of the total budget. With more systematic attention to funding, design issues, and regular reporting, TA development programs can enhance their ability to understand the needs of their users, continuously refine their program offerings, document their effectiveness to decision-makers, and inform the profession of the effectiveness of various ways to help TAs as teachers.

REFERENCES

Abbott, R. D., Wulff, D. H., & Szago, C. K. (1989). Review of research on TA training. In J. D. Nyquist, R. D. Abbott, & D. H. Wulff (Eds.), *Teaching assistant training in the 1990s.* New Directions for Teaching and Learning, No. 39. San Francisco, CA: Jossey-Bass.

Bogdan, R. C., & Biklen, S. K. (1998). *Qualitative research in education* (3rd ed.). Boston, MA: Allyn and Bacon.

Boice, R. (1989, October). *Results of the 1989 survey of faculty development practices among POD members.* Handout distributed at the meeting of the Professional and Organizational Development Network in Higher Education, Jekyll Island, GA.

Carroll, J. G. (1980). Effects of training programs for university teaching assistants: A review of empirical research. *Journal of Higher Education, 51* (2), 167-183.

Centra, J. A. (1976). *Faculty development in U.S. colleges and universities.* Princeton, NJ: Educational Testing and Services. (ERIC Document Reproduction Service No. ED 141 382).

Chism, N. V. N. (Ed.). (1987). *Institutional responsibilities and responses in the employment and education of teaching assistants.* Columbus, OH: The Ohio State University, Center for Teaching Excellence.

Chism, N. V. N., & Lumpkins, T. (1995). The great TA program evaluation question: The pragmatic response of one center. In T. A. Heenan & K. F. Jerich (Eds.), *Teaching graduate students to teach: Engaging the disciplines.* Urbana-Champaign, IL: University of Illinois, Office of Conferences and Institutes.

Chism, N. V. N., & Szabó, B. L. (1996). *Research report: A study of how faculty development programs document their usage and evaluate their services.* Columbus, OH: The Ohio State University, Office of Faculty and TA Development.

Clark, J., & Bekey, J. (1979). Use of small groups in instructional evaluation. *POD Quarterly, 1,* 87-95.

Davey, K. B., & Marion, C. (1987). Evaluating TA development programs: Problems, issues, strategies. In N. V. N. Chism (Ed.), *Institutional responsibilities and responses in the employment and education of teaching assistants.* Columbus, OH: The Ohio State University, Center for Teaching Excellence.

Duba-Biederman, L. (1991). Changes in teaching behavior reported by teaching assistants after a midterm analysis of teaching. In J. D. Nyquist, R. D. Abbott, D. H. Wulff, & J. Sprague (Eds.), *Preparing the professoriate of tomorrow to teach.* Dubuque, IA: Kendall/Hunt.

Ferren, A., & Mussell, K. (1987). Strengthening faculty development programs through evaluation. *To Improve the Academy, 6,* 133-143.

Ford, W. (1993). Identification and validation of training needs for teaching assistants. In K. Lewis (Ed.), *The TA experience: Preparing for multiple roles.* Stillwater, OK: New Forums Press.

Gaff, J. G. (1975). *Toward faculty renewal: Advances in faculty, institutional, and organizational development.* San Francisco, CA: Jossey-Bass.

Gardener, E. S. (1985). *The relationship of student and teacher interaction, teacher training, and student perceptions of teaching effectiveness for university teaching assistants.* Unpublished doctoral dissertation, Texas A&M University, College Station, TX.

Heenan, T. A., & Jerich, K. F. (Eds.). (1995). *Teaching graduate students to teach: Engaging the disciplines.* Urbana-Champaign, IL: University of Illinois, Office of Conferences and Institutes.

Jerich, K. F. (1993). The use of a clinical supervision model for the training of graduate teaching assistants. In K. G. Lewis (Ed.), *The TA experience: Preparing for multiple roles.* Stillwater, OK: New Forums Press.

Jerich, K. F., Leinicke, L. M., & Pitstick, T. M. (1995). A comparative study of the instructional development of two groups of graduate teaching assistants in accounting. In T. A. Heenan & K. F. Jerich (Eds.), *Teaching graduate students to teach: Engaging the disciplines.* Urbana-Champaign, IL: University of Illinois, Office of Conferences and Institutes.

Lenze, L. F. (1993). Assessing the learning outcomes of instructional preparation seminars for TAs. In K. G. Lewis (Ed.), *The TA experience: Preparing for multiple roles.* Stillwater, OK: New Forums Press.

Levinson-Rose, J., & Menges, R. J. (1981). Improving college teaching: A critical review of research. *Review of Educational Research, 51* (3), 403-434.

Lewis, K. G. (1997, May). *Training focused on postgraduate teaching assistants: The North American model.* Invited paper presentation for a series of joint research seminars held by the Society for Research into Higher Education and the Committee of Vice-Chancellors and Principals of the Universities of the United Kingdom. London University, London, England.

Lewis, K. G. (Ed.). (1993). *The TA experience: Preparing for multiple roles.* Stillwater, OK: New Forums Press.

McMillan, J. H. (1975). The impact of instructional improvement agencies in higher education. *Journal of Higher Education, 46* (1), 17-23.

Menges, R. J., & Svinicki, M. D. (1989). Designing program evaluations: A circular model. *To Improve the Academy, 8,* 81-97.

Nyquist, J. D., Abbott, R. D., Wulff, D. H., & Sprague, J. (Eds.). (1991). *Preparing the professoriate of tomorrow to teach*. Dubuque, IA: Kendall/Hunt.

Oppenheim, N. (1996). *"Living through" an intercultural experience: Undergraduates learning from nonnative English-speaking teaching assistants*. Unpublished doctoral dissertation. University of Texas, Austin.

Piccinin, S., & Fairweather, D. (1996-97). A local analysis of TA training needs. *The Journal of Graduate Teaching Assistant Development, 4* (1), 23-33.

Rubino, A. N. (1994). *Faculty development programs and evaluation in American colleges and universities*. Unpublished doctoral dissertation, Western Michigan University, Kalamazoo, MI.

Scriven, M. (1973). The methodology of evaluation. In B. Worthen & J. Sanders (Eds.), *Educational evaluation: Theory and practice*. Belmont, CA: Wadsworth.

Smith, C., & Beno, B. (1995). Evaluating staff development programs. *Journal of Staff, Program, & Organization Development, 12* (3), 173-184.

Smock, R. (1980, October). *The development and impact of the campus teaching program*. Paper presented at the conference of the Professional and Organizational Development Network, Berkeley, CA.

Svinicki, M. D., Kristensen, E., & Menges, R. J. (1995, June). *Team visitation: A model for evaluating faculty development programs*. Paper presented at the National Conference on Assessment and Quality, American Association for Higher Education, Boston, MA.

Weimer, M. (1990). *Improving college teaching*. San Francisco, CA: Jossey-Bass.

Weimer, M., & Lenze, L. F. (1991). Instructional interventions: A review of the literature on efforts to improve instruction. In J. C. Smart (Ed.), *Higher education: Handbook of theory and research, 7,* 294-333. New York, NY: Agathon.

15

TA Certificate Programs

Stacey Lane Tice, Patricia H. Featherstone, and Howard C. Johnson

American postsecondary institutions have been growing increasingly concerned with the quality of education they provide. Locally initiated assessment efforts and public outcry have led faculty and administrators to reexamine both undergraduate and graduate curricula. To enhance the quality of graduate education, many institutions are developing programs to better prepare graduate students for their careers, including careers as faculty. As a result, many institutions are developing Preparing Future Faculty programs, described in Chapter 16. One possible component of these programs is a certificate in college or university teaching.

Purposes and Benefits of Certificate Programs

While the reasons for establishing a certificate program are dependent on several contextual variables, including the nature of the institution, the field of study, and the department or academic unit, the following are the most often cited reasons:

- To extend existing TA training efforts

- To reconceptualize graduate education to include preparation for both the creation of knowledge (research) and the dissemination of knowledge (teaching)

- To provide a more systematic preparation of graduate students for all phases of academic careers

- To involve faculty in the preparation of graduate students for academic positions

- To enhance the collaboration between centralized and departmental efforts to prepare graduate students for teaching

- To document teaching effectiveness

- To provide a tangible award that recognizes the completion of a formal preparation for college or university teaching

By going beyond traditional TA training programs, certificate programs offer other advantages. In many disciplines, the academic job market is very tight, and institutions are looking for ways to better prepare their graduates so that they will obtain positions. A certificate program can prepare participating graduate students to step into junior faculty positions with an awareness of what such positions entail, and the knowledge and experience to succeed. It is also necessary for graduate students to be well prepared to do both research and teaching. Certificate programs are well placed to address this need, particularly when they have an interdisciplinary component. Seminars and workshops can be offered to students from across campus or from all departments within a school or college. When such seminars are supplemented with department-specific workshops, students benefit from the expertise and experience of the best researchers and the best teachers that the wider resources make available.

When certificate programs incorporate these kinds of activities, they are well placed to provide graduate students with a systematic preparation for all aspects of academic careers. Enhanced collaboration between departmental and centralized components of graduate education is likely to be an additional benefit. Because of their focus on teaching, certificate programs require a mentored teaching component that often goes beyond the typical TA experience, requiring faculty involvement as mentors. The kind and extent of mentoring varies across, and sometimes even within, departments. There are, however, common elements; e. g., class observations and follow-up discussions, videotaping of classes, graduate students visiting their mentors' classes, and—perhaps most importantly—discussions about teaching both within and across departments. Certificate programs can also encourage the documentation of teaching effectiveness. A teaching portfolio, or in some cases a professional portfolio, is the most widely used documentation (see Chapter 13).

IMPLEMENTING CERTIFICATE PROGRAMS

In determining whether or not a certificate program is appropriate for an institution, there are several factors to consider:

1) The rationale for establishing a certificate program may vary depending on the needs of the institution. The specifics are not as important as ensuring that the design, development, and implementation are appropriate for the rationale. For example, in order for a certificate program to be a useful tool in the reconsideration of graduate education, the graduate faculty must be intimately involved in the development and implementation of the program. While administrators and graduate students can play an important role, it will be impossible to alter curricula or the ethos of a department or institution without significant contributions from the faculty.

2) Certificate programs can be used to extend existing efforts but should take advantage of the strengths of preexisting efforts. They often provide an opportunity to build on strengths and rethink practices. Given this strategy, it is imperative that there is "buy in" or investment in the new efforts from those who are involved in current TA training programs.

3) As a means for documenting teaching effectiveness, a certificate program is only as valuable as the assumptions and definitions of what constitutes effective teaching. In fact, it is optimal to design a certificate program that initiates and sustains discussions about what constitutes effective teaching.

4) In order for a certificate program to promote the professional readiness of graduate students for academic careers, it must be integrated into the graduate curriculum. In other words, if preparation for university teaching is to be given due consideration, it should be included in the student's program of study.

5) For a certificate program to be sustainable, it should be flexible enough to allow for evolution.

TYPES OF PROGRAMS

In recent years, certificates in university and college teaching have gained popularity. In the mid-1980s, the University of California,

Davis, established a seminar series titled "A Closer Look at University Teaching," which culminated in a certificate of completion (Davis, 1987). This effort served as the basis for the Program of College Teaching, developed in 1990 (Baker & Davis, 1993). Since that time, many institutions in North America have developed and implemented certificate programs, while many other institutions are in the process of doing so.

The certificate programs that universities have in place vary in a number of ways and have different components developed to suit each university's institutional, disciplinary, and departmental needs. There are, however, some common elements. One is some kind of mentored or supervised teaching experience. Another is the construction of a teaching or professional portfolio. Most programs also include workshops, seminars, or coursework, organized and run by a central office such as the graduate school or by academic departments or programs. The time at which the certificate is awarded also varies from program to program.

Academic Degree Program

One type of certificate program is the academic degree program such as the University of New Hampshire's Master of Science in Teaching with a major in college teaching. Academic degree programs require course work, perhaps as much as 32 credit-hours in approved courses, some of which are required and some of which are electives. The courses typically cover such issues as teaching at the college and university level, teaching in the student's discipline or field, and other subjects related to preparation to be a faculty member. Another important component of degree programs is a supervised teaching experience that involves classroom visits and meetings with a teaching mentor. The construction of a teaching portfolio is also a component of most degree programs.

University-Wide with Disciplinary Variation

A second type of certificate program has university-wide standards but allows for disciplinary variations. For example, the Graduate Teacher Certification Program at the University of Colorado at Boulder is offered by the graduate school, which sets the requirements, keeps the records, and offers through the Graduate Teacher Program the workshops that students must complete for certification. The discipline-specific component requires teaching assistant training courses or workshops and a documented faculty/teaching assistant mentoring relationship, but departments can handle these aspects of the program in a variety of ways. The University of California, Davis's year-long Program in College Teaching is similar. At its core a mentored teaching experience, it also requires participants to design a set of individualized learning contracts and to participate in a series of teaching roundtables. It is interesting to note that this program, like the one at the University of Wyoming, combines centralized activities and individual student plans.

University-Wide with Departmental Standards

A third type of program is university-wide with departmental standards, such as we find at the State University of New York at Binghamton and Syracuse University. At Binghamton, individual graduate programs decide whether or not their students are eligible to participate in the program, which consists of four components: 1) university-wide workshops, which include the teaching assistant orientation, professional development meetings, and colloquia on issues related to teaching; 2) discipline-specific activities, such as teaching practica, courses on pedagogical theories, and professional development meetings; 3) guided teaching; and 4) the teaching portfolio, developed in consultation with the program advisor or teaching supervisor. The Syracuse University program is described in detail later in this chapter.

University-Wide with Option of Student Design

A fourth kind of program is university-wide but allows students to design their own programs within the university guidelines, such as the Program in College Teaching at the University of Wyoming.

EXAMPLES OF CERTIFICATE PROGRAMS

University of New Hampshire

The University of New Hampshire offers a university-wide Future Faculty Program, coordinated by the office of the dean of the graduate school, which involves the University Teaching Excellence Program and faculty from across campus. The program is designed to better prepare graduate students for careers in higher education, focusing in particular on their future roles as classroom instructors and faculty members in colleges and universities. The program is also designed to complement and enhance existing degree programs by providing students the opportunity to develop formal competencies in college teaching. The Future Faculty Program offers two academic programs: 1) the Cognate in College Teaching, and 2) the Master of Science in Teaching (MST) with a major in college teaching.

The Cognate in College Teaching. The cognate program emphasizes the development of classroom teaching skills in a specific field or discipline. Doctoral students add the Cognate in College Teaching to their degree; they are eligible for admission to the program after one year of graduate study and upon recommendation of the coordinator of their graduate program. (Special permission is required for students to add the cognate to a master's degree.)

Awarded with the doctoral degree, the cognate requires the satisfactory completion of 12 academic credits from three components: 1) a core requirement of three credits earned in the one-credit course, "Issues in University Teaching," which is offered each semester and in the summer; 2) an approved three-credit course related to teaching in the student's discipline; and 3) a teaching requirement, a three-credit teaching praxis course which is taken twice and which is supervised by a faculty committee appointed by the dean of the graduate school.

The Master of Science in Teaching with a Major in College Teaching. This program builds upon the classroom teaching emphasis included in the cognate and adds to it courses related to the broader role of the professor as teacher, scholar, and member of the academy. A 32 credit-hour program available to Ph.D. students as a joint degree, it has four components: 1) the "Issues in University Teaching" course, 2) the "Research in College Teaching" course, 3) a field or disciplinary requirement, and 4) the teaching portfolio. The degree is awarded after all requirements for the Ph.D. have been completed.

Syracuse University
In 1991, Syracuse University established the Future Professoriate Project, which entails three initiatives: 1) seminars to assist faculty in their efforts to better mentor graduate students for future faculty positions; 2) an advanced teaching apprentice experience, called a teaching associateship; and 3) a Certificate in University Teaching.

Certificate in University Teaching. The Certificate in University Teaching was created in order to provide an organized, well-defined program of professional development which culminates in 1) a teaching or professional portfolio, a document that contains evidence of teaching effectiveness; and 2) a tangible award which documents the student's accomplishments. It provides a means for formalizing the process of preparing graduate students for future faculty positions, a process which emphasizes high-quality interactions between supervising faculty and teaching associates.

The Certificate in University Teaching is awarded to teaching associates who pursue a program of professional development that results in the documentation of their preparation to assume a teaching position at a college or university. While the certificate is awarded jointly by the graduate school and the teaching associate's academic department, the specific requirements for the certificate are established by the faculty of each academic department. Requirements of the teaching associates often include: 1) working closely with a faculty teaching mentor in advanced teaching assignments, 2) having the mentor observe and formally critique their teaching, 3) coordinating teaching workshops for the department, 4) mentoring new teaching assistants in their department, 5) developing a teaching or professional portfolio, and 6) requesting a comprehensive written assessment of their performance from the faculty teaching mentor(s).

As a key element of the certificate, the portfolio has become an important component of the graduate education of those students who are interested in pursuing academic careers. The value lies in both the process of developing a portfolio and the final product. Often, through portfolio development, faculty members and graduate students engage in substantive discussions about pedagogy and other issues of professional development. While the specific content of a portfolio varies from discipline to discipline and individual to individual, some common elements include a reflective statement about teaching or a philosophy of teaching; copies of syllabi, examinations, course materials, and critiqued student papers; student, peer, and faculty evaluations of teaching; teaching awards; evidence of special teaching-related projects; and videotapes of teaching.

Completed portfolios are reviewed by the faculty of the academic department and the graduate school prior to the awarding of the certificate. The graduate school has a library of over 100 teaching and professional portfolios.

In telephone interviews of over 70 Syracuse University alumni who participated in the Future Professoriate Project, virtually every participant commented about the value of assembling the portfolio. Over 50% noted that they had used all or part of their portfolio when they were on the job market, and they felt that it was helpful to them. Some typical comments follow: "The most positive aspect of the portfolio was as a tool of reflection," "Constructing a portfolio helps to organize thinking and helps one speak coherently about accomplishments," "The process of assembling my portfolio was very time consuming yet valuable," and "I assembled the portfolio by myself, but I looked at another student's in the department for some ideas. My mentor was very helpful; she looked over my portfolio a number of times. It was a growing process. It was thin when it started, but now it is quite large."

The University of Wyoming

Program in College Teaching. The University of Wyoming offers the Program in College Teaching, which is a cooperative effort between the graduate school and the Center for Teaching Excellence. The program is a self-designed, one-credit-per-semester program that consists of five components. Designed to help master's and Ph.D. students become better instructors while they are graduate students at the University of Wyoming, and also to prepare them to enter the classroom with high-level teaching skills when they become college or university faculty, the certificate is awarded upon the successful completion of the program requirements. The certificate, which includes a general description of the program and a summary of the student's individualized program plan, is typically awarded approximately halfway through the degree program.

Students are eligible to apply to the program after they have completed their first semester of study at the university. They submit an individualized plan to the program advisory committee through the dean of the graduate school or the director of the Center for Teaching Excellence and then meet with the committee to orally present their plan and explain any modifications to the basic design. Students are expected to consult with their graduate advisors or selected mentors as they develop the plan of action.

The program has five components:

1) Participation in an extensive teaching seminar for new teaching assistants, held at the beginning of each academic year

2) A set of five agreed-upon activities designed by each student in the

context of his or her own goals. The students design a plan of action that describes what they plan to do for each of the selected activities, how they will document these activities for their supervisors and their portfolio, and who the supervisor will be. The five activities are selected from the following:

- Preparing to teach, including course design and syllabi, teaching strategies, and evaluating student learning

- Accommodating diversity and providing equality in the classroom

- Helping students outside the classroom, including office hours, academic advising, and personal counseling

- Considering the ethics of the academy

- Planning professional development, including institutional, disciplinary, and professional resources

- Understanding the academic career

- Continuing to develop a personal teaching philosophy

3) A mentored teaching experience where an approved faculty mentor works one-on-one with the student to review the teaching experience.

4) A "reinvestment" agreement, in which the student agrees to share with a designated audience a teaching technique, a newly discovered process, a result from research conducted during the activity agreement, or some similar outcome.

5) The development and maintenance of a teaching portfolio. No specific format for the portfolio is required, but it should take into account the individual student's goals and preparation as a teacher and reflect the student's growth and effectiveness as a teacher. At the conclusion of the program, the portfolio is made available to the advisory committee. There may also be an opportunity at the end of the year to share the portfolio with other program participants.

In addition to these five components, participants must enroll for one credit-hour in the "Practicum in College Teaching." Participants in the program must be regularly registered graduate students and must complete all requirements, with the exception of the teaching seminar, while they are admitted members of the program.

LIMITATIONS OF CERTIFICATE PROGRAMS

As just described, certificate programs have been successfully employed on several campuses. It is also true that several institutions have explored the possibility of initiating a certificate program and have elected to accomplish their goals through other means. Indiana University, for example, had developed a certificate program but decided not to implement it when they joined the Preparing Future Faculty program. Others have been concerned about one or more of the following:

- That certificate programs are too job-market oriented and have become more about learning how to make oneself look good and less about professional development

- That in the attempt to document effective teaching it becomes too easy to focus on measurable pedagogical skills instead of the more illusive "scholarship of teaching"

- That involvement in certificate programs may result in graduate students taking longer to complete their studies

- That variations among certificate programs make it unclear what they represent

- That a lack of evidence about the effectiveness of certificate programs may limit their job market value

- That there is a lack of certainty about what exactly is being certified beyond completion of a program

On the other hand, well-conceived certificate programs have the potential of serving as a tool for promoting professional development and of being an asset on the academic job market. In a personal letter of April 8, 1997, one recent graduate of the Syracuse University program wrote that the Certificate in University Teaching was "one of the things that set me apart from the other two, equally qualified candidates under consideration."

CONCLUSION

As postsecondary institutions look for ways to ensure that their graduates are as well prepared as possible for their future careers, in particular careers in the academy, they are moving beyond the TA training already in place. Many institutions are finding that certificate programs are an effective way to meet this need. Because such programs are formalized, they provide a structure for systematic preparation in all phases of graduate professional development. They also enhance collaboration between centralized and departmental efforts. Certificate programs involve faculty in the students' professional development, especially as mentors but also in the increased number of conversations about teaching that take place within departments and in campus-wide seminars and workshops. An important component of certificate programs is the development of a teaching portfolio, which students can use to document their teaching effectiveness. Although the main rewards for student participants in certificate programs are intrinsic—many students report that participation itself enables them to compete for positions with the knowledge that they are well prepared as researchers and as teachers—there is also a tangible reward, a certificate that recognizes the completion of a formal preparation for college or university teaching.

REFERENCES

Baker, J. B. II, & Davis, W. E. (1993). Beyond the teaching assistantship: Mentoring the next generation of faculty. In K. G. Lewis (Ed.), *The TA experience: Preparing for multiple roles.* Stillwater, OK: New Forums Press.

Davis, W. E. (1987). TA training: Professional development for future faculty. In N. V. N. Chism (Ed.), *Employment and education of teaching assistants.* Columbus, OH: The Ohio State University.

INSTITUTIONAL CONTACTS

Below is a selective list of institutions that offer certificate programs in university teaching.

Binghamton University
Name: Susan Strehle
Address: P.O. Box 6000
        Binghamton, NY 13902-6000
Telephone number: (607) 777-2070
Email address: sstrehle@binghamton.edu

The University of California, Davis
Name: Will Davis
Address: Teaching Resources Center
        One Shield Ave.
        Davis, CA 95616
Telephone number: (530) 752-6050
Email address: will.davis@ucdavis.edu

The University of Colorado at Boulder
Name: Laura T. Border
Address: Graduate Teaching Program
        Box 362, Norlin S461
        Boulder, CO 80309-0362
Telephone number: (303) 492-4902
Email address: border@spot.colorado.edu

Cornell University
Name: Katherine Gottschalk
Address: J. S. Knight Writing Program
        159 Goldwin Smith Hall
        Cornell University
        Ithaca, NY 14853
Telephone number: (607) 255-4061
Email address: kkg1@cornell.edu

Florida State University
Name: Tracy J. Bestor
Address: Ctr. for Prof. Devel.
        Florida State University
        Tallahasee, FL 32306-1640
Telephone number: (850) 644-7550
Email address: tbestor@cpd.fsu.edu

Loyola University, Chicago
Name: Marie Rosin-Dittmar
Address: School of Education
        1041 Ridge Road
        Wilmette, IL 60091
Telephone number: (847) 853-3323
Email address: mrosind@wpo.it.luc.edu

The University of Manitoba
Name: Beverley Cameron
Address: 220 Sinnott Bldg.
        70 Dysart Road
        Winnipeg, MB R3T 2N2
Telephone number: (204) 474-7025
Email address: bcamero@cc.umanitoba.ca

The University of Minnesota
Name: Janice Smith
Address: Center for Teaching & Learning
        120 Fraser Hall
        106 Pleasant St. SE
        Minneapolis, MN 55455-0433
Telephone number: (612) 625-3389
Email address: pff@tc.umn.edu

The University of New Hampshire
Name: Lee Seidel
Address: UNH Teaching Excellence
        Program
        11 Brook Way
        Durham, NH 03824
Telephone number: (603) 862-0233
Email address: teaching.excellence@unh.edu

Syracuse University
Name: Stacey Lane Tice
Address: The Graduate School
        Suite 303 Bowne Hall
        Syracuse, NY 13244-1200
Telephone number: (315) 443-5012
Email address: sltice@summon.syr.edu

University of Wyoming
Name: Donald Warder
Address: The Graduate School
        P.O. Box 3108
        Laramie, WY 82071-3108
Telephone number: (307) 766-2287
Email address: dwarder@uwyo.edu

16

PREPARING FUTURE FACULTY PROGRAMS: BEYOND TA DEVELOPMENT

Stacey Lane Tice, Jerry G. Gaff, and Anne S. Pruitt-Logan

The quality of graduate preparation for the professoriate is of growing concern. Over the past decade, at least two initiatives have addressed the preparation of students who aspire to the professoriate—teaching assistant (TA) development programs and Preparing Future Faculty programs. An examination of these programs indicates that they both focus on graduate students—one on support for the teaching that graduate students do at their universities and the other on the preparation they receive for their future careers. This chapter examines two types of programs for points of intersection and offers suggestions for making the transition from a TA development program to a faculty preparation program, which we regard as both possible and necessary.

TEACHING ASSISTANT DEVELOPMENT PROGRAMS

A significant portion of introductory courses offered at research universities are taught by teaching assistants (Eble, 1987; Syverson & Tice, 1993). For many years, teaching assistantships were regarded as a means of providing financial support for graduate study as well as an inexpensive way of augmenting the supply of instructors. Little regard was given to the impact of TAs on undergraduate education or to how this experience could prepare them for future academic careers. Recently, public demand for improved quality and greater accountability in undergraduate education has made the quality of teaching a major concern. At the same time, interest has developed in the potential of teaching assistantships for the preparation of faculty.

In the 1970s and 1980s, in response to requests from teaching assistants for more support for their classroom responsibilities, many universities organized TA training programs. These programs, which became prototypes, provided a valuable introduction to teaching and came to be regarded as a necessary first step in TA development. As TA development efforts have matured, becoming campus-wide and centralized, greater numbers of universities are offering comprehensive year-round programming on a variety of teaching and learning topics. The programs include university-wide and departmental seminars and workshops, mid-semester feedback surveys, outstanding TA awards programs, consultation services, TA newsletters, teaching portfolios, and certificate programs (Lambert, 1993)—the wide range of activities that are the subject of this book. According to Boyer (1990), "Teaching assistant programs, perhaps more than any other, are crucial in the preparation of future faculty" (p. 71).

Beginning in 1986, the National Consortium on Preparing Graduate Students as College Teachers began a series of biannual national TA conferences. These forums provided opportunities to discuss graduate education and examine programs designed to promote the education and employment of graduate teaching assistants. These conferences have evolved to include more of a disciplinary focus, involving faculty, graduate students, and deans from many different fields of study. The TA development programs featured components of cognitive learning theory, pedagogical issues, attention to the learning environment, and the diversity of the student population (Weimer, Svinicki, & Bauer, 1989; Chism, Cano, & Pruitt, 1989).

The 1990s brought a more intentional focus to preparing graduate students for future faculty positions—not as a by-product of TA development, but rather as an integral part of their doctoral studies. This shift was signaled by the 1991 survey of the Council of Graduate Schools membership and publication of *Preparing Graduate Students to Teach: A Guide to Programs That Improve Undergraduate Education and Develop Tomorrow's Faculty* (Lambert & Tice, 1993). Sponsored by the Council of Graduate Schools, TIAA-CREF, and the Pew Charitable Trusts and published by the American Association for Higher Education, the guide analyzed programs to support graduate students in carrying out their current teaching responsibilities.

The study revealed that most universities had some type of TA development program, and that virtually every institution had some combination of centralized and departmental efforts (Syverson & Tice, 1993). At that time, 83% of the centralized programs were less than ten years old, with nearly 60% having been developed in the past one to four years. In contrast, the departmental programs had a longer tradition, with 51% in existence for more than 11 years. Most comprehensive programs focused attention on both content and how the content was presented to maximize student learning (Lambert, 1993). Leadership for centralized programs came primarily from one of three sources: faculty and TA development centers; graduate schools; and, less frequently, schools of education. Longer-standing departmental programs were established and often led by one or two faculty members in the department (Syverson & Tice, 1993). When asked about barriers to carrying out their programs, leaders of TA development cited the ethos of the university and/or department, the hegemony of research, and the low regard accorded teaching in research universities. Faculty leaders of TA programs in particular have commented about their feelings of isolation and belief that their departmental programs would be crippled if they did not continue their personal involvement (Hutchings, 1993).

PREPARING FUTURE FACULTY PROGRAMS

Increasingly, leaders in TA development and national educational organizations have determined that discussion needed to focus not only on graduate student preparation for their current teaching but on their professional development for academic careers, of which teaching is only one component. Gaff and Lambert (1996) write:

> Traditional doctoral study prepares graduate students to be better students, in the classic sense of the term, that is, to conduct studies. TA training prepares students to be better teaching assistants, and to the extent that the assignments are meaningful and support is provided, perhaps better college teachers. Preparing Future Faculty programs prepare graduate students to be better assistant professors, an outcome that subsumes the other two (p. 44).

Further, a serious mismatch exists between the research universities where faculty members are trained and the institutions where they will work. Only 102 research universities award 80% of all doctorates. Most faculty positions are in the over 3,000 other institutions with very different missions, student bodies, and faculty roles than those at research universities. Acquainting graduate students with this variety of institutions is important in helping them clarify their career options since fewer than 10% of new Ph.D.s secure faculty positions at research universities. Clearly, the students need to know how to succeed in those other settings (Gaff & Lambert, 1996).

Doing original research is a necessary but not sufficient condition for faculty success. Boyer's publication of *Scholarship Reconsidered: Priorities for the Professoriate* (1990) prompted faculty members to discuss and expand the meaning of scholarly work. Many people agree that in addition to original research in a particular discipline, scholarly work includes integration of knowledge across fields, application of knowledge to practical problems, and knowledge about effective teaching and learning strategies in the discipline. Efforts to remake the reward structures to address this broader definition of scholarly work are being undertaken within disciplines and on individual campuses (Adam & Roberts, 1993).

Regardless of the institution, virtually all new faculty members rate their work as stressful, primarily because of the pressure of finding enough time to get everything done (Boice, 1992; Turner & Boice, 1989; Fink, 1984; Sorcinelli, 1992; Whitt, 1991). To some extent this time pressure results from the sense that everything is equally important and an inability to set priorities. The cost of recruiting new faculty, decreased mobility in academic careers, and the stress on new faculty hires all argue for better preparation and careful selection. Graduate students can begin learning to integrate teaching, research, and service during their graduate years and thereby can be prepared to assign relative value to different priorities when they take their first position.

Several programs have been specially designed to help socialize future faculty and to create a smoother transition from graduate school to a faculty position. These programs seek to better prepare graduate students for research, teaching, and service responsibilities. They include:

- Preparing Graduate Students for the Professional Responsibilities of College Teachers, sponsored by the Association of American Colleges

- Preparing Future Faculty, sponsored by the Council of Independent Colleges

- Future Professoriate Project, sponsored by Syracuse University

- Compact for Faculty Diversity, sponsored by the New England Board of Higher Education, the Southern Regional Education Board, and the Western Interstate Commission for Higher Education

- Preparing Future Faculty, sponsored by the Association of American Colleges and Universities and the Council of Graduate Schools

- Preparing Future Professors: A New York State Consortium Project, a collaboration with Cornell University, New York University, the State University of New York at Binghamton and at Stony Book, and Syracuse University

  Each of these initiatives received substantial support from the Pew Charitable Trusts or the Fund for the Improvement of Postsecondary Education.

The programs share several elements including:

- Mentoring of graduate students by faculty members (Gaff & Lambert, 1996)

- Attention to the developmental stages of the graduate student (Sprague & Nyquist, 1991)

- Increasingly independent and varied teaching experiences (Gaff & Lambert, 1996)

- Development of portfolios to demonstrate the range and effectiveness of professional experiences (Lambert, 1996; Seldin, 1997)

- TA training efforts that serve as the groundwork (Pruitt, 1996)

- Efforts to achieve a balance of research, teaching, and service demands (Gaff & Lambert, 1996)

In addition, the Association of American Colleges and Universities (AAC&U) and the Council of Graduate Schools (CGS) Preparing Future Faculty (PFF) program includes partnerships between research universities and clusters of diverse, primarily undergraduate institutions. According to Gaff and Pruitt (1996), "This arrangement brings the consumers of Ph.D. programs into contact with the producers and provides opportunities for graduate students to gain personal experience with different types of institutions, faculty cultures, and student bodies" (p. 12). Each of the clusters develops programs tailored to its own particular needs and circumstances. All programs incorporate a broader vision of graduate preparation and provide graduate students with experience in often overlooked aspects of faculty life. Mentored experiences with faculty members from partner institutions allow graduate students to experience firsthand the expectations and values inherent in university teaching and service, particularly in the university's governance system. Classes and seminars also introduce students to central academic traditions, such as academic freedom and tenure, the concept of shared governance, and the idea and practice of liberal education.

Examples of Preparing Future Faculty Program Activities

Each PFF cluster of institutions has developed its own specific activities. The activities are located in individual departments, across the university, and on partner campuses. Some require relatively short time commitments, such as attending a series of seminars in the course of the academic year. Others are extensive and require enrollment in courses, weekend activities, and routine travel to another campus.

Examples of departmental PFF activities include:

- Forums for faculty members to describe and analyze their professional lives

- Discussions with doctoral alumni about how their careers do or do not connect with what they did in their graduate program

- Courses on teaching specific disciplines

- Seminars on professional issues

- The revision of doctoral program guidelines to provide PFF experiences for students planning academic careers

- Forums to discuss faculty histories, career paths, and alternative professional lifestyles

- Supporting graduate students who attend professional meetings and make presentations with faculty

> *There are a couple of things my mentor did that sort of inspired me. One was going to a local conference of our national association. As a graduate student, I simply had not made it a high priority. It really helped quite a bit to go to one of these conferences with someone who had gone before and knew people and had a connection to that experience. That was an important part of the mentoring experience that I realized I would like to pass on to my students. [A doctoral student in archeological studies and religion at the University of Minnesota (Pruitt-Logan & Gaff, 1996).]*

Campus-wide PFF activities include:

- Seminars on general issues in college teaching

- Seminars on professional and career issues taught by faculty and administrators from different institutions and held on different campuses

- Discussing teaching in a multicultural setting

- Certificate programs in PFF or teaching and noting these accomplishments on students' transcripts

- Reviewing academic governance systems and inviting graduate students to attend faculty meetings or committee meetings

- Providing TAs with "promotion" opportunities with titles and pay to reflect expanded responsibilities or professional growth

- Helping students develop portfolios documenting expertise in teaching, research, and service

- Training faculty how to mentor students in areas beyond research

> *My mentor took me to these meetings of women who were either coming up for tenure or who had just gotten tenure. It was really useful to hear. It was really reassuring. It was nice to know that there's a support network. It was a chance to go up and talk to these women who were deans. [A doctoral student in geography at the University of Minnesota (Pruitt-Logan & Gaff, 1996).]*

On partner campuses, graduate students:

- Discuss the distinctive institutional missions and different academic cultures

- Work with a teaching mentor

- Teach a unit or entire course and get feedback

- Attend faculty, committee, or departmental meetings and discuss their interpretations

- Shadow professors or academic administrators and discuss the activities observed

- Discuss the graduate school experience with undergraduate students

- Participate in faculty development activities

> *I came to understand how important and how small faculty committees can be. I didn't realize until I got there (a partner campus) that they were deciding the actual curriculum for everyone. . . . It was pretty neat topic—a computer requirement for the students, regardless of discipline. [A doctoral student in physics at the University of Minnesota (Pruitt-Logan & Gaff, 1996).]*

Because they seek to redefine graduate education to include a more balanced preparation for a faculty position, faculty preparation programs necessitate changes in the graduate curriculum. Thus, the dean of the graduate school, as well as departmental faculty, typically provides leadership for these programs. The success of these efforts may be directly tied to the ability of the graduate dean and respected departmental faculty to elicit the support and involvement of other faculty in their departments and at partner institutions. These contributors often work closely with the director of the TA or faculty development program.

Successful faculty preparation programs provide graduate students with a better understanding of faculty roles and of diverse institutions. This understanding, in conjunction with participation in a strong TA development program and collaboration with faculty mentors, results in graduate students who are better prepared to succeed as future faculty members. An investment in such programs during graduate study has the potential to decrease stress among new faculty, to enable greater contributions at an earlier time, and to save hiring institutions the time and money invested in hiring new faculty who are not prepared to succeed in their institutions.

BENEFITS OF FACULTY PREPARATION PROGRAMS

Early assessment results from Syracuse University's Future Professoriate Project (FPP) and the AAC&U and CGS Preparing Future Faculty (PFF) program indicate that graduate students are reaping benefits from involvement in both these programs. At Syracuse University, telephone interviews with more than 70 alumni who had participated in the Future Professoriate Project revealed that over 90% had secured employment in the type of position they were seeking. Virtually every participant said they believed that their involvement in the FPP had been helpful to them in securing their positions and succeeding in them. In both the PFF and FPP programs, the participants said that they developed greater sophistication about the professoriate. One student cited the most valuable benefit as "Listening to and taking part in a sustained, complex, and meaningful discussion of the profession from a number of institutional perspectives" (Pruitt-Logan & Gaff, 1996).

In fact, it was not uncommon to hear that involvement in these programs was one of the highlights of participants' careers as graduate students. In the words of an English student,

> *My experience as a graduate assistant with the PFF project has been one of the highlights—if not the highlight—of my doctoral study.... To be honest, I was a little uncertain how the experience would pan out, considering that I was an advanced doctoral candidate finishing up my dissertation. I expected that I would be hearing a number of things I had already heard.... What I soon learned, however, was that [the university's] mission was not the mission of many other colleges and universities. In the end, I believe it was my participation in the PFF project that was the key factor in my being offered a tenure-track assistant professor position in the English department at [a comprehensive state institution]. (Pruitt-Logan & Gaff, 1996)*

The PFF program conducted surveys of graduate student participants in 1995 and 1996. The students regarded the program as worthwhile; out of 357 surveyed, all but three said that they would recommend the PFF program to other students. Many noted the value of working with partner institutions in improving their teaching. Their experiences highlighted the need for good teaching, and work with their faculty mentors enabled them to learn about their own strengths and weaknesses. For instance, one student said the greatest benefit he gained was that "I have improved my teaching skills and my understanding of the needs of students," and another cited "Confidence regarding my own teaching methods" (Pruitt-Logan & Gaff, 1996). They also noted an increased understanding of the nature of faculty work and, in particular, the need to juggle varied responsibilities. Representative quotes include: "Demystified the multiple roles of professor," "gained knowledge of the job search," and "learned more about diverse institutions," "... about liberal arts colleges," "... about community colleges" (Pruitt-Logan & Gaff, 1996). Others reported the value of working with faculty members and graduate students in their own academic department as well as in other departments on campus (Pruitt-Logan & Gaff, 1997).

The PFF program also inquired about the experiences of faculty members at partner institutions. At first blush, it might appear that faculty at other institutions have little to gain by mentoring graduate students. But it has turned out to be a valuable stimulus to the professional development of the faculty. One said, "I view it as a 'generative' activity—passing information, ideas, expertise to the next generation of scholar-teachers" (Pruitt-Logan & Gaff, 1996). Other predictable benefits were cited: "the intellectual stimulation," "the challenge of 'sharing' a course," "stimulated my thinking about my own pedagogy," and "energized my teaching" (Pruitt-Logan & Gaff, 1996). Graduate faculty, too, mentioned several benefits, including "a reminder to make sure our students learn more than how to do research," "have met some interesting new colleagues," "new ideas," and "made teaching a more prominent department concern" (Pruitt-Logan & Gaff, 1996).

Early indicators are that these programs have a positive effect on recruitment of top quality graduate students to institutions that offer a faculty preparation program; on retention of graduate students as they become more fully involved in their department; and on placement in an academic position (DeNeef, 1996; Gaff & Pruitt-Logan, 1998).

In sum, while TA development programs assist students in their work with undergraduates, faculty preparation programs increase the competence and confidence of graduate students as teachers. Further, they give graduate students the opportunity to expand their teaching repertoire by teaching in other institutions with different missions and student bodies and to learn more about faculty life in a number of institutions.

INTERSECTIONS OF FACULTY PREPARATION AND TA DEVELOPMENT PROGRAMS

Perhaps the most important commonality in both programs is that they seek to improve the quality of undergraduate instruction. Motivated by this common purpose and the importance of preparing future faculty to be well-rounded teachers, the lines between the programs may blur and the rhetoric may mask differences. What one institution identifies as a TA program might be considered a faculty preparation initiative on another campus. Thus it becomes important for program leaders to share specific program content, successes, and disappointments as widely as possible to allow educators to fully grasp the commonalties and distinctions between the two programs.

TA development may very well be a necessary component of a faculty preparation program. If neither is in place in a department or university, one can begin with an effective TA development program. Most departments have faculty members who are committed to teaching and mentoring graduate students in their teaching assistant assignments. As the program evolves, program leaders can then establish a faculty preparation program. In most cases, TA development is more appropriate than faculty preparation efforts in the early stages of graduate study (Pruitt, 1996). It has been shown that graduate students with the foundation of a TA development program are better prepared to succeed with more advanced teaching experiences and are better suited to work with faculty mentors as junior colleagues (Sprague & Nyquist, 1991).

In addition, both types of programs tend to benefit from a combination of centrally organized and departmental components; assessment of graduate students' effectiveness as undergraduate instructors; the use of teaching portfolios; strong faculty role models in the department; attention to the institutional climate in which they operate; and graduate student participation in planning and development.

MAKING THE TRANSITION FROM A TA DEVELOPMENT TO A FUTURE FACULTY PROGRAM

Faculty preparation programs may be structured in a number of ways. In many cases, universities have built PFF programs upon successful TA development programs (e.g., the Universities of Kentucky and Washington). Some, like the University of Minnesota, have subsumed the TA development program under the broader rubric of preparing future faculty. Others have established new PFF programs that operate more or less independently of the TA development program (e.g., Northwestern University and the University of New Hampshire). However they are structured, the following factors should be considered when establishing a Preparing Future Faculty program.

Establishment of Partnerships with Diverse Institutions

Faculty preparation programs require that the program leaders create and manage an interinstitutional cluster of diverse institutions. This requires the involvement of local undergraduate institutions. The more diverse the undergraduate institutions, the richer the experience for the graduate students. Graduate or other academic administrators typically do the recruitment of partner institutions, although often faculty-to-faculty recruitment is also essential. Agreement to participate requires commitment from chief academic officers and faculty from selected departments at the partner institution. We have found it valuable to establish a steering committee, composed of all constituents, to meet to plan the program and keep lines of communication open. Once the program has been established, it is essential that someone manage the day-to-day operations of the efforts. Several universities, such as Arizona State, have found that graduate student coordinators can maintain communication among the various institutions involved, including coordination with leaders and mentors at partner institutions. This can be particularly challenging when dealing with several institutions and multiple departments in each institution. Respecting the diversity of the institutions, keeping communication flowing, and providing a flexible framework for implementation may help with this challenge.

Faculty Involvement and Leadership

Faculty involvement and leadership are necessary if the ethos of the department and institution is to support future faculty programs. It is important for the graduate dean to establish contacts and elicit the support of key departmental faculty members. Involvement of senior faculty respected by their colleagues is critical. Faculty members with this stature are well positioned to lead departmental discussions about what needs to be modified, eliminated, or added to the graduate program. They are also well positioned to garner support for the initiative from their faculty colleagues and, in some cases, the chair of the department or of the graduate program. Department chairs may be helpful in recruiting support from the appropriate senior faculty. Faculty at the doctorate-granting universities are very helpful in recruiting colleagues in their disciplines at partner institutions. One of the benefits from these clusters is the relationships forged among professionals on different campuses.

Opportunity to Work with Multiple Faculty Mentors
Opportunities to be mentored by faculty need to be available to all graduate students involved in the program. A list of expectations or general guidelines available for all program participants is important to clarify for both mentors and graduate students the nature of this special relationship. Howard University requires that the graduate student and faculty member prepare a "contract" setting forth parameters of the relationship. It is not safe to assume that all faculty members are equipped to mentor students. Seminars, workshops, or consultations should be offered for faculty members who want to explore strategies and/or issues related to mentoring. At Syracuse University, nearly 200 faculty have been involved in learning to be effective teaching mentors, essentially learning from each other. In most cases, we have found that graduate students benefit from working with multiple faculty mentors, not just the traditional research mentor.

Access to Advanced Teaching Assignments
Some senior teaching assistants already have access to advanced teaching assignments, including curriculum development, student advising, independent teaching, or working with an upper division course. In order for faculty preparation programs to be successful, participants must routinely have access to these experiences. Often these may be found at partner institutions where students have the opportunity to teach courses or units that are not available to them at their universities.

Opportunities to Participate in Academic Service Activities

Faculty preparation programs introduce and explore the multiple roles and expectations of junior faculty, such as serving on faculty committees, attending faculty or department meetings, or participating in faculty development activities. They also provide opportunities for graduate students to gain practice and receive advice about balancing these activities with other responsibilities. Graduate students have done such things as organize a forum on race relations, participate in a study of the university in the 21st century, attend a board of regents meeting, and participate in a public discussion on the future of tenure.

Access to Professional Development and Career Development Programs

Faculty preparation programs offer seminars and encourage discussion among graduate students and faculty mentors about alternative career opportunities and preparation for the academic job search. We have found that deans and faculty members at partner institutions are very articulate about their various missions and their implications for faculty work. Providing occasions for such conversation is informative to the graduate students and graduate faculty, and they legitimate talking about careers in the full range of colleges and universities, conversations that are sometimes discouraged otherwise.

These areas are intended to provide guidelines, not to prescribe a model to be replicated from one institution to another. Both faculty preparation initiatives and TA development programs must be tailored to the institution's or cluster's unique climate. While it is likely that we can learn from successes and failures at other institutions, there is no single template that can be used to establish successful programs for every institution.

CONCLUSION

For decades, the opportunity to be a graduate teaching assistant has provided valuable learning for future college teachers. In recent years, TA development programs have enriched this experience and expanded this learning. Today, faculty preparation programs add to TA development programs by emphasizing work with a teaching mentor, preparation for service responsibilities, and experiences at diverse partner institutions. Together, TA development and faculty preparation programs hold the greatest promise of more fully preparing graduate students for life in the academy.

That is why several institutions that have worked with both TA development and faculty preparation programs are "scaling up" the latter to add to the benefits of the former. For example, Florida State University has expanded its department-based PFF programs from four to ten departments, and Indiana University has increased the number of departments involved from three to nine. University-wide programs are expanding too. Since 1995, Syracuse's Future Professoriate Project has been absorbed into the university's budget and currently has about 200 graduate teaching associates and 200 faculty teaching mentors. It has awarded over 60 certificates in university teaching. The University of Minnesota operates its PFF program in the form of courses that provide tuition support to provide base program expenses. About 200 graduate students are currently enrolled, and 250 have completed the Minnesota program. With 77 of the 110 doctoral programs involved, the program has over 200 faculty mentors from 11 campuses. The institutions that have gained experience with faculty preparation programs are moving beyond demonstration projects to a new way of preparing graduate students.

We conclude this chapter with three policy recommendations.

- Every university and department that offers a doctorate should offer a faculty preparation program.

- All graduate students interested in exploring a career in the academy should have access not just to a graduate teaching experience and a TA development program but also to a faculty preparation program.

- Current TA development programs should add a faculty preparation component or subsume their TA work under the broader rubric of a faculty preparation program.

Given what we have learned about the power of such programs—even if we do not have definitive long-term results—it almost seems irresponsible to not work toward these goals.

REFERENCES

Adam, B. E., & Roberts, A. O. (1993). Differences among the disciplines. In R. M. Diamond & B. E. Adam (Eds.), *Recognizing faculty work: Reward systems for the year 2000.* New Directions for Higher Education, No. 81. San Francisco, CA: Jossey-Bass.

Boice, R. (1992). *The new faculty member: Supporting and fostering professional development.* San Francisco, CA: Jossey-Bass.

Boyer, E. L. (1990). *Scholarship reconsidered: Priorities of the professoriate.* Princeton, NJ: Carnegie Foundation for the Advancement of Teaching.

Chism, N., Cano, J., & Pruitt, A. S. (1989). Teaching in a diverse environment: Knowledge and skills needed by TAs. In J. D. Nyquist, R. D. Abbott, & D. H. Wulff (Eds.), *Teaching assistant training in the 1990s.* New Directions for Teaching and Learning, No. 39. San Francisco, CA: Jossey-Bass.

Committee on Science, Engineering, and Public Policy Report. (1995). *Reshaping the graduate education of scientists and engineers.* Washington, DC: National Academy Press.

DeNeef, A. L. (1996). *The lessons of PFF concerning the job market.* Washington, DC: Association of American Colleges and Universities and Council of Graduate Schools.

Eble, K. (1987). Defending the indefensible. In N. V. N. Chism (Ed.), *Institutional responsibilities and responses in the employment and education of teaching assistants.* Columbus, OH: The Ohio State University.

Fink, L. D. (Ed.). (1984). *The first year of college teaching.* New Directions for Teaching and Learning, No. 17. San Francisco, CA: Jossey-Bass.

Gaff, J. G., & Lambert, L. M. (1996). Socializing future faculty to the values of undergraduate education. *Change, 28* (4), 38-45.

Gaff, J. G., & Pruitt, A. S. (1996). Experiences of graduate students, faculty members, and administrators in preparing future faculty programs: Year 1. *CGS Communicator, 29* (1), 1.

Gaff J. G., & Pruitt-Logan, A. S. (1998). Preparing college faculty. In M. S. Anderson (Ed.), *The experience of being in graduate school: An exploration.* New Directions in Higher Education, No. 101. San Francisco, CA: Jossey-Bass.

Hutchings, P. (1993). Preparing the professoriate: Next steps and what we need to do to take them. In L. M. Lambert & S. L. Tice (Eds.), *Preparing graduate students to teach: A guide to programs that improve undergraduate education and develop tomorrow's faculty.* Washington, DC: American Association for Higher Education.

Lambert, L. M. (1993). Centralized TA programs and practices. In L. M. Lambert & S. L. Tice (Eds.), *Preparing graduate students to teach: A guide to programs that improve undergraduate education and develop tomorrow's faculty.* Washington, DC: American Association for Higher Education.

Lambert, L. M. (1996). Building a professional portfolio. In L. M. Lambert, S. L. Tice, & P. H. Featherstone (Eds.), *University teaching: A guide for graduate students.* Syracuse, NY: Syracuse University Press.

Lambert, L. M., & Tice, S. L. (Eds.). (1993). *Preparing graduate students to teach: A guide to programs that improve undergraduate education and develop tomorrow's faculty.* Washington, DC: American Association for Higher Education.

Nyquist, J. D., Abbott, R. D., & Wulff, D. H. (1989). The challenge of TA training in the 1990s. In J. D. Nyquist, R. D. Abbott, & D. H. Wulff (Eds.), *Teaching assistant training in the 1990s.* New Directions for Teaching and Learning, No. 39. San Francisco, CA: Jossey-Bass.

Pruitt, A. S. (1996). *The Preparing Future Faculty Program and teaching assistant training: Building bridges.* Washington, DC: Association of American Colleges and Universities and Council of Graduate Schools.

Pruitt-Logan, A. S., & Gaff, J. G. (1997). *Assessments of preparing future faculty programs.* Washington, DC: Association of American Colleges and Universities and Council of Graduate Schools.

Pruitt-Logan, A. S., & Gaff, J. G. (1996). [Survey of PFF participants]. Unpublished raw data.

Pruitt-Logan, A. S., & Gaff, J. G. (1998). *Impact: Assessing experiences of participants in the Preparing Future Faculty Program 1994-1996.* Washington, DC: Association of American Colleges and Universities and Council of Graduate Schools.

Seldin, P. (1997). *The teaching portfolio: A practical guide to improved performance and promotion/tenure decisions* (2nd ed.). Bolton, MA: Anker.

Slevin, J. E. (1992). *The next generation: Preparing graduate students for the professional responsibilities of college teachers.* Washington, DC: Association of American Colleges.

Sorcinelli, M. D. (1992). New and junior faculty stress: Research and responses. In M. D. Sorcinelli & A. E. Austin (Eds.), *Developing new and junior faculty.* New Directions for Teaching and Learning, No. 50. San Francisco, CA: Jossey-Bass.

Sprague, J., & Nyquist, J. D. (1991). A developmental perspective on the TA role. In J. D. Nyquist, R. D. Abbott, D. H. Wulff, & J. Sprague (Eds.), *Preparing the professoriate of tomorrow to teach: Selected readings in TA training.* San Francisco, CA: Jossey-Bass.

Syverson, P. D., & Tice, S. L. (1993). The critical role of the teaching assistantship. In L. M. Lambert & S. L. Tice (Eds.), *Preparing graduate students to teach: A guide to programs that improve undergraduate education and develop tomorrow's faculty.* Washington, DC: American Association for Higher Education.

Turner, J. L., & Boice, R. (1989). Starting at the beginning: The concerns and needs of new faculty. *To Improve the Academy, 6,* 41-55.

Weimer, M., Svinicki, M. D., & Bauer, G. (1989). Designing programs to prepare TAs to teach. In J. D. Nyquist, R. D. Abbott, & D. H. Wulff (Eds.), *Teaching assistant training in the 1990s.* New Directions for Teaching and Learning, No. 39. San Francisco, CA: Jossey-Bass.

Whitt, E. J. (1991). Hit the ground running: Experiences of new faculty in a school of education. *Review of Higher Education, 14* (2), 177-197.

INDEX